San Francisco's
HALLINAN
Toughest Lawyer in Town

Hallinan at the time of his personal defense against three street muggers (1973).

San Francisco's
HALLINAN
Toughest Lawyer in Town

James P. Walsh

PRESIDIO PRESS

Library of Congress Cataloging in Publication Data

Walsh, James P., 1937–
San Francisco's Hallinan.

1. Hallinan, Vincent.   2. Lawyers—California—
San Francisco—Biography.   I. Title.
KF373.H27W34   1982   349.794'61'0924 [B] 82-15023
ISBN 0-89141-167-4   347.946100924 [B]

Jacket design, Kathleen A. Jaeger
Interior design, Lyn Cordell
Printed in the United States of America

Dho Patrick Walsh agus Nellie Murphy Walsh

Le buíochas ó bhur gclann mhac atá
ag fuireacht leis an lá nuair a bhéas an
teaghlach uile go cionmhar buil a chéile. Is mór
faoi chomaoin díbh muid as ucht an tsaoil nua sa domhan úr.

Books by James P. Walsh

The San Francisco Irish, 1850–1976 (1978)
The Irish: America's Political Class (1976)
Ethnic Militancy: An Irish Catholic Prototype (1972)

Contents

Foreword

Vincent Hallinan, whom I have been proud to call my good friend over the years, may well be the toughest lawyer in town, but he is also much, much more. To say that he is "astute" would be grossly to understate. He's that and more. He's an intelligent, imaginative, and perhaps above all, a courageous lawyer who has been a dominant force before the courts of San Francisco over the last sixty-three years.

I doubt if any lawyer in any city has left such a trail and such a list of accomplishments as has Vince. He could love a rich man as well as a poor one, but commitment brought him mostly to the side of the poor. He represented minority and ethnic causes long before it became fashionable to do so.

Indeed, the cases are legion in San Francisco in which Vince established law for the least of us, and did it in a grand and unforgiving manner.

Hallinan came to the bar in San Francisco before I did. I came out of Boalt Hall, the University of California at Berkeley, in 1933. He graduated from St. Ignatius long before it became the University of San Francisco, and he even defended his first case before having earned his degree or having passed the bar. The law then was far different from the law at the present time; it was horrendous—that is if you were the plaintiff in a personal injury case, the defendant in the criminal case, or in anyway on the side of the minority. I wonder how ordinary people received any semblance of justice in criminal cases, and I know with certainty that no one received adequate awards in civil cases.

Vince Hallinan began in San Francisco what I have advanced in more recent years. From the start, he waded in against street railways, banks, insurance companies, and those who now would be President Reagan's most staunch supporters. In the 1920s and 1930s these institutions held all the cards and their influence over the courts bordered on absolute control.

Capital punishment was the order of the day. Non-suits in civil cases were regularly granted. Verdicts were reduced by trial judges even after the most modest of judgments. Vince attacked all of this.

I remember well when Judge Deasy died. Hallinan asked the court to recess out of memory to his honor. After all, Vince pointed out, all of the Market Street Railway streetcars were carrying their flags at half-mast. And well they could. Deasy never decided a case against the Railway, and if a jury came in for the plaintiff against this entrenched octopus, Judge Deasy would grant a new trial. If today lawyers and ordinary citizens are required only to convince disinterested courts of the justice of their case, Vince Hallinan was the one who made it so in San Francisco.

He was not loath to go before the grand jury on petite jury selection. He challenged bar associations, commissions, supervisors, the federal government, even the Catholic Church.

On the latter, some say Vince is an atheist. Maybe he has said so himself. But, and he probably will hate me for saying this, I think he has a deep religious feeling, at least for his fellowman. His lifelong commitment could only come from an appreciation of the teachings of our Lord.

Vince has done some writing but most of his best work has been forensic, before judges and juries, both civil and criminal.

I don't believe a lawyer deserves the title of trial lawyer unless he can try all types of cases—criminal, capital punishment cases, will contests, personal injury, land frauds, everything. From the start Vince has been an exquisite trial lawyer. Through his long and abundant career he has tried everything, and he has been at home with all types of cases. In mid-career he even was defense counsel at political trials, which created the radical dimension that has characterized his more mature years.

He has defended numerous cases of a spectacular nature which are recounted in this book. Through the excitement of vivid prose, Professor Walsh has delineated a most remarkable life and legal career. In so doing he has placed Hallinan within his own exciting ethnic tradition and related it to the evolution of our nation's most exciting twentieth-century city —San Francisco.

I wrote at length in my *Modern Trials* of the use of the extended opening statement. Vince was one of the very few lawyers doing just this when I came to the bar. He told me, "Mel, a good opening statement makes the jury want to go out and vote for your side right then without listening to your opponent!" Long before disclosure proceedings became standard, Hallinan's thorough case preparation and extreme confidence allowed him to spread his defense in front of the jury before he heard the prosecution. This was daring and effective.

Vince never was adverse to brawling, scuffling, hand fighting. Only his client was always right. If someone would hazard otherwise, he would hardly believe that possible and on more than one occasion he substantiated his views with his fists.

His final arguments, like his opening statements, were works of art and young lawyers used to crowd into the San Francisco courtrooms to hear him, whether it was a criminal summation or a plea for damages in a personal injury case.

I remember when Hallinan and Jake Ehrlich, another old, great lawyer friend of mine, would argue pure points of law in demurrers or law motions. The repartee among counsels and court over the then-technical rules of law was a delightful excursion into forensic endeavor for us all to see and hear. In 1919, on the day President Woodrow Wilson signed the Paris Peace Treaty ending World War I, Hallinan began a unique legal career. Today he remains the "toughest smart guy" in San Francisco. I invite you to read, enjoy, or be outraged by what happened in between.

Melvin M. Belli

May 19, 1982

Introduction

The primary power of this biography comes from its compelling—and frequently infuriating—protagonist: a man in whom a number of paradoxical and sometimes contradictory impulses come together to create a public personality of enormous importance in the history of the American Left. Here, among other paradoxes, is a Jesuit-trained attorney who has waged a lifelong guerrilla action against the Roman Catholic Church, showing in the process a superb range of Jesuitical skills, to include a devastating logic and a forensic ability based solidly in the four-hundred-year-old Jesuit tradition of controversial argument. Here is a self-made millionaire who has spent his life on the outer edges of the Far Left. Here is an iconoclast, a foe of the orthodox establishment in all its phases, who has made a near-religion of family life. Here is a gut-fighter whose compassion for the downtrodden, whose rage for social justice is possessed of powerful authenticity. Here is a man who is both loved and hated, but never ignored. Here is Vincent Hallinan.

This biography has both the vivid detail and the narrative power usually associated with fiction. With investigative exactitude, James P. Walsh, an academically trained scholar of history, has spared no effort in recovering and dramatizing the milieu and context of Vincent Hallinan's extraordinary career. This biography is as unique as the life it chronicles, but it draws its strength from a wider context as well.

It is, first of all, an Irish-American story, hence touched by the perennial Irish-American imperatives of family and religion, or in this case, family and militant disbelief, which is religion's opposite face. It is, secondly, a San Francisco Irish-American story, hence animated by that special civic passion, that sense of being solidly at home in one's own city, that makes the story of the San Francisco Irish somewhat different from the story of the Irish in the East.

It is also an important contribution to the San Francisco annals of bench and bar, a genre first pioneered in the 1870s and 1880s by Oscar Tully Shuck, Hall McAllister, Francis J. Heney, Garret McEnerney, Jake Ehrlich, George T. Davis, Melvin Belli, and James Martin MacInnis. Down through the years, San Francisco has been graced by many gifted attorneys. Some of them were Irish. Some were notorious. Some, such as Vincent Hallinan, were both notorious and Irish. San Franciscans have always celebrated their colorful legal personalities because these gentlemen of the bench played such a major role in the early organization of the city. San Francisco, after all, emerged in the mid-nineteenth century as the legal capital of the entire Far West. Here sat the major federal courts outside of Washington, D.C.; and before the San Francisco bench, state and federal, were argued the landmark cases of western American society.

Throughout his lifetime, Vincent Hallinan has carried on a lover's quarrel with the world, as every Irish person of passion and intelligence must. In his case, the quarrel has been decidedly political and on the Far Left. Professor Walsh gives us in this biography the career of an important American radical, whose protest and resistance spans every major phase of Far Left involvement since the First World War, to include running for the presidency in 1952 on the Progressive Party ticket. In and out of these pages come and go a cast of fascinating left-wing Americans, from Dr. W. E. B. Du Bois to Paul Robeson, Marion Bachrach, and Harry Bridges.

It was Harry Bridges, in fact, who once made in a speech a most telling comparison between Vincent Hallinan and his predecessor in protest, the San Francisco labor leader and fiery prophetic radical, Father Peter C. Yorke (1864–1925). At this point, the circle is circled: the vigorously anti-Catholic Hallinan being compared to the priestly radical of an earlier era. Personally, I like Harry Bridges's comparison, savoring its aptness and its sly irony, a quality for which Harry Bridges is famous. Like Peter Yorke, Vincent Hallinan has never feared being a pain in the neck when the time and the cause were appropriate. Both men drew great strength from their immediate environment: their city, their Irish heritage, their family or, in Yorke's case, the extended family of a working-class urban parish. Both men were possessed of an apt and bituminous eloquence and a capacity for close skirmishing. Both men had within themselves a deep, deep anger that they were constantly trying to civilize by joining that anger to the suffering and injustice of the world and making it work productively.

Few readers of this biography will agree with many of Vincent Hallinan's opinions. Few readers, in fact, will put this book down, believing that the world needs more Vincent Hallinans. For the time being, one Vincent Hallinan has been enough—and very necessary; for one need not be on the Far Left to recognize that the Left does a valuable American work when it challenges the Center and the Right to take seriously the promise of America. Vincent Hallinan has spent a lifetime making such challenges, and American society is the better for his impassioned resistance.

Kevin Starr

Preface

Vincent Hallinan disdained orthodoxy right from the beginning. He defended his first court case in 1919, one year before he passed the California Bar Examination and two years before he completed law school. In 1982 he continues winning difficult cases, those which afford him maximum opportunities to demolish expert witnesses in open court. He has spent the intervening sixty-three years building up an unprecedented legal career.

Through sheer durability Hallinan overwhelmed and outdistanced all of his contemporaries. No other presently active American trial lawyer argued a case on the day that President Woodrow Wilson ended World War I and signed the Treaty of Paris. Hallinan's professional debut preceded the establishment not merely of the United Nations, but the League of Nations.

Today Hallinan ranks as a master of the American courtroom. His success and survivability within the highly competitive legal profession have established him not only as an outstanding attorney to his generation, but to the following generations.

The major obstacles which interfered with the exuberant pursuit of his calling were successive jail terms and legal suspensions. Both sprang from the provocative quality of his courtroom advocacy.

The skill and relentlessness with which Hallinan practices law, in part, account for both the spectacular success he has achieved and the hostile opposition he has encountered. His clients have hardly ever constituted an attractive segment of society. For the most part they were outcasts, persons publicly scorned and privately disturbed. Sometimes they were very guilty as well. Yet, Hallinan did for each of them what no other attorney of the day could, or perhaps would, do.

Hallinan ingeniously designed and aggressively advanced challenging defenses which normally aroused judicial displeasure, hostility, and even prejudice. Never did he relent in his assertion that the creation of the most compelling and, therefore, most challenging defense possible was every citizen's right. This became Hallinan's corollary to the legal right to plead not guilty.

As a young lawyer in his twenties, Hallinan refused to be silenced by a judge who, at best, was inadequately prepared for his place on the bench and, at worst, was hostile to the accused. Thereafter, contempt citations, or even denial of the right to practice law itself, never intimidated Hallinan.

The man's mental and professional vigor, however, explain only the less exciting fraction of Hallinan's life. Unstructured and unabridged, the life of Vincent Hallinan is one of drama. His response to the flow of history has been quite unlike any other nationally known twentieth-century attorney. Each time the clamor for repression arose — in any context from law to politics, economics, religion, or foreign policy — so too did Hallinan. Still, Hallinan remained consistent and vocal in his dissent. Predictably, he expressed the unpopular side of the issue cogently, always with candor and frequently with wit.

His commitment to opposing whatever he considered to be against the national interest might properly be measured by his efforts in 1952 when he ran for president against General Dwight D. Eisenhower and Governor Adlai Stevenson. For Hallinan, the fact that he was not going to win was entirely irrelevant. His coast-to-coast travels allowed him to articulate a well-reasoned alternative to the nation's then forming military-industrial complex. When most Americans were scarcely aware of the problem, Hallinan was. When they had no understanding of its potential significance for our time, Hallinan grasped an opportunity afforded few

Americans and told all who listened and more who would not.

Back in his school days young Hallinan had fleetingly considered the priesthood, but he received scant encouragement from his Jesuit teachers. In fact, the prefect of discipline considered Vincent to be some "sort of a crazy genius." His intellectual sparkle came wedded to a spontaneous unpredictability which those sworn to lives of obedience, poverty, and chastity considered unsuited to the requirements of religious conformity and subordination.

This "crazy genius" component of the boy thrived in Hallinan the man. Perhaps only in California, San Francisco at that, might a personality such as Hallinan's find a near-comfortable environment. Even so, Hallinan and his perpetual defense of the unpopular became tolerable to the city's masses belatedly when, at the age of seventy-seven, he violently resisted a mugging. Only the radical few among his fellow Irish Americans applauded at his eighty-fifth birthday party when Hallinan dubbed Margaret Thatcher, Britain's pro-NATO Prime Minister, "a Ronald Reagan in drag."

Such distaste for authority was the sole legacy his immigrant father left Hallinan. Even though his own challenges never approached the terrorism of his father's generation, the defenders of the status quo considered them threatening enough. For Vincent the courtroom and the public forum took the place of the strike and the assassination. Research, a nimble mind, and an agile tongue replaced the club, the pike, or the gun. Within a transformed arena Hallinan did battle for his clients, his own causes, and for the advancement of what America, in his vision, ought to be. Throughout, the judiciary became a point of encounter between Hallinan's mature radical idealism and the system he both manipulated and tried to change.

His biography is the story of a unique American.

James P. Walsh

San José State University
March 20, 1982

1. Prologue: Friday Morning, December 27, 1973

Dry breakfast food, or his mother's old Irish porridge, had carried Vincent Hallinan successfully to lunch every day for seventy-seven years. The only exceptions were his two stretches in the federal penitentiary. One spoon of government mush was enough; it left him with the same taste as licking stamps. Ever since his release, whenever he stamped an evelope rather than have his secretaries use the office postage meter, his mind jolted back to those periods of confinement. Though insufficiently motivated to find out, he often wondered if contracts for jail food and stamp glue went to the same government vendor. The stuff his mother used to boil up kept him till noon, but the federal mixture stuck with him sometimes for days.

Finishing off his only course, Hallinan poured a second cup of black coffee and reached for the morning paper. Rose would be arriving soon to enforce her own discipline upon the rebellious kitchen and transform the rest of the well-appointed home into that ordered serenity Vivian enjoyed sharing with their frequent dinner guests.

Vince could not remember who were expected that night although his wife must have told him. He hoped it would not be a celebrity fop to whom Vivian was obligated for helping her advance some social cause. Maybe it would be a small party he had scheduled long in advance, perhaps a progressive judge or two, some congenial attorneys, or a few old radicals. Just so there were good looking and smart women included, any assortment would do.

Hallinan turned the pages of the *San Francisco Chronicle* as carefully as his disfigured left hand allowed and scanned President Richard Nixon's "enemies list." The unrepentant old radical felt disappointed at being omitted and disgusted at how respectability was closing in on him. He had not changed but the times and the issues had. He could not remember, in fact, the last time an antagonist yelled, "Communist," at him in public.

Lately, as the media was becoming less hostile toward him, Hallinan jokingly told reporters that at age eighty he expected to receive full absolution from Rome. Privately though, he hoped for just one more unpopular cause to come along so he could outrage all the old respectables who assumed he was dead or safely installed in a suburban rest home.

Intentionally, he skipped over the obituary page without a glance, since the friends and foes of even his middle years were gone. A generation ago he had concluded that life was a fickle bitch, that happiness really was impossible. Death, like life, was beyond his comprehension and, despite his Irish heritage, he ceased attending wakes.

Folding the *Chronicle*, Hallinan moved quickly into the expansive living room, dropped to the floor, and clicked off some push-ups. The soapy fragrance that ascended from the carpet reminded him of the dinner party that evening. Evidently Rose had Pedro shampoo the luxuriant, white Chinese rug.

At the count of twenty he went down for another half, then rolled over for a quick sit-up out of which he sprang to his feet. He stepped briskly to the hall closet and slipped into a well-worn coat. Through habit he paused at the mirror and adjusted his necktie. He ignored the rain gear Vivian had put out for him the night before.

Considering his age and the life he had lived, Hallinan still looked good, better than several forty-five year olds he had saved from the California gas chamber. Except during his newlywed years back in the 1930s, he had kept his weight down. And, since his seventy-fifth birthday, he had been cutting back even further.

He still had all his own teeth, though heavily inlaid with gold. Age, plus the facial exercise he had developed during his last stay in prison, made the paralysis of his left cheek less noticeable. The self-designed therapy took some of the twist out of his smile and made him look less sardonic. If a few more wrinkles developed, he might even appear benign to those who did not know better.

He smoothed his thick wavy hair, buttoned up, and contemplated another damp San Francisco morning. Before he opened the door though, he scribbled a note to Vivian not to accept any deposit for the sale of one of her downtown properties. A priest from nearby St. Boniface parish had called his office about it. Hallinan hoped his wife could unload the dump on the Catholic church.

Vincent Hallinan always did his best thinking while on the move. He assumed it had something to do with the natural and easy rhythm of the body in motion. Whatever the physiological reasons, his three-mile walk from Pacific Heights to his downtown law offices did pay dividends.

In recent years his growing hatred of things such as automobiles was spreading to include his desk. When he sat at it for any period of time, without conversation or reading, he felt like twitching or scratching. Young receptionists at first apologized when they failed to screen out phone calls from the kooks that San Francisco enjoys in such abundance. But Hallinan seemed not to mind. He listened attentively to their tales and sometimes offered free advice or directions. If one of these non-clients became abusive, he gave him a verbal flip-off and slammed the phone. Usually he was glad for the distraction and slightly invigorated by the encounter. In time, the more experienced staff ceased worrying about the occasional weirdos and just plugged them in. Hallinan talked to anyone.

Formal case preparation no longer captivated him the way it did during his maturing years. Now he had to discipline himself to do what used to be fun. Because he could not rely solely upon experience to keep winning difficult cases, he prepared all the harder. No longer could he consult with those older Irish and Jewish attorneys from whom he had learned the tricks and peculiarities of the San Francisco courts. Those shrewd brokers in human frailty were all gone.

Gone too was the caution, and the guidance, they provided Hallinan in so many of his spectacular, no-win undertakings. Gone was the restraining influence these older men exercised over his radical idealism. Practical, but sentimental too, Hallinan gathered in all the wisdom they left behind and regretted their passing. He even ignored the fact that these wily but honest court veterans had remained silent and aloof when he challenged the powerful interests that corrupted the California courts.

As the years hastened past, Hallinan absorbed new legislation and decisions as they materialized. He continued to read deeply and widely. And from a media he despised, he seized whatever information he found useful. For strictly legal research, he had leaned for some years on clerks. But now he had his own sons practicing law, and it felt good having them in close for the years ahead.

This combination of walking and planning paid off handsomely in the Stulsaft case. Every Saturday morning, with a little note pad in his shirt pocket, he used to take off for his sister's house, eleven miles away. During those weekly walks he created for Lillian Ryan Stulsaft the whole story they would use in court. It did not come in one shot; that was the stuff of papier-mache television lawyers—the pretty boys. No, Hallinan worked out Lillian's story over a month and a half. He was methodical, comprehensive, and wily. He took advantage of every prop of evidence and accounted for everything the other contestants to the will of his client's husband could use against his scenario. He tried out his fiction on anyone who would listen, noted their criticisms, and revised his story to cover each flaw. As with every case, when the trial opened, his story was believable because it accounted for the evidence and anticipated the opposing argument.

The walking, the thinking, the story creation; that was the source of his satisfaction now. An insightful flash in the actual presence of a jury was no reason for congratulations. It was reason for reproach. Thinking of it in advance would have allowed more telling use of the knowledge. Winning was in the preparation.

Yes, this walking and thinking let him polish and tighten the script he created for clients like Stulsaft. In her case, after he dropped the bomb of a second will, shaky as it was, her sisters-in-law offered an even million dollars for an out-of-court settlement. At first they pretended to be magnanimous, a useless posture, given Hallinan's cynicism. He held out for three million and got it; two were for his client and one, for himself.

As Hallinan moved briskly along his usual route past the Presidio Heights playground, he saw the same governesses already out deforming the lives of their little charges. Each morning he suppressed the urge to tie these women up with the children's starchy new jump ropes and liberate kids whose only crime was having been born into the confinement of inherited wealth.

Every time he saw them he embellished his plan, much as he did the stories he created for his clients. After freeing the children he would run with them all the way down to the Marina Greens to skinny dip. On the way back he would give a prize to the kid who broke the most windows at Military Police Headquarters in the San Francisco Presidio. Those who effected a clean get-away would get all the hotdogs they could eat and brownies too. He still remembered the recipe.

Acting out this fantasy might have been worth ending up as a three-time loser — except for that mush served in prison. So he passed on, leaving the little ones innocently to their fate. His private amusement, fleeting as it was, provided enough satisfaction for the moment.

With deliberation, Hallinan turned south on Baker Street and stepped up the pace to his normal, rapid stride. In minutes he left behind the hill-clinging mansions and plunged into the black ghetto.

It was getting close to mid-morning but he saw no familiar faces. Maybe the threat of showers kept indoors the older members of the black community who knew and liked Hallinan so well. Young people, particularly unemployed youth, were hanging around storefronts, but few of them knew him personally. Even the new, educated young blacks at San Francisco State would have to be persistent to discover his name buried in the statistical tables of Morison and Commager's *Growth of the American Republic.* Even there the history text gave no assessment of Hallinan's precedent-making political association with black Americans.

Every day the same depressing thought caught up with him as he crossed Fillmore Street at Turk. In the name of a now-stalled urban redevelopment program, the wrecking ball had laid waste to the neighborhood. What had escaped appeared ready to collapse of its own weight. The hideous Pink Palace, a prototype housing project, was the only exception. Yet even there his discerning eye observed the evidence of urban crime, violence, and decay.

It made him wonder which was greater, the waste of human lives through unemployment or the waste of real property through physical neglect. Here were two fully compatible and harmonious needs which the American system could not mesh to mutual advantage. Instead, the dilemmas of the nation's social, political, and economic structure glared at one another across littered and rat-infested streets.

The Fillmore validated his long-held conviction. Nothing the present system could devise could make America sound again. San Francisco, like the rest of urban America, stood in silent witness to the crumbling obsolescence of the capitalistic system.

Distracted by the physical surroundings, Hallinan had not noticed the three black men who were following him. Fortunately, even when not conscious of his imperiled security, he was wise in the ways of the urban combat zone. His appearance offered no suggestion of his great personal wealth. He wore no jewelry and the only gold he carried was in his teeth. So he kept his mouth shut. Since his last imprisonment he cut his work load back to just those cases that interested him. That limited his preparation to office hours and the long walks around the city. He took no work home, left his briefcase at the office, and walked the city streets with free hands.

Suddenly he did notice the blacks. They were getting closer. The biggest darted into an opening in the concrete project which extended for much of the block.

Vince always walked down Turk Street because it was one-way. The traffic flow allowed him to see into each approaching car. Just as when lunching in the workingmen's restaurants with his back to the far wall, he watched what was coming.

Turk was one-way all right, but it was the wrong way now. This was Friday, a work day, so all the morning traffic headed downtown toward Market Street. Turk ran in the opposite direction, away from Market and back toward the avenues and the Ocean Beach. It was deserted now. Nobody was around.

By then the two blacks were on him. The little guy pushed Hallinan into a stairwell where the biggest of the bunch had circled around and was waiting. Hallinan hardly expected to hear, "Stand and deliver," the famous salutation of the early English highwayman, Dick Turpin. Yet, the absence of all verbal communication surprised him completely. The trio said not a word, nothing, not even, "Give us your money, you old mother fucker!" Nothing. Finding a senior citizen alone on a ghetto street, they seemed to attack him in mute premeditation.

Hallinan's response was automatic. All those years of weight control and exercise piled on top of a tough upbringing brought things together. His combative disposition welcomed the quick adrenaline boost which shot through his circulatory system.

The old street fighter instinctively took advantage of the momentum the first kid gave him. Adding a right lead to boot, he caught the big fellow with a surprise punch square on the face where his broad nose met his left cheek. Stunned and hurt, he hit the step. He was not out, but he was down and down hard.

As Hallinan turned around to meet the others, the third mugger, a real dude of about twenty, whacked him across the face with a walking stick. It tore his flesh and the blood oozed swiftly into his right eye. The cane was unweighted, luckily, so it did not put him down or even drive him up against the wall.

More angry than stunned, Hallinan grabbed the stick. Twisting, he broke it in two. Rather than grappling with his opponent, Hallinan drove the bone of his right elbow deep into the adam's apple of his scared foe.

Vince had always been a headhunter, but so was the short kid who gave him the first push. Never reaching five feet, ten inches himself, even in his prime, Hallinan identified with short people, particularly when they were smart and tough besides.

The gladiator emeritus never got a clean shot at this little punk though. He was too fast. With brass knuckles on his right fist, the shortie caught Hallinan square on the left cheek bone. "Christ almighty, my head must have been made out of brick." The punch drove Hallinan back out of the stairwell onto the sidewalk. He swayed but still stood.

If any welfare mother watched the action from the Pink Palace, she knew enough to remain in the grandstand. No one bothered the police.

The weighted knuckles opened the other side of Hallinan's face, creating a crudely balanced blood flow. The lesion on the right side, however, pumped more crimson. It flowed freely down his neck and over his collar and tie.

For the moment he felt no pain; the excitement was too intense. Even the concussion effect from the broadside with the loaded fist had its compensation — pride in still being able to take it.

Later he recalled, "All I had was a couple of dollars on me. If they asked, I'd probably have given it to them. But they didn't. They just tried to put me down. All three of them.

"What was I supposed to do?"

Once he was out in the open again, Hallinan knew the longhaul advantage would be with him. Even though the trio had no idea who he was and would not believe that he had more ghetto friends than they had, their street smarts would not let this become an extended battle. The police occasionally cruised down Golden Gate Avenue and back up Turk, so they could not keep after him out in broad daylight.

He had no option but to stand his ground. Hallinan certainly was not egging them on. He had that much prudence at least. But he knew he could not turn and run either. He never was a sprinter and he would have no chance at all with his back turned and moving away. The lightweight with the knuckles could overtake him and beat him to the ground. Once he was down this bunch was quite capable of finishing him off. Old age would be bad enough without the added incapacity and pain of invalidism.

As the big man was picking himself up off the concrete step, Hallinan realized he still held the bottom half of the dude's cane.

The good-looking black flashed a knife as he pulled himself out of the stairwell and came slowly forward. He was powerfully built and showed no sign of alcohol or drug abuse. He should have been doing better things than this, but right now his eyes were fixed on his uncooperative victim.

Vince looked up and down Turk Street. Empty or not, he had no intention of dying face down in the gutter.

He took a deep breath and switched the broken cane to his right hand, holding it like a rapier. His sidewalk rival, knife held like a dagger, started closing in on him at the curb.

When his assailant lunged with his blade, Vince sidestepped in a way his old boxing coach would have applauded. Then he countered to the face with the jagged and splintered cane stump. Headhunting was still best, but on the first pass Hallinan missed his target, the eyes.

If he could keep this up for a few more thrusts and parries without letting the other two move around behind him, he could wind the big guy easily.

His shirt and coat continued to sponge up blood but he

did not care. He knew from his studies in physiology that the body had many more quarts left. Besides, he was flying. Since he never drank liquor, this was Vincent Hallinan's best high in years.

Carefully he backed off the curb onto the street. To reduce the height advantage of the knifer and to keep shorty in front of him too, Hallinan moved further out into the desolate thoroughfare, drawing the pair off the curb and into the gutter.

Fortunately the dude contented himself with watching from the doorway.

Then with all the suddenness of the initial attack, it ended. Not with eight inches of steel in his stomach and a wince of pain, but with a fierce yell.

When contact broke off momentarily, Hallinan used the disengagement to holler for help. The three could not fight this duffer forever in the middle of Turk Street and from his looks up close, his wallet was not worth the risk. They turned and ran.

What a seventy-seventh birthday! But for the carnage to his face by the cane and the brass fittings, he would almost believe this was a custom gift dreamed up for Vivian and the boys by one of those San Francisco specialty outfits that provides the ideal present for the man you love who already has everything. It surely sparked more excitement than the desk set the office staff forced on him the week before.

He doubted the remote possibility that he could go into shock after this beating. But he had experience in cases where such things happened. So much sweat was running down his back that he thought it might be blood from another, unnoticed wound. Maybe he ought to take it easy; certainly a doctor's examination would be prudent.

Dripping profusely, Hallinan picked up his normal pace just short of a trot and cut over one block to Golden Gate Avenue heading to the main cross street, broad Van Ness Avenue. He noted that his breathing had returned to normal but wondered about his blood pressure.

Central Emergency Hospital, across from City Hall and the Civic Auditorium, was eight blocks away. He knew he would make it with ease so he decided to bypass the office. One of his sons or a staff member might get a glimpse of him looking the way he was. He was late already and in recent years their concern was becoming more than just polite.

The Hallinan boys had tempers just like his. Only they were all still young, and strong, and wild, if you believed *Time* magazine. To see the lads later would be more prudent, after the red seepage from his face had been sewn shut and the indignity of a tetanus shot forgotten.

The attack, actually, was too short to be frightening. Now that it was over Hallinan recognized it for what it was, an adrenaline boost and a newsworthy incident, newsworthy because it happened to him, a celebrated San Franciscan, rather than some Iowa tourist on the vacation of his lifetime.

This sort of coverage always converted easily into new clients and new opportunities. Increasingly important now, he also wanted this for his sons. He wanted to transfer the family legal mystique to them. Sure, he still liked what he was doing and intended not to give it up, but they had fresh careers ahead and the stronger the name identification, the better. Events like this attracted more good work for all the Hallinans.

When Dr. Alan Petit discharged him from Central Emergency in good condition at 11:35 A.M., he hurried to his office near the Opera House. Already the reporters and the police had the news and the phone was ringing for interviews and photographs.

Of course he would meet members of the press. Why not?

No, he did not feel bad at all. Sure, he could give an exclusive; he could give one to everybody.

He had only two points for each journalist to get straight.

"I'm Hallinan. And I won."

After that each reporter was free to ask whatever came to mind. And sure, he would be happy to put up his dukes too and show the cameramen how he defended himself.

What impact did this beating have on his frequently announced liberal views on Negroes and civil rights?

None. "These guys didn't do that mugging because they

were black and I was white. They did it just because they were poor and needed money.

"They were seduced by television, by all that fantasy, seduced into believing they could have some of those wonderful things for themselves. The fact of the matter is they can't have those things. Never.

"Poverty, illiteracy, and unemployment are rampant. They don't have those things and will have no chance of ever getting them. Our system won't allow it.

"They needed my money and I even beat them out of that."

Now that that fact had surfaced, it made him distinctly uncomfortable, but the reporters let it pass.

Would Mr. Hallinan be walking home in the evening on the usual route?

"Of course, my dear." Why the hell not, he thought to himself.

"If anyone here wants to see the San Francisco that tour buses avoid, meet me out front at quitting time.

"If there are no more questions, I am sure we all have things to do. Good afternoon!"

At five o'clock the lumps hurt. His face was feeling the way it had looked since before noon. For a Friday it had been exciting enough, only he had accomplished next to nothing. Most of the judges had slid into the easy habit of curtailing court schedules on Fridays to the point where it was hard to get new business transacted with so few of them around. Hallinan liked to use it as catch-up day around the office.

To be ready again on Monday, he had immersed himself in the week-old paper pile and completely forgot his intention to go home early to talk business with Vivian. Now it was late so he quit.

Outside, the sidewalk was empty, just as he expected. He understood the reporters as well as they understood him. The evening papers were on the streets for an hour and even the writers for the morning editions had more attractive things to do than risk it on foot in the Fillmore after dark.

He turned left at the bottom of the steps to start up

Franklin Street when he heard the characteristic purr of a well-tuned Mercedes idling in the lot close beside the law offices.

As soon as he sensed it he knew he was about to be picked up, and by a good-looker, too.

Already he felt refreshed.

Vivian got the story from the boys even before it hit the evening newsstands. They had reassured her lest the synoptic radio flashes should frighten Rose out of the kitchen with a garbled account to their mother upstairs.

"Hey, big boy! How about a ride? I hear you had a heavy day."

Vince eased himself in beside her and they embraced. Then he settled back, deep into the comfort of soft leather.

Vivian cancelled the dinner and gave Rose the evening off. They were to be alone together that night.

Property and priests were never mentioned.

2. Out of the Irish Tradition

No sooner was Patrick Hallinan strong enough to hold to the back of his father's saddle than Black Mick carried him off to the cattle fairs. Besides the adventure, young Pat loved the escape from the tedium of copy books and lessons. At age nine he rode a Connemara pony, at eleven, a chestnut mare. The gift of his first black stallion told Pat that his father was not so displeased when he and school parted with words and a fight.

Land was the thing in nineteenth-century Ireland. Black Mick and his father before him understood that well enough. By holding their piece of County Limerick, they clung to security, to status, and to life itself. Relentless English exactions, even the Great Famine, had made them tenacious sharers of the ultimate worldly value of the peasant class below them. They too would endure any privation so they might retain their patch of ground. The Hallinan world included more, though, a dynamic ingredient. For them a coin was an opportunity, not merely an inert buffer against greater political or natural disasters which might take from them their holdings.

Land was the thing, to be sure, but Ireland remained so unsettled that only a fool assumed the permanency of much beyond his next breath. Black Mick was not a counter of what he had; he was a gatherer of more. His shrewdness was at business. Breeding and horse trading brought him to the provincial fairs where he gathered in a modest profit. That

14

was the margin which kept the Hallinans from sinking into the class of landless men who had once been their equals, men endowed with stolid endurance but not Hallinan cunning.

As soon as Pat could sit the stallion father and son rode off as master and apprentice to trade and to drink, the tradition-sanctioned rituals of rural Ireland. Pat could not learn any sooner how to trade up and then sell off prize stock for money. To barter up to a sporting animal and then be stuck for its winter feed would not do. Risk was in the game. Yet, Black Mick knew there was money in it too.

In 1882, as Black Mick traveled about the West of Ireland, he knew the country was restive again, and for good reason. A flood of cheap American grain was depressing the value of Ireland's crops. The potato blight that starved and drove away half of Ireland's people during the Famine was reappearing. The desperate tenant farmers, unable to meet both the exactions of absentee landlords and the needs of their families, would turn to violence rather than be driven from the land. Black Mick had already seen frightened women and hungry, bawling children put out upon the roads by well-fed men in English uniforms. While neighbors watched and resentments smouldered, the soldiers put fire to the thatch, then withdrew to the security of the barracks.

Black Mick was an anomaly. He built modest cabins for his own tenants and treated them with a decency seldom offered by a man who spoke from horseback. During the intense agrarian unrest, Hallinan, instead of closing ranks with his landholding class, led the local resistance movement. He led the Land League and supported the nationalist Charles Stewart Parnell. So strong was his advocacy that it brought him into conflict with the most powerful element in Irish life, the Catholic clergy.

On a Sunday morning Hallinan placed a makeshift table in front of Rathkeale Church to collect for Land League agitation and victims of a recent, brutal eviction. No sooner were the first coppers down than the parish priest ordered him to remove his table and take himself into mass. When he refused to obey, words flew and the priest kicked the table into sticks. In front òf the gathering parishioners Hallinan cursed his priest. On the next Saturday evening Black Mick tried to confess his blasphemy but was refused absolution, so foul had been his sin, compounded a hundred-fold by public scandal. Unwilling to grovel and yet fearful for his soul, Hallinan staged a one-man sit-in there in the confessional box, a test of wills which lasted through the night.

That year, 1882, was a fateful one for his boy. Its events smashed Black Mick's plan and determined the remainder of Patrick's troubled life.

Early in the spring the Invincibles, a Dublin-based terrorist fringe of the Irish Republican Brotherhood, began recruiting among the wilder country lads. The Hallinans encountered two activists at the Ballinasloe horse fair. Mick and Pat joined in draining a glass to "Ireland for the Irish," then hastened off about their business. As a landholder himself, Black Mick thought Parnell's organization was radical enough and he warned his son to stay clear of strangers from Dublin.

Wild and young, Pat Hallinan did not share his father's caution. Before he began the thirty-mile trek back across the Shannon to Ballingarry, he had taken the oath. He became a pledged member of a secret society and he intended to carry out whatever orders would follow.

The Invincibles announced themselves to a stunned English ruling class by stabbing to death Lord Frederick Cavendish, the newly appointed Chief Secretary for Ireland, and his Permanent Undersecretary, Thomas Henry Burke. Terrorist attacks on rack-renting landlords and their agents began in the West of Ireland, first with the assassination of a particularly odious aristocrat at Ardrahan, then by a second killing at Loughrea. Both acts took place within riding distance of the Hallinan farm.

Patrick Hallinan's authenticated participation in terrorism was closer to home. His target, Nolan, was the local agent of an absentee rack-renter. With three others, he set out on this murderous task. Pat and one of the quartet stationed themselves where they could intercept the victim while the other two proceeded a half-mile further on the road just in case Nolan escaped the first ambush. When the agent's horse and trap approached the first outpost the two men sprang out and seized the reins, upon which Nolan, with great presence of mind, cried out, "Christ, boys, don't bother with me! I have nothing, but that fellow Nolan is only minutes behind me and he has a bag of money! I saw him with it at the fair!"

His gullible assailants mumbled an apology and allowed him to proceed with a brief reprieve.

One of the second duo knew him by sight and as his horse galloped onto the next village, the hapless agent's body crumpled to the floor of the trap. Nolan was dead, his face blown away by shotgun blasts.

Patrick Hallinan's desperate act all but replicated a family tradition instituted by his clansmen, Hugh and Henry O'Halinan, in 1313. Patrick, rather than testing his father's reputed talents before the courts, fled to America instead, to a life of hopeless regret.

Black Mick lived on until 1925, dying at age ninety-nine. The only happiness to punctuate his declining years was the Easter Rising of 1916 and the advance of Irish independence under the leadership of Eamon de Valera, the son of his wife's first cousin. As his final days dragged on through sickness to death he saw the land fall to Timothy Mullins, the son-in-law he did not like. The land should have become Patrick's; it should have remained Hallinan. "Twas a shame he and Anne Coll had but one son, and he gone to America. The land was lost.

The San Francisco cable cars provided Hallinan his major employment. Affable, quick and compelling, he did not mind, at least at first, the weeks full of twelve- and fourteen-hour days. In a pre-automobile age all sorts of interesting people climbed aboard his Nob Hill car. Wealthy and stylish gentlemen descended to their banks and counting-houses in the financial district below. Later in the day smartly uniformed cooks and maids came aboard, going shopping and on errands. If Pat missed collecting the fare of an Irish servant girl, sure enough he would engage her in plenty of talk before he assisted her from the platform on the return trip.

That was how he met Elizabeth Sheehan. When they married in the parish church, she gave up the starched cottons and fashionable address for a rented room, a few sticks of furniture, and the bed. Pat was thirty-one and his bride was twenty-two. Age concerned them so slightly that both believed they were a year younger than they were. Later, when the date of birth became a statistic one was expected to know, Pat Hallinan patriotically selected St. Patrick's Day, 1863, a year and ten days late. His wife never bothered herself with any choice.

As Elizabeth's children started arriving with near-yearly punctuality, Hallinan's marginal living standard plummeted. Pat moved them through a series of rented flats in the Western Addition north of Market Street, none large enough for the growing family. With never enough to go around, Pat found what solace he could in drink. When the drop was in him, instead of becoming happy and lighthearted with his wife and eight children, he turned mean and abusive. Vincent, the oldest, remembered four children to a bed and the pathos which permeated his first recollection of his father. He ran to his mother because a strange man was on the bed. "It was my father, home from work, sick. I didn't know him. He went to work before his children awakened and came back after our mother put us to bed. He never had a day off then and existed to support a raft of kids he brought into the world who didn't even know him."

Each of the six girls and two boys were born at home. The last was born in 1916, when Elizabeth was two months short of her forty-fifth birthday. She resented that pregnancy as an imposition but doted over the child of her waning years with a fondness born of pride. Thereafter Patrick never shared the bedroom again. He was displaced by little Patricia who lingered first in her mother's bed and remained in the same room until adolescence.

At his prime Pat earned twenty-seven and one-half cents

an hour. To log twelve hours a day on broken shifts required fourteen or more hours at work. He looked to politics for a way out. In 1896 he voted for James D. Phelan, an Irish Catholic Democrat, for mayor. In the long run Phelan's ethnic and religious bond to the Irish laboring class did not compare with his membership in San Francisco's monied class. During the teamsters strike of 1901 the millionaire mayor used the police to protect strike-breaking scabs. Disillusioned, Hallinan agreed with his favorite priest, Father Peter C. Yorke. In the campaign of 1896, Yorke had placed his hand on Phelan's shoulder and called him friend. After the strike, Yorke called him "Jimmy the rag, a politician who is as much help to labor as a towel on the end of a pole."

Pat reacted by joining the newly organized Union Labor party, which amazed and threatened the city's conservative business interests. Hallinan was a peripheral figure who never became a confidant of Abe Ruef, the political manipulator who used the sincere but untutored union men for his own enrichment and the corruption of San Francisco.

The workingmen in the party chose Pat Hallinan as their 1902 candidate for state senator in the Twenty-second District. Hallinan out-polled the Democrat but lost to the Republican, whose November majority was a slim 767 votes. Pat spent nothing on his campaign because he had nothing. Since Ruef's interest was limited to city offices he provided no support for Hallinan. Even Yorke, the pro-labor, militant priest, remained neutral in his weekly *Leader*. Burned once by Phelan, Yorke abandoned politics in favor of the trade union movement. The *Chronicle*, however, was far from neutral. Its election-day editorial called for such an overwhelming Republican majority that "agitators and demagogues shall not again dare to seek their personal ends by appeals to passion. . . ."

In 1902, Hallinan stood and fell on his own. It was his only try for office. Thereafter he followed Yorke into militant trade unionism.

When the 1906 earthquake and fire struck, Pat and Elizabeth had seven children, ranging from Annie at twelve through Emily, who was not yet a year old. Vincent was nine. Pat paid twelve dollars a month for a four-room cottage, and whatever else he brought home, Elizabeth used for food and clothes. The physical devastation of the city did not touch their home, but the massive spiral of inflation which followed, did. The owner ordered them out so he could rent to tenants capable of paying more. The rest of the city lay in ashes and, outside of refugee camps, there was no place to go.

Faced with catastrophe, Pat decided to dig in. He stopped paying rent altogether and had his kids collect from the disaster relief stations all the free food they could store.

Next, Pat Hallinan joined the most violent streetcar strike in American history up to that time. His Carmen's Union walked out when the United Railroads refused to pay three dollars for an eight-hour day. Patrick Calhoun, grandson of the South Carolina justifier of slavery, was president of the traction company. He fired the strikers and imported armed, professional strikebreakers. Meanwhile he fortified the car barns and stockpiled food, bedding, and ammunition.

At night Pat joined the union attacks.

The strikers shot into the barns, hurled bombs through the shattered windows, and then put the buildings to the torch. At dawn the haggard scabs rolled the lumbering cars out through the mouths of the charred structures and rammed the barricades rather than risk dismounting to clear the tracks. Those strikebreakers who broke clear had to endure salvoes of bricks and mortar which union carpenters hurled down from the post-fire construction sites that lined the tracks.

By the end of the summer Calhoun's estimated loss exceeded one million dollars. In the riots and sieges 239 men were wounded—mostly scabs—and 3 union men were killed. But as long as the disorders continued, the Hallinans ate free and lived free. Pat's nights outside the barns were far more interesting than all the days he spent collecting fares. He did not even mind returning home over the back fences to avoid the process server. Besides, he had no real alternative. Calhoun and his stockholders surely would win, but at least the union men "gave the bastards a fight."

Pat had taken a few drinks the night he brought down a strikebreaker. The straggler was late getting back into Calhoun's carbarn so Hallinan hit him with a right hand to the face. In all the excitement and yelling he did not notice the swelling around his broken knuckles. As he bent over to get a loose cobble that would finish the job properly, a big man in a uniform clubbed Pat, tearing open his scalp. He struggled to draw himself upright but the club cracked its heavy way forward; the last blow closed Hallinan's left eye.

That night, Pat could not make it over the neighbor's fence. In fact, an older Irishman had a hard time getting Pat up the front steps. The stranger was coughing blood and looked worn out himself but knew enough not to stay. Elizabeth did what she could to wash away Pat's caked blood and the accumulated dirt so the children would not see their father like that in the morning. But Pat himself no longer cared. His militancy was gone. The best he managed was a curse for Calhoun and the broken strikers who accepted his terms: no union and the previous conditions of employment. Pat never went back on the cars.

Eviction and family disruption followed. Left unattended by any physician Pat mended slowly with a permanently deformed right hand and a scar from his hairline to his left eyebrow. He drifted about working as he could until he settled into driving a horse and wagon for a city department. Unable to rent a flat for his own family, he became a lodger among those slightly more fortunate than he. Elizabeth took the children and moved to Petaluma, a rural town north of San Francisco. There, for six dollars a month, they settled into a cottage devoid of gas and electricity. The running water was cold, but the kids hardly minded because the bathtub was unconnected. Elizabeth used it to store potatoes. By then Vincent had earned his first day's pay, a dollar for cleaning old bricks. He gave the money to his mother.

Petaluma was a happy interlude for Elizabeth. Surrounded by her brood of healthy little barbarians, she was freed from Pat and from the string of pregnancies which, with time, starchy foods, and beer, encased her once thin young frame in excess flesh. She raised her own chickens, much as her mother had in County Cork, and a few heads of cabbage too. Pat sent what money he could and occasionally arrived with bags of good, used clothes from a wealthy German, who had befriended the family since the cable-car days, when Pat used to save him an indoor seat on wet mornings.

At age twelve Vincent became a sustaining family member, a role he was destined to fill and expanded for over seventy years and four generations. It began humbly enough at the J. A. McAllister grocery store for $1.50 a week in 1909. After school he delivered the groceries on the run until his legs grew long enough to ride the red delivery bike. In the summers he worked all day, every day except Sunday, but for exactly the same pay. Each Saturday night Vincent received his $1.50 and all he could carry from among the produce that would spoil by Monday morning. "I always got the biggest box they had. The more it hurt my shoulder, the happier I was." Once he even dragged a packing crate most of the two miles home. "McAllister exploited me but if he fired me, I would have committed suicide."

As each child reached school age Elizabeth would take another trip over to the Sisters of Charity at St. Vincent's Academy even though the public school was closer and free. Vincent entered all the school and parish-related activities as naturally as all the other students. He served at mass, distinguished himself in all his subjects, and, in the eighth grade, he published his first poem. The occasion was the restoration of a local adobe structure dating from California's Spanish period. He celebrated the event with "Sonoma's Old Adobe," a seven-stanza blend of history, nature, and romance.

The photograph that appeared with his complete work in the Native Sons of the Golden West magazine showed him as small, sturdy, and resolute. He was dressed well in a white shirt, his confirmation tie, and a dark suit; undoubtedly they were hand-me-downs from Pat's benefactor. His first published work showed a mastery of meter and rhyme and its sixty lines suggested an orderly and sensitive mind.

The nuns told Elizabeth that her boy was brilliant and

that he should continue on for as much education as possible. Sister Emerenciana suggested Saint Ignatius in San Francisco, but Elizabeth stayed in Petaluma until a local factory owner offered Vincent full-time employment. Under the threat of wasting her son's life at factory work, Elizabeth returned to Pat and San Francisco.

On July 30, 1912, the stalwart J. A. McAllister handed his best worker the same $1.50 he had earned every week for three years. Without any smile or show of warmth he also slid an unfolded letter across the counter. As sparing with words as with cash, the Scotsman recommended Hallinan as "a steady, willing and consciencious [sic] worker."

Vincent Hallinan passed the bulk of his formative years in the care of the Society of Jesus at St. Ignatius: three years in high school, then the B.A. and LL.B. degrees from the college and law school. He entered as a pugnacious and precocious boy and left as a man confident in his destiny. Those intervening years were normal and happy, if extremely active.

Hallinan got along very well with his teachers. They respected him as a manly fellow free of those "bad habits" prefects of discipline constantly looked for. He won the perpetual mathematics medal so often that Mr. Louis O'Brien, the Jesuit Scholastic who taught the class all subjects, gave him the medal to keep.

He knew all the answers and won the highest grades in religion class. He wrote clearly, logically, and forcefully. Next to poetry and fist fighting, oratory became his greatest love.

In Golden Gate Park he listened to florid old Irishmen sprinkle their St. Patrick's Day orations with snatches of poetry. When the English executed another young rebel, Kevin Barry, Hallinan stepped confidently into the Irish poetic tradition. He gave honor and glory to the boy who died so that Ireland could be free.

> Who sat with you through that dreary night,
>   Boy with soul of flame——?
> That night when the sentry's footsteps fell

> Like death notes rung on the tocsin bell,
> And you waited and watched in a prison cell
>   Till the dread morning came?
>
> Did Wolfe Tone stand beside your cot,
>   And Connelly's murdered shade?
> Came Lucan's soul across the wave;
> Did Emmet speak for the vanished brave,
> Or Pearse from the sleep of a quick lime grave
>   To tell you "Be unafraid!"
>
> When the dread morning called you forth;
>   Oh, lad, so proud and fair!
> Did they whisper a comrade's last good bye;
> Did they point to the softening eastern sky
> Beyond where the gallows lifted high
>   And say, "We shall meet you there."?

Emotional nationalism aside, Hallinan learned one permanent lesson from these Irish men of words. They convinced him that the heart, not the mind, was the surest of targets. If Vincent strained logic and credulity too, he began not to care. Tears, laughter, and sympathy for a cause — these became his imperatives.

The premier event of Hallinan's nine Jesuit years, he always remembered vividly. It was Hallinan vs. the "Greek." No one recalled how his opponent, the son of an Italian fish dealer, acquired the misnomer. Hallinan was a small youngster made strong by work. Heartiness and daring preserved him from beatings to which his propensity for physical violence seemed so frequently to propel him.

When the Greek, a powerful upper-classman and the school bully, amused himself and his hangers-on by cuffing around little "Ducky" O'Connor, Hallinan reacted characteristically. He rushed the Greek and landed a solid punch on his jaw. Outraged and astounded, the big fellow growled, "You son of a bitch! You know I'll get expelled if I get in another fight. I'll see you in the park at noon!"

The shock wave spread quickly through the school but the excitement at the prospect of witnessing its culmination was not shared by Vincent's friends. Their sole concern was to prevent the fight. Not only had Vincent no chance, but the Greek, who was three inches taller and thirty pounds heavier, might hurt him badly.

Hallinan brushed aside their concerns with a defiant, "I'm not afraid of him!" Finally, an upper-class boy who had boxed at his father's club intervened.

The hasty lesson that ensued assumed that the Greek, still enraged and confident of an easy victory, would rush his smaller foe and make himself an excellent mark for a straight left. The assumption proved prophetic when the whole student body assembled in Golden Gate Park for what promised to be an unequal but interesting scrap.

Scarcely had they shed their coats when the Greek rushed Hallinan to finish the fight with a single rain of blows. Vincent, having braced himself firmly, put his whole weight behind a classic left jab which caught the Greek full on his nose. As if only fired further by this insult, the big fellow hurled himself forward again only to collide with the same blow. This time, as he recoiled, a flow of blood from his nostrils brought a cheer of mingled surprise and elation from the crowd of spectators, redoubled when a third charge brought more blood. Now Vincent pressed ahead, scoring again and again while blocking or evading the Greek's powerful but clumsy blows. In desperation, the Greek seized him, trying to change the format to a wrestling match, but the upper-classmen broke his grasp and warned him to fight fairly. What followed, however, was anything but fair to the Greek. Boys he had bullied took advantage of the occasion to kick, trip or shove him.

Exhausted, and bleeding, the Greek received the coup de grace from a spectator. From the overhanging tree a freshman member of the Sanctuary Society urinated on him. At that, the crowd broke up the scrap and hailed Vincent as the victor. Tradition thereafter enshrined "Hallinan vs. the Greek" as the classic of Ignatian fist fights.

On the athletic field Hallinan was not among the swift; he was just the most enduring. At rugby and football he played the whole game and usually stayed to kick the ball around with the little boys who admired his uniform. To compensate for his lack of size and speed, he figured things out in advance, "scientific-like," not caring what people thought about his novel expedients. On President's Day no classmate would enter the mile run against two local champions. The bronze medal looked good to him hanging on its red and blue ribbon so he signed up for the event. Since he was the third and final entrant, the stars lapped him, but he brought home a nice prize. Instead of humiliation, he earned respect. He, not the first- and second-place winners, earned the most good-natured applause. "People can go for the underdog. If you give them a show, they'll remember you."

Hallinan was in both the last rugby game and the first football game ever played at St. Ignatius College, the future University of San Francisco, but his most notable distinction was the ability to survive any game until the gun ended the carnage. Occasionally his team beat the one from Davis Farm. (Davis Farm later became a campus of the University of California.) The Ignatians regularly brawled themselves to close losses at the hands of Santa Clara, their rival Jesuit college down in the valley near San Jose. For those intra-faith bloodlettings the rules for football were as easily suspended as those for rugby. Sports were rough but innocent then. The big stadiums were for the future. And fun could be had by anyone crazy enough to wear a soft leather helmet and a shirt with extra cotton sewed around the shoulders.

Hallinan's spiritual life passed almost unnoticed at St. Ignatius. He did belong to the Sodality of the Immaculate Conception and pious classmates recalled that he availed himself of early dismissal with those who wished to make their confessions on the eve of First Fridays.

Privately, Hallinan even considered the priesthood, only he received none of the encouragements that the younger Jesuits dispensed to their selectees. While he was moral enough, his strange unpredictability, his impetuosity, made him unacceptable. He was, the prefect of discipline confided to an inquisitive neighbor, "a sort of crazy genius."

The priests chose him to edit the *Ignatian* during his last two years in college even though it normally was a one-year assignment. During his tenure he expanded the literary portion of the combined magazine, yearbook, and school paper; he improved the quality of its physical appearance; and he placed the publication on a secure financial footing. After graduation, just as after football games, he stayed around; he accepted an assistant editorship as younger students assumed the role of editor. He liked the work and liked being around. All the while he continued writing news, poems, and short stories; some he composed on the way to the printer just to prevent a page from remaining blank.

World War I was the first event to puncture the insulating cocoon of Hallinan's Irish Catholic world. He grew up hating England for what she had always done to Ireland. Yet, in 1917 President Woodrow Wilson brought the United States into the war on the side of the British Empire. Beset by conflicting loyalties, Hallinan rode both horns of the Irish-American dilemma, careful not to get gored himself. He patriotically called for full support of the war by college men and denounced the slackers as "renegades." At the same time he joined in smuggling guns to the Old Country, so Irish rebels could kill English soldiers.

When his own prospects of being drafted to fight on England's side appeared probable, he joined the navy, the service least likely to shoot Germans. Additionally, he signed up for a series of training schools that he cautiously figured would outlast the war. They did. In effect, he missed all college classes during the fall term of 1918 but he passed the examinations anyway. He also missed the war.

Studying law became his new obsession. It promised money for the family and excitement for him. In his junior year in college he enrolled concurrently in night law classes where instruction was informal, offered part-time by practicing attorneys. The students, like Hallinan, came from working-class families and recognized law as their best chance to move up.

Hallinan's doubts about the adequacy of the training prompted him to look beyond the classroom for actual experience. For his tutor he chose carefully and well.

Daniel A. Ryan was a politically active and experienced

lawyer. Vincent read about him in the papers and watched him in court before he pushed his way into Ryan's office and asked for work. Hallinan was likeable and after a while at clerical work, he was allowed to try Ryan's minor justice court cases. There one did not have to be an actual attorney to speak for people. Ryan also let Hallinan sit with him at the defense table when he handled major cases in the superior courts. He shared his trial tricks with his eager young pupil and explained basic psychology, human nature, and the real interests behind the legal puffery. Ryan paid him forty dollars a month and threw in the education for free.

Admission to legal practice in California before 1919 had been a rather casual affair. In rural counties a judge would question a young aspirant on law he had read under the erratic supervision of some local attorney. Not infrequently, admission to the bar was a virtual gift presented on the applicant's twenty-first birthday, age being the only absolute requirement. In San Francisco the judges gave written exams that were hardly more rigorous. After World War I the California Bar Association assumed responsibility and held the state's first written examination. Since the obvious purpose was to tighten up the monopoly, Hallinan's fellow students despaired.

Made confident by having passed college and law school exams without having attended the courses, Hallinan disagreed. He thought that the public controversy surrounding the shift made the state bar appear self-serving. He said nothing and signed up with the correct assessment that the first examinations would be more than fair. On February 11, 1920, he and his friends saw his name on the list of those who were admitted to California practice. It was the first anyone knew that he had taken the test.

That evening at probate class Mr. William Breen smiled warmly. "Good evening, counselor. Would you begin the discussion of the California statutes on *causa mortis* gifts?"

Everyone laughed and congratulated him on his success, even Breen, who gave him a D in the course for poor attendance. Hallinan was pleased by his coup, passing the bar before completing law school. He was also smart enough to understand that he really did not know very much law. He decided to stick close to Ryan for a while, even though a rival firm offered him three hundred dollars a month for the same work.

Between evictions, dog bites, rumpled fenders, and drunks, Hallinan watched and learned, not just from Ryan, but from a fading generation of men, not a few of whom lived as much by their wits as their learning. Jimmy Carroll, a San Francisco legend, was one.

He was obviously not an accredited lawyer but practiced as one and no one cared. Jimmy may never even have studied law. When a suspicious young assistant district attorney asked him to repeat the case citations he so glibly offered to support a disputed point, Carroll brushed him aside. "Never mind, son. . . . It won't do you no good to look in those books. There are no pictures in them." Nearly blind from years as a fighter, the shadowy Jimmy subsisted on half of the cash in the pockets of persons arrested for minor infractions of the law. The other half he offered to the arresting officer if he would change his story. When the police would not co operate, Carroll would return his client's money and advise him to obtain other counsel. Carroll and a score of more circumspect men were the lawyers who created the environment from which Hallinan began his own career.

When they were prepared, these men could cut down smarter opponents. Too often, though, even the quick-witted Ryan entered court without adequate research and investigation. Hallinan's own preference was to bury even the dog-bite cases in facts, laws, witnesses, and experts. At first, he overprepared to compensate for inexperience. Because he won, he kept it up the rest of his life. Thus began what was to become an enviable record and an awesome reputation in both civil and criminal law. For being a continuous celebrity, for his success with unpopular cases and clients, and for the sheer duration of his central position in the courts he has no American equal. His criminal defenses brought him fame and hatred.

Money came primarily in civil actions and it came immediately and plentifully. Hallinan promptly purchased a two-story, eight-room house in the respectable middle-class neighborhood near Haight and Ashbury streets. He stuffed it with rugs and furniture from fashionable Sloane's, with one of those new radios, and then a victrola. Annie was twenty-eight, Patricia was six, and everyone was still at home with Pat and Elizabeth. As they drove away from the old flat in Vincent's "new" used car, he promised his mother that the weeks at $1.50 and all the spoiling produce they could eat were gone forever. They were rich now and he would never let them be anything else again.

Elizabeth's response revealed the psychological defense mechanism that had sustained her through hard times. "Why, Vincent," she said, "we've never been poor."

Pat was realistic. He celebrated his son's good fortune by telling his foreman what he could do with the old wagon, and with the nag that pulled it too. From moving day until his death at age eighty-eight, Pat devoted himself mostly to poetry, prayer, and just puttering.

"This was the worst case of legal lynching I ever saw through sixty years of active trial practice."

— Vincent Hallinan
July 13, 1979

3. The First Big One: The Windmill Murder Case, 1925

Earning money never constituted a problem for Hallinan even at the start of his legal career. Vince quickly discovered that he could not accept every case that made its way up the steps, even on a regular workweek of seventy-two hours. Early and resolutely he decided, "I'm in this business to make money." Years later, he admitted, ". . . if there was a chance for a great amount, I wasn't too concerned back then about . . . morality or ethics. . . ."

At the same time he could not kill the soft spot that made him accept cases of limited or no value when the person was right and in need. He was particularly vulnerable to Old Country Irish laborers who sustained physical injuries, all the more so when they had a flat full of children and otherwise reminded him of his father and his own family situation. During the height of Hallinan's unpopular years, those old retirees offered quiet, but enduring testimonials to the man who had settled their claims and then threw them out when they asked for his bill. Patrons of San Francisco's saloons and parish vestibules learned that if Hallinan did not extract cash or your signature in advance, anything he won would be yours.

31

As the years passed he assumed more work without fee or for token amounts, mixed occasionally with extraordinary settlements. Civil cases, particularly the personal injury suits, launched Hallinan's career. In most cases the clients needed no cash to put up but had to agree to share the settlement, if he got one for them. Usually he earned one-third for cases of ordinary complexity, and one-half for the difficult or expensive ones. Hallinan and client either won or lost together. When he failed to deliver a verdict, they got nothing, and he lost his time and expenses. But he usually won. Besides the money, he earned a reputation for challenging powerful interests that corrupted the courts for private gain.

These civil cases could have kept him active for an entire legal career, and at the end certainly Hallinan would have little to regret and nothing for which to apologize. Yet, they could not hold his restless attention. He liked the money that the civil actions brought, but he craved excitement.

The spring of 1925 brought the first of what was to grow into a life-long list of spectacular criminal cases, mostly murders. Hallinan's real debut, the Windmill Murder Case, was a nightmare rather than a coming-out party.

Early that year the San Francisco papers had dispatched reporters to Hanford, California, a dusty agricultural community down in the Central Valley where a young rancher named Lee Camp had fallen to his death. He had been working on the roof of a tank house dismantling the windmill machinery when he apparently lost his footing and slid off. There was no hint of foul play, as the accident took place before noon on a Sunday morning adjacent to a well-traveled road. Camp's foster-mother, Jenny Laura Brown, was grief-stricken and others at the ranch were visibly shaken. The coroner's jury ruled that his unfortunate death had been accidental.

Camp's will subsequently disclosed, however, that his life had been inordinately insured, with some policies including double indemnity clauses for accidental death. Camp left the entirety of his estate to Mrs. Brown, except for a five-dollar bequest to his estranged sister, Pearl Camp King, who resided in the community.

Normally, nothing so exciting happened in the stifling, hot little town and the disclosure of the estate prompted gossip to spread like dust clouds. The insurance companies ceased paying off and dispatched a detective who helped reopen the case. Camp's sister promptly challenged his will. Murder dominated town talk. And the local paper for once celebrated a home-grown sensation worthy of its established fixation for violent crime and legal actions. The rural county grand jury responded by indicting not just Mrs. Brown for the murder of Lee Camp, but everyone who lived on the ranch except her invalid husband. This included the foreman, a teenage boy the Browns were bringing up, and Mrs. Brown's uncle, Johnny Tipton.

Tipton had moved down from San Francisco to be with his niece after her husband's stroke, earning his keep as a ranch mechanic. His advancing years did not reduce his general awareness at all. He determined quickly enough from the questions put to him before the grand jury that he needed some legal help, only he did not know any lawyers, particularly around Hanford. One of his San Francisco friends, Tim Kelly, who happened to be the Hallinans' milkman, brought Tipton and Elizabeth's son, the lawyer, together.

Since Hallinan did not believe the newspaper accounts and could not free himself from scheduled court appearances, he sent his associate and friend, Melvin I. Cronin, to Hanford to find out precisely what was going on. As a favor to Vince, Cronin took Pat Hallinan along. Vince wanted his father to have a little trip as much for his own amusement as for Elizabeth's relief. Pat had been a relatively steady, though hardly abundant, provider during his working years. Retired and with little to do, he was difficult. In any case, Cronin did not mind the company.

In Hanford the two incongruous city slickers tagged along to the Brown ranch and closely watched the grand jurors examine the death scene. To their surprise, neither the district attorney nor the foreman of the grand jury was in charge. Instead, a stranger named Hamilton Fields seemed to be managing things. He was an agency detective who was retained by one of the insurance companies. When Cronin and Pat Hallinan reported the details back to Vince, he immediately realized that the grand jury had seriously violated proper legal procedure. Not only should Fields not have conducted the session, neither he nor Hallinan's emissaries should have been present. That they were, however, assisted the defense because it specifically violated California law.

In early May, Hallinan entrained for Hanford alone, armed with affidavits from Cronin and his father, a briefcase full of case citations, and the pertinent code covering grand jury proceedings. In the morning he met with the four local lawyers retained for the other three co-defendants only to discover that none of them understood that the indictment was improper and contrary to California law. It was news to them all. Concerned that they would be the senior members of the impending defense team, Hallinan asked them to join in his motion that the entire murder indictment be set aside, a move that they gladly joined.

These country lawyers were all older men apparently used to a slower pace of a rural county court system, unfamiliar with the law in the case itself, and insufficiently energetic to have read up on it before being retained. Only one of his new-found associates, J. C. C. Russell, appeared interesting, and less for his legal acumen than for his exceptionally handsome young daughter, Mercedes. So when Mr. and Mrs. Russell hospitably insisted that the city boy stay with them for the duration, how could he refuse?

Hallinan's instant adjustment to the amenities of small-town life turned to culture shock on the first day in court, however, as he tried to explain to the judge, K. Van Zante, how the indictment was contrary to law. Before finishing with the impropriety of the grand jury, Hallinan added that its transcript amounted to a "mess of suspicion, a monumental malice and a monumental ignorance." As a record, the document only disclosed that Lee Camp was dead. The only relevant evidence it contained showed that the respected and experienced University of California criminologist, Edward Oscar Heinrich, maintained that death was accidental. Van Zante calmly took it all in, then turned to the attentive and equally youthful district attorney, William R. McKay, and asked him what he thought of Hallinan's motion for dismissal.

The mild mannered schoolteacher-turned-prosecutor asserted that the grand jury session that the outsiders attended was not actually "in session" and therefore did not have to be secret. He disagreed on the role detective Fields played and argued that the presence of the outsiders presented no irregularity. Therefore, the indictment was proper. To illustrate his contention that the meeting at the death site was informal McKay maintained that he and the jury reporter arrived a half-hour after the grand jurors.

Hallinan did not expect that even an inexperienced district attorney would agree and join in his dismissal motion. As he prepared to rebut McKay's argument, Hallinan got his first surprise of the case, one that terminated any apprehension the young out-of-towner may have had about being alone among weak co-counsels. John F. Pryor, a slight man bordering on middle age, unexpectedly demanded that McKay cite from the grand jury transcript where it said he arrived late. When the district attorney failed to respond to his inquiry, Pryor actually hit him in the mouth with the heavy transcript and drew blood. Hallinan hardly shared Pryor's depth of feeling, at least not yet, but his solidarity with the defense prevented him from interfering, even when Pryor followed up by throwing a brick-like law book at McKay.

By that time the sheriff intervened and, in the ensuing scuffle, knocked the attorney's glasses off and cut his face. Restrained and forcibly reseated near Hallinan, Pryor reached for another book but the sheriff and bailiff both held him back. This was the same man who, before Hallinan entered the case, seemed unaware of precisely how the grand jury was supposed to conduct itself.

Besides Hallinan, the second stranger in town for the big event was a former Alameda County prosecutor named Preston Higgins. Hallinan had never heard of the man before he swung down off the train from Oakland but after that he never forgot him. He was brought in as a special prosecutor to supersede the regular district attorney for the trial. To the still impressionable Hallinan, Higgins became a life-long symbol of the loathsome prosecutor hell-bent on conviction despite the rules of evidence and despite decency itself.

Higgins displayed a confidence based on a personal history of sixty-six convictions blemished by only one acquittal. He was proud of that record and had come back out of private practice in order to extend it by one more guilty verdict. Immediately he met the local reporter and informed the news-conscious townsfolk that Hanford had been doubly victimized, once by unpunished criminals and then by defense attorneys. Those "certain attorneys" were the "malefactors" that Special Prosecutor Higgins was intent on "squashing."

Slightly amused to read this, Hallinan wondered if he were included among such abusers of Hanford even though he had never heard of the place until his mother's milkman mentioned it. The interview left Hallinan wondering precisely what interests Higgins actually represented.

Hallinan was twenty-eight years old and while his police court experience represented a valuable bonus, still he was only five years away from having passed the California Bar. The other men had never taken a written examination but enjoyed, nevertheless, well-established local reputations. Their success, Hallinan quickly concluded, rested on their close identity with a small town clientele and an innate sharpness of intellect, rather than a thorough grasp of the rules of law and legal technicalities. This time his colleagues were definitely out of their domain.

The older men initially assigned Vincent the task of offering objections to inadmissible testimony and to the alarming misconduct of the special prosecutor. Though they first thought his youth made him a bit green, his knowledgeable initiative in the pre-trial motion for dismissal encouraged them sufficiently to assign him the responsibility of the major defense motions for the entire trial. Besides these, Hallinan delicately assumed one more chore, the instruction of his senior colleagues in the legal refinements bearing upon a murder case. Throughout, he deferred naturally to their seniority and treated them with the politeness he normally reserved for older men and thereby succeeded in not arousing ill will. He taught by example rather than proclamation so the relationship developed into one of easy collegiality.

As the trial progressed, all patronizing thoughts about a greenhorn turned to wide-eyed astonishment as Hallinan incessantly objected to the prosecutor's evidence, regularly on technical grounds with which the others often had been quite unaware. Always he offered lists of cases and laws to support his objections.

Their antagonist, Special Prosecutor Higgins, was an interesting though entirely different type of attorney. Outside the courtroom Higgins appeared to be quite personable. He looked to be about ten years older than Hallinan, in his late thirties, certainly no more than forty. Stocky and handsome with a wavy head of hair, he had the appealing looks of a mellowing All-American. But once the judge gaveled court to order he became altogether transformed.

A rather basic problem directly confronted Higgins as special prosecutor. Even though an atmosphere of lynch law prevailed which proclaimed guilt and prompted a hanging, no crime had actually been committed. Nor did the prosecution have anyone sufficiently willing to perjure himself by claiming to have witnessed one. Higgins overcame this disadvantage by opening the case with an inflammatory eruption. He simply assumed murder, then spread guilt by insinuation through a succession of witnesses who offered hearsay evidence over Hallinan's objections. The court, in reversible error, overruled every single objection and sustained the prosecution on all points. This was a situation Hallinan had not encountered even in fixed cases up in San Francisco.

Going a step farther for Higgins, Judge Van Zante

silenced the objections of all five defense counsels until the
prosecutor had finished and thus had made his full impact
upon the jury. Only then did the court entertain cumulative
objections. The judge refused altogether Hallinan's arguments on the issues that he had prepared and was unconcerned with Hallinan's citations of law and analogous cases.

Van Zante himself was rather new to the bench and
quite deficient in formal legal education. The son of Dutch
immigrants, he had acquired his initial exposure to the law
as a traveling salesman for a law book publishing house. A
correspondence course augmented his meager training of
half of a year at law school. But qualified or not, he presided
over Kings County Superior Court by virtue of popular
election.

The deceased's sister, Pearl Camp King, was the first star
witness Higgins brought before Van Zante's court. She and
her brother, Lee, had been abandoned as infants in Hanford.
After their first adoptive parents died, the Browns took them
in. That was around 1900 when both were still small children. Higgins alleged that Mr. and Mrs. Brown were motivated not by sympathy and kindness but by desire to exploit
the waifs. If that were not enough, he accused Jenny Brown
of having tried to kill Pearl by feeding her phonograph
needles and mercury-laced breakfast cereal. When those
bizarre ploys failed, she tried to work the girl to death. At
least that was Pearl's testimony against the heir to her
brother's substantial estate.

Sex found its way into the prosecution scenario too. The
prosecution claimed that as Lee matured, Mrs. Brown traded
the joys of his childhood for the pleasures of her adultery.
The inevitable crisis arose when he reached the age of thirty-
four, at which time she conspired in his murder, the prosecution maintained, because he was becoming serious about a
young girl from the neighboring farm. If they married, Lee
undoubtedly would substitute his wife for his adoptive
mother as his chief beneficiary. By 1925 his ample estate
consisted of an estimated $80,000 in real property, as well
as $130,000 in insurance policies.

Throughout this recitation defense exasperation built to the point of explosion. To no avail Hallinan objected to the remarks as prejudicial to the rights of the accused and assigned misconduct to the prosecution. The one time he was allowed to do so, he heatedly argued an objection for forty minutes, meticulously listing the cases in support of the defense position. Hallinan again astounded his co-counsel by basing his argument for the inadmissibility of evidence on the ground that Higgins "failed to show that the defendants knew anything about such evidence." Hallinan observed that Camp's insurance meant nothing to defendants who remained unaware of its existence and magnitude.

He was well-prepared and also overruled. At that point Hallinan decided to be more emphatic with Van Zante. No *corpus delicti* had been established. No evidence of a crime had been entered, yet the court was accepting hearsay evidence, prejudicial statements of guilt over persistent defense objections. This was, Hallinan concluded, a "travesty on judicial procedure."

His direct approach got him nowhere.

The next thing Hallinan knew, he was back in his chair, pushed there by his excitable associate, Pryor. He liked and respected the man and did not even object to the shove, particularly when he heard Pryor demand of Van Zante, "Does the court know the law?"

Before the mildly stunned jurist could respond, Hallinan bounced back up to assign "the court's prejudicial misconduct."

The temperature in Hanford climbed to ninety-six and would reach one hundred and four before the jury reached a verdict. Inside the courthouse Van Zante reconsidered, ordered a recess, and perused Hallinan's citations while the defense counsels smoldered. By that time the prosecution and the court had been charged with misconduct. The judge's professional competence had been questioned and Hallinan had been warned by Van Zante about his aggressive behavior, a normal preliminary before an attorney is cited for contempt of court. The only ones who seemed to enjoy the

whole event were the three-hundred spectators compressed
into the large but stifling upstairs courtroom. They were
watching the best show in town.

The unrelenting, arid heat did not bother Hallinan as
much as it did the others. He sported a fashionable bow tie
and maintained his outward expression of respect for the
court by wearing his suit coat at all times. The other attorneys came to court similarly attired but by ten o'clock every
morning had discarded what they could in a futile search for
physical relief.

As the weeks melted into months the initial hostility of
the special prosecutor compounded the community's
assumption of guilt. Defense efforts responded by concentrating on building a strong appeal record for what appeared
to be an inevitable conviction. Hallinan did not disagree at
all with the prospects but his basic legal metabolism, abetted
by the energy of youth, required more of himself.

His chance came when Higgins entered into evidence a
letter which threatened a Catholic family living near the
Brown ranch. Their daughter supposedly was the girl Camp
intended to marry. The document itself had been signed,
"KKK," and was delivered at a time when the Ku Klux Klan
experienced its national revival and exhibited sporadic
activity in California. The prosecution's handwriting expert,
however, attributed the letter not to the reconstituted forces
of bigotry, but to Mrs. Brown. The graphologist was
Chauncey McGovern, a court-wise professional who held up
so well under cross-examination that, in disgust, senior co-
counsel relinquished him to the resourceful young San
Franciscan.

First, Hallinan moved to the window hoping to catch a
draft of fresh air, but there was none. Unrefreshed, he turned
back on McGovern, a man about whom he already knew
something. Hallinan had consulted the expert once before
in San Francisco concerning a document from an earlier
case. He remembered that "the first thing McGovern asked
me when I walked into his office, before he even looked at my
document, was 'Whose side are you on?'" The professional

wanted to know the relationship between his employer and his testimony. Now Hallinan had him on the stand so he probed him with a few questions about how much he was being paid by the prosecution for his testimony.

Fifty dollars a day plus expenses, he said.

Then came the knife. "Isn't it a fact," Hallinan twisted, "that if you had been offered seventy-five dollars by the defense, you would have testified that the letter was not written by Mrs. Brown?"

McGovern's professional veneer blistered with a yell, "That's a lie!" Hallinan suspected from the appearances of the jurors that most of the twelve men had never seen that much cash money in their lives, so he certainly was not hurting the defense any. Besides, he was getting McGovern's goat so he persisted.

The angry objections from Higgins also helped. They spread smiles down the length of the defense table for the first time since the trial began. And getting a kick out of McGovern's discomfort, he pushed in a little deeper.

"Isn't it a fact," he asked the expert, "that you are employed and being paid by an insurance company, the same as Prosecutor Higgins?"

Higgins's anger turned to outright rage. He called Hallinan a damned liar and McGovern parroted it even louder. Neither of the two persisted in the corridor during recess however. McGovern knew Hallinan's reputation for personal settlements of such disputes and tried to drop the matter. To avoid being slugged he apologized in front of the reporters. Hallinan's rejoinder ("Stick it up your ass, fatso!") never made the Hanford paper though.

The *Morning Journal* admired Higgins's master plan; it liked the way he was "forging the links in the chain of circumstantial evidence . . . to bring about a conviction." When confronted with Hallinan's objections to what was a chain of hearsay, gossip, and other normally inadmissible testimony, Higgins argued that what he introduced was for the purpose of showing motive, design, and conditions at the Brown ranch at the time Camp died. For accepting this argument and allowing the trial to continue along this line, Judge Van Zante was later cited for judicial error.

Incapable of letting the case run its course, Hallinan prepared a five-part omnibus motion over an extended week-end recess during which the district attorney was married. He had the motion ready when Higgins rested his case. The first four parts struck at major sections of the prosecution case and were based upon the same grounds as his regular objections. The last part moved that all testimony whatsoever be stricken from the record on the grounds that the *corpus delicti* had not been proven and that the prosecution had not shown that Lee Camp had been murdered or that any crime had been committed. Hallinan concluded that "all evidence submitted tends to prove the contentions of the defense. It was an accident."

Long before the prosecution rested, the defense lawyers abandoned their initial impression that Hallinan was a young greenhorn. Instead they conceded to him on all legal points. Yet they knew the Hanford court. As they predicted, Van Zante listened and shook his head. By denying Hallinan's motion, the court shifted the burden of proof to the defense. Van Zante now required Hallinan and his senior colleagues to prove that no crime had taken place.

From the start of the trial, the court and the pervasive atmosphere had been unfriendly. By mid-trial the element of intimidation became manifest. After the introduction of the Klan letter, rumors of lynching surfaced. Whenever Hallinan became separated from the Russells, the locals sized him up, undoubtedly wondering if he would be as truculent alone behind the corner filling station as he was before the crowded Hanford court. The sense of personal threat prompted Hallinan to stick close and to formulate his Hanford street strategy. He walked mid-way between the opened doorways and curbed automobiles, and he kept his hands free.

Hallinan was a city boy beset for the first time by the paradoxes of small-town life. Russell and his family represented open-armed personal acceptance and all that was warm and fine in the community. The specter of the Klan represented the opposite extreme. In between, he concluded, was "a whole lousy town filled with hatred for defendants who had never done any of those people any harm."

Undoubtedly small-town America had its impressions of Hallinan too. In the middle of the roaring twenties, he was all too visible an example of what repelled an older, nativist America. He was young and handsome, from immigrant stock, a fast thinker and articulate speaker. He dressed smartly, obviously had cash in his pocket, and could look forward to the new urban America, which certainly had a place for him and his kind. Already he bore the cast of the city. He had attended Catholic schools as a boy. Unmarried at twenty-eight, he probably practiced free love when he could get away with it. Most galling of all, his success with the girls followed from these very attributes that prompted the townsfolk's enmity.

The defense called its first witness, R. L. Boyd, who owned a filling station not far from the Brown ranch. The co-counsel carefully developed Boyd's testimony in order to counter specific prosecution allegations and, in doing so, asked Boyd to relate a conversation he had had with Camp before the latter's death. Immediately Higgins objected to this as hearsay, the very grounds Hallinan used unsuccessfully to object to Higgins's entire case.

Judge Van Zante sustained the objection! The defense was not allowed to offer testimony identical in character to that placed before the jury by the prosecution.

Hallinan exploded for the first time in what was to become a celebrated career of eruptions at major trials. Van Zante ordered him seated, and when he persisted, the judge restated his order with a renewed threat of a contempt citation. Unperturbed and still standing, Hallinan pointed his finger at Van Zante, saying, "I assign misconduct of the court," a statement destined to fall often from his lips at critical moments in the many years ahead.

If the prosecution could enter hearsay, he protested, it was unjust to deny the defendants equal rights. He evaded the contempt citation but got nowhere with his protestation. The only tangible result was increased spectator hostility.

All attempts for evenhanded treatment having failed,

the defense pushed on through its other witnesses as best they could, thwarted at every significant point. They rested their case with Professor Heinrich, the Berkeley criminologist, who was not permitted by the court to state the conclusion of his study, which the prosecution had commissioned, that Camp died accidentally by falling off the tank-house roof.

Intimidated by the special prosecutor's brazen misconduct, which the judge sustained, the local attorneys reconciled themselves to efficient compilation of a strong appeal record. Not Hallinan. He had to go all out for his client, old man Tipton. Perhaps Higgins first convinced himself that he was simply performing a required public duty by advocating guilt, about which a jury would decide, and then he got carried away. But Hallinan saw too many little signs that suggested a far worse conclusion. If this were a true conspiracy to commit murder, why would so many diverse people be involved? Why would Mrs. Brown drag in a teenage boy? Higgins had been around longer than Hallinan and should have asked himself that too. Worst of all, if it were a conspiracy of four, why did the special prosecutor not offer each of them immunity from prosecution in exchange for direct testimony against the other three? Not only did this not happen, the four accused became united in their unarticulated courage. Hallinan sensed what he later considered absolute: there never was a conspiracy of four people in which one of them did not turn state's evidence.

Hallinan decided to do more than build an appeal record for another reason. At this stage of his life his loves and hates were very personal things that guided his behavior every bit as much as principles. In Hanford, Higgins kept him from throwing in the towel because he came to despise the special prosecutor. "Higgins was an abuse I couldn't stomach. He perverted justice with the complicity of a marginally competent court, and together they were hanging my client."

During his rebuttal, which followed the defense witnesses and preceded the final arguments to the jury, Higgins acted improperly again by reopening his own case in a particularly vicious manner. He brought in new testimony on entirely untreated aspects of the case. With a new witness he smeared Hallinan's co-counsel by claiming that attorney Brown had visited the ranch at the very time Camp sustained his fatal injuries.

"The prosecution should not be allowed to reopen their case," Hallinan all but yelled. "To do so is manifestly unfair."

Van Zante, unable this time to gavel him into silence, shouted back, "Mr. Hallinan, I don't want any such language from you or any insinuation that this court is unfair."

Hallinan refused to back down and restated his charge, whereupon Van Zante cited him "guilty of contempt of court for continually talking back!"

In the studied terms that were to be repeated in celebrated cases of each decade to come, Hallinan told Van Zante, "I take exception to those statements in the presence of the jury. The court is unfair."

At the start of the case Pryor had questioned the judge's knowledge of the law, and at the end Hallinan repeatedly challenged Van Zante's honor itself. For that the twenty-eight-year-old was found guilty of contempt a second time, a not unanticipated comeuppance, but one that still could not silence him.

He declared, "I am, your honor, going to continue to make any objections which I see fit and am not afraid of any statements or threats of the court." For the first time, but not the last, he refused to remain silent when so instructed by lawful authority gone wrong.

He wondered what he had gotten himself into. At a separate hearing Van Zante gave him the choice between a five-hundred-dollar fine or eight months in jail. He would appeal, but that was like "a mouse complaining to two cats about the way another cat treated him." The San Francisco courts had been tough, sometimes corrupt, but nothing like this. "This was even more raw than the famous case of Tom Mooney, the labor radical. It was," Hallinan believed, "a legal lynching."

His last turn to address the court came following noon

recess. "It was hotter than hell" when he looked at the bulb-nosed Van Zante but still he kept his coat on and even straightened his tie. The older men had covered all the substantive issues and had pinpointed each of the prosecutor's abuses in their own summations, but apparently it meant nothing to the judge. Co-counsel, with their careful chronicles of prosecution deficiencies, appeared to have no impact on the jury either. Their appeal to community fair play likewise was hopeless.

Hallinan decided that he would restate the abuses as they related to Tipton and review the prosecution's evidence in all its weaknesses, particularly in relation to the rules of law and the technicalities that had escaped the older country lawyers. And one thing more. He would make it personal. The special prosecutor had earned the right to be singled out for individual consideration. Hallinan had three hours in which to do it.

He began scorching Higgins for his allusions to Mrs. Brown, the chief defendant, as a "foster-mother for hire." She and her husband had brought up the Camp children and two other foundlings besides. Hallinan asked the special prosecutor not only to apologize to Mrs. Brown and to the court, but to the memory of Lee Camp, above whose body lying in the Hanford cemetery Higgins was raising a "monument of shame."

Hallinan sopped local pride with gratuitous remarks about the popular young district attorney. Even though in his inexperience he abandoned the case to Higgins, Hallinan knew from the events surrounding McKay's wedding that the locals liked their boy. He invested the former country schoolteacher with whatever nobility they thought the District Attorney's Office possessed. He was not a gutless educational product of Stanford and California. No, he was a judicious servant of the people who saw both sides of the case. Higgins? He was something altogether different. Not impartial at all, he was in it for the pay and the ugly gratifications that convictions brought to those employed by special interests. He was the mercenary.

Dramatically, before the hostile but not yet incited throng of incipient lynchers, Hallinan assaulted extra-judicial interests which stood to gain by this conviction but remained in the shadow of their hand-picked accuser. "Did you know," Hallinan asked the jury, "that insurance companies had approached a high-minded attorney to be a special prosecutor who did not believe the accused parties were guilty? And that he indignantly spurned the offer?"

"That attorney," Hallinan announced, "was Frank Curran of Fresno. And this is the case." Curran, of course, had respect in Hanford.

Three hours and ten minutes later the young Hallinan retook his seat. His reasoning had been clear and his grasp of the law and evidence sound. He spoke well, far better than the more seasoned co-counsels who had attained their best years. His summation was the third time over much the same ground, Pryor and Russell having preceded him. Yet, his dramatic and articulate presentation kept everyone attentive, almost mindless of the climbing afternoon mercury. Only protestors left. And at the end his coat remained buttoned and his youthful dignity intact.

Seated, he could claim two satisfactions. He had argued Tipton's case as well as any attorney could. Even if he lost his expense money and the contempt fine along with four pounds to Hanford dehydration, Hallinan knew he could face the milkman on the back steps. He was satisfied that he could not have done better even if Mrs. Brown would pay him for Tipton's defense only after the fact. Also, he had spoken his mind about Higgins and showed the folks how an attorney from the big city went about that indelicate task.

Unknown to himself, Hallinan had set both the groundwork for a successful appeal as well as foolishly offending deep local prejudice. When reviewing the history of wrong convictions based upon circumstantial evidence such as that before the jury, he lingered unnecessarily on the case of Tom Mooney, the San Francisco radical then serving time for bombing a World War I preparedness parade in 1916, a crime he did not commit. Quite obviously the popular mind

that accepted Mooney's conviction in 1917 was duplicated
in Hanford just eight years later. Hallinan's plea for Tipton
in light of Mooney, who was then confined to San Quentin on
perjured testimony, may have been valid but very unwise
given his audience. To those listeners, Mooney deserved what
he got and, therefore, Tipton would deserve it too. In the heat
of the moment Hallinan satisfied his own emotional commitment to justice at a possible cost to his client. If a favorable
verdict had been possible, perhaps he would have been more
circumspect, otherwise this statement could have been a
critical misjudgment.

Those who walked out at Mooney's name departed
almost unnoticed from the press of human flesh. Those who
remained were all but literally on Hallinan's back, crowding
at the barrier, which surrounded an arena rather than a
court of justice. The only person exercising any freedom of
movement seemed to be a vendor surreptitiously dispensing
soda pop to the hot and irritated spectators. Other than him,
Hallinan detected only one calculating mind within the
whole crush. A little boy, maybe six or so, in tattered though
well-washed overalls, sold his front-row seat for a dollar.
Since the prosecution shared its table with a friendly San
Francisco reporter, Hallinan thought of bringing the little
guy up front with him but lost sight of the lad when a woman
fainted and he streaked for her seat next.

A few of the big boys undoubtedly were having a good
time also. Two women, when they emerged from the grasp-
ing pack, screamed hysterically. Their skirts were gone. At a
San Francisco party Hallinan would have enjoyed the laugh,
but the picture here was not so funny.

The junior counsel's summary argument also had permanent and positive results that far outweighed the Mooney
indiscretion. By hitting Higgins where he was soft, Hallinan
provoked from the special prosecutor an uncontrolled reply,
which the appeals court was to cite in its reversal of the
inevitable conviction.

Higgins confirmed the court in its ultimate indignity
in his final argument for conviction, which he actually yelled

at the jury. "I have observed prosecutors of all kinds, in all sorts of cases, and in wide varieties of atmospheres," Hallinan recalled years later. "Some committed felonies in order to obtain their convictions. That day in Hanford I thought it would be impossible ever again for me to witness such a call for innocent blood. Now, with sixty years of trial experience, I can say, in that, I was right. If I believed in the devil, I would say the prosecutor became possessed."

He began by wrapping himself in the glory of American patriotism and local pride and called God down from heaven as his witness. His argument, the appellate court ruled, "bristled with prejudicial insinuation, or worse." It "patently savored of animosity and personal venom."

Higgins could not ignore Hallinan's accusation that an honorable lawyer had spurned the job he grasped for corporate money. Instead he met Hallinan's charge and replied in kind, a reply that the appellate court ruled "was unjustifiable on any ground."

Sarcastically he dismissed the testimony of the chief defendant's crippled husband. Was it any wonder, Higgins snarled, that "Saint Brown" did not see intercourse between his wife and Lee Camp? "That is such a crime that you seldom get any eyewitness to it. Do you believe that carnal relations . . . are practiced in a public court or park while a band is playing and a couple of thousand people are aroused watching it?"

The sudden, hushed attention marked the sweating throng's titillation.

Well before ten that morning Higgins dropped his coat mindlessly over his chair. Already perspiration glued the shirt to his broad back. Before noon he began breathing hard for air in the stifling room. He loosened his necktie, but the redness of his face remained. By afternoon the tie joined candy wrappers and discarded bottles as mounting residue of the event.

"You have the witnesses to this crime," Higgins bellowed in flagrant disregard for the trial record, "and it is time that somebody was brought in." If the jury did not convict someone, Higgins directed Hanford citizens to "prepare to take the law in your own hands."

In his final climax the demagogue turned from the crowd which, in five hours and fifty-five minutes since the opening of his harangue, he had transformed into a seething mob. He ceased his incessant pacing and looked at the jury of humble, unpretentious farmers.

"Now, what are you going to do about it, gentlemen? What are you going to do about it?"

Fatigued and approaching exhaustion from the long hours of excitement, Higgins ended in oratorical orgasm. Hanford's court needed no band to accompany its special prosecutor. In solo he stimulated himself as well as the mob until passion exploded.

It was not a matter of the guilt or innocence of those charged. The lives of Hanford children were now at stake and depended upon a conviction. "Gentlemen," he eased back and whispered, "do your duty and fear no one."

The courtroom went berserk.

Approaching the bench in order to be heard above the roar, Hallinan moved that the courtroom be cleared. But the shouting and foot stamping prevented him even then from being heard. When he penetrated the noise barrier, his motion was denied.

The special prosecutor, spent by the long debauch, languished listlessly in his chair, his castoff garments laying where gravity carried them. Pryor crouched down at the ear of the court reporter and continued to document his assignment of misconduct and error. Hallinan, for the only time in his legal career, was speechless, surrounded as he was by noise and disorder. He did not know if the defendants had heard the rumors of lynching or if they grasped the full meaning of Higgins's suggestion to the mob. But a virtual lifetime later he could still see their faces. "There they were, two old people, a teenage kid, and a simple ranch foreman. All of them frozen to their chairs, frozen in fear. This was our America."

Amidst all of this Van Zante became isolated in chaos.

He had lost physical control of the court until, at last, the San Francisco reporter who stuck so close to Higgins throughout the case restored order by leaping up on top of the prosecution table and, with outstretched arms, quelled the incited rabble.

The judge refused defense demands that he instruct the jury as to the special prosecutor's misconduct. According to the appeals court, "the entire harangue remained with the jury, unqualified, and stamped with the approval of the trial court."

Russell took Hallinan back to his house in town that evening for the special dinner Mercedes had prepared, which neither of them more than picked at. Then they waited in the study for the verdict that could come at any time. As the hours slowly passed and the crowd outside the courthouse swelled, Hallinan decided no mob would lynch any client of his while he stood idly by. Russell, who had been stigmatized by the local paper as "too fat to fight," then proceeded to load two heavy caliber revolvers. Hallinan picked the larger of the two off the desk and Russell pocketed the other. Together and armed they skirted the noisy crowd overflowing the lawn outside and pushed their way back into the upstairs courtroom.

"With that gun in my pocket I didn't think of the Irish. I was too caught up in the impending tragedy, but I could have. We Irish are used to dying in youth, in promise, and in violence. But isn't that what serious protest against injustice is all about? Those prisoners had to be protected no matter what. If the ostensibly unarmed sheriff carried a concealed weapon, he could have stood with me or faded into the mob. It was all the same to me. Besides, how could you slide off this one and let Tipton get lynched to save your own skin? Life isn't worth that."

Near midnight the jury returned a verdict explainable only by the stark reality of intimidation. The entire prosecution rested upon an elaborately contrived theory of conspiracy, yet the jury brought in a conviction for murder in the second degree, murder without premeditation.

The sheriff moved in immediately and ordered the prisoners to their feet as the ashen-faced Tipton whispered pleadingly, "Stay close to me, Vince." Hallinan scanned the holsterless officer's loose-fitting uniform for the tell-tale bulge of a weapon but detected none. With the sheriff in the lead, Hallinan pushed a path for the old man through the courtroom crush and down the stairs. Together they looked out across the expansive lawn, which now separated them from the temporary safety of the jail. It was after midnight but still the townsfolk and those gathered in from the outlying farms stood in solid formation, all for who knew what. The noise ceased as they stepped from the courthouse and came into the clear view of the crowd, but the silence was more deadly than any demonstration. Hallinan walked straight ahead examining the men the way a yet uninvented radar would scan the sky. His left hand tight on Tipton's wrist kept the old-timer moving rapidly in the sheriff's wake. His own right hand remained free as the bounce of Russell's revolver in his hip pocket increased with Tipton's accelerating pulse.

Hate filled the eyes of those whose gaze he met, yet they divided as the sheriff moved into the assemblage, creating a four foot path to the jailhouse door. Apparently the word "guilty" had been enough, even in the second degree. Neither did the acquittal of the teenage boy provoke an attack.

On the train back to San Francisco Hallinan knew that the appeal would be successful and, all in all, he had not fared that poorly. He received no fee as anticipated. He would pay the five hundred dollars rather than go to jail. And he lost three months of remunerative trial work in the city along with his expenses. On the positive side he discovered something insightful about himself. Well before the higher court reversed the conviction and cited Hallinan's initial motion on improper grand jury procedures, he realized just how fortunate he was to be able to return Russell's weapon unused and unnoticed. That incident told him that he would risk everything, including life itself, when an ultimate conviction was at stake.

He also could have fared less well at the hands of Russell. His daughter was a lovely small-town girl who found Hallinan's company pleasant and exciting. When her father produced his revolver collection, Vincent was not unduly worried but still felt relieved when he loaded two weapons rather than just his own.

As the train sped closer toward San Francisco the young Hallinan looked forward longingly to the invigorating summer fog and a night of dancing with city girls whose fathers he intended never to encounter. To save precious time later, he ducked into the men's compartment for a quick shave. He managed it without excessive bloodshed even while scanning a copy of the *Hanford Morning Journal* which had been discarded in the next wash basin. The editorial on page two caught his eye:

> Without doubt Kings County has a right to congratulate itself upon the election of Judge Van Zante to the superior bench. Under him people are assured that . . . equal and exact justice is meted out to all, and under him society will feel that it is amply protected.

Hallinan splashed on some cologne, zipped up his shaving kit, and relocated the newspaper to the adjoining stall. Its tissue supply had been exhausted and certainly the next occupant would appreciate the courtesy.

4. The Toughest Smart Guy in Town

The Hanford windmill case taught Hallinan a lesson he never
allowed himself to forget: the entire legal apparatus surrounding the court could be capable of cooperating in an
unjust prosecution. Perhaps the greater the injustice, the
greater the drive for conviction by constituted authority.
Subsequent cases reinforced this belief until it became fixed
among Hallinan's most enduring convictions.

These early years also marked substantial development
and change in Hallinan's thinking and activities beyond his
professional concerns. He found an outlet for his physical
energy; he rejected religion; he belatedly left his parents and
adopted a lifestyle quite out of keeping with Irish tradition
and his new-found opportunities as San Francisco's most
prominent trial lawyer. Shortly, too, he launched his crusade
against corruption and unsuspectingly took his first step
toward becoming the city's famous radical lawyer.

In the summer of 1925 Hallinan returned home to San
Francisco, first, to immerse himself in the affairs of his
parish, St. Agnes. He was anxious to discover what progress
his friend, Father Stephen Barron, had made with his Catholic social club for young adults. Barron had served as chap-

54

lain to California troops in Europe during 1918, and when he returned home he devoted his considerable organizational skills to creating the Agnetian Club. At first Barron limited membership to the unmarried young people of St. Agnes parish. When it became popular among Catholic youth, he opened it to those from across the city, until it became the pride of Catholic San Francisco. The home Hallinan bought for the family was three blocks away from the parish complex and as the 1920s advanced Vince observed property values inflating. Before he went down to Hanford, he advised Barron to buy up some lots along Haight Street and build a permanent clubhouse. It would be a useful move and an inflation hedge for the Agnetian treasury.

Father Barron was less interested in financial schemes than he was in the religious and social purposes of the club. Their monthly dances and annual Halloween extravaganzas at the Civic Auditorium all made money. Some of their musicals received better reviews than performances of professional companies downtown. And the success of the sports program could stand as a model for urban youth directors. But profits and publicity meant nothing to Father Barron. He remained intent on channeling the boundless energies of a pivotal immigrant generation into wholesome and productive activities.

He ran the club as a friendly confessor, modest cultural attache, and Barry Fitzgerald matchmaker. He insisted on strict attention to religious observances and regular participation in sponsored events. The social network he developed helped those who did not have white-collar jobs to move up, through the contacts of those who did. While so much of San Francisco's youth roared through the Prohibition era, not one among the two thousand young Agnetians came in conflict with the law. Drinking seemed not to be a problem.

Hallinan never attended the Communion masses but threw himself into the other Agnetian Club activities with his accustomed abandon. He hounded Barron to invest and expand. He delighted in the sparkling musical successes put on by the handsome young men and women. Privately he practiced the violin with the fond hope of overtaking those who had taken lessons from childhood. But all these and even the many fine young girls, were peripheral to Saturday football.

Hallinan had joined the Agnetian Club in 1921 when it fielded a football team. He had been captain of his college squad and played center for the Golden Gate Post of the American Legion, which won the state American Legion championship in 1920. He proved a vital addition to the band of somewhat unpromising recruits that turned out for the first Agnetian practice. Given their average size and experience, two thirds of them would today be turned away by any first-class high school team. But 1921 was in that transitional period that marked the demise of football as an amateur sport and its incorporation into the highly remunerative realm of spectator entertainment.

Despite its paucity of material, the Agnetian Club plunged into the football world with abandon. It hired a coach—Bart Macomber, an All-American half-back from Illinois—and signed an ambitious schedule of six games with formidable opponents. The opening game was against the Olympic Club, which prided itself as the leading athletic club in the country. Its boxing teams consistently returned from national tournaments with two or three gold medals and its football team played, and frequently defeated, the leading Pacific Coast college teams.

Agnetian practice sessions did nothing to reduce the apprehensions of Coach Macomber and Captain Hallinan. Most of the team had played very little organized football before. They were young accountants, first-year teachers, and civil service employees; all were enthusiastic, but none had the weight to sustain the battering the Olympic stalwarts regularly dispensed. In those days the standard strategy mingled an occasional end run with pounding various parts of the line. Whoever could hit harder on offense and take the heavier beating on defense normally won.

To compensate for their dangerous lack of weight, Hallinan invented a new defensive tactic, the "roving center." On each of the opponent's plays Hallinan would stay at center only if the ballcarrier was coming at him, otherwise he would pull out of the line and follow the play, thus adding his strength to the threatened position.

The opening game drew a crowd of several thousand, mainly from the Catholic community. They paid twenty-five cents each in hope of seeing their co-religionists work a miracle against the mercenaries fielded by the exclusive men's club to which few Irish Catholics belonged. In this they were disappointed since the Olympians won by a score of 49–0. They did witness a dramatic and far-reaching innovation in the game however. The Agnetians' roving center accounted for fully half of all the tackles made by his team. Next day, the sympathetic newspaper account of the game stated: "Hallinan, Agnetian center, was a star for his team, playing a wonderful defensive game."

The team ended the season with a perfect record, no wins and six defeats. They scored one field goal against Hallinan's old American Legion champions and had 172 points scored against them. Their worst punishment came on the road against the University of Nevada. The players were tired from the trip, and the dry heat and high altitude wilted them in the first quarter. The only consolation for the city boys was that in Reno nobody knew them. They lost 54–0.

In 1922 the Agnetians increased the schedule to seven games but omitted the Olympic Club. The season wound up with two victories and five defeats. Again Hallinan played every minute of every game. However, his fiercely competitive streak, which propelled that personal record, started clouding the picture. He could endure the public beatings every Saturday. What he hated and what he refused to endure further was the exasperation of defeat.

California's undefeated "wonder team" had capped its 1921 season with a stunning 28–0 defeat of Ohio State in the Rose Bowl. That victory marked the culmination of the collegiate careers of many Cal stars who had introduced Saturday football in the roaring twenties. And it was out of this development that Hallinan detected opportunity.

In order to maintain Olympic Club preeminence on the

coast, Coach Bob Evans offered the former Californians free memberships. His deal fell apart when the players reserved the right not to take the field against their alma mater. When Hallinan heard this he contacted Webster "Fat" Clark, reputedly the brainiest of the California warriors, and offered him the august job of Agnetian playing coach at $50 a game, and $150 if he could bring with him teammates "Brick" Muller and Cort Majors. Clark liked the idea.

The next two seasons saw the Catholic club filling the stadiums with spectators, and the sports pages with photos and accounts of its illustrious personnel. The Agnetian Club won the Pacific Coast Club Championship in 1924; its sweetest attainment was the 14–0 victory over the Olympic Club.

However, the end of the 1924 season witnessed the decline of the amateur teams. Professional football had spread from the East to the San Francisco Bay Area, quickly drawing off the more publicized players from the club teams. The depleted Agnetians took the field once in 1925, then disbanded.

Hallinan had captained the team during its entire history and played every minute of each of its twenty-eight successive games. Ripley's "Believe It Or Not" commemorated his endurance record in 1928 and designated him "The Iron Man of Football." His enduring contribution to modern football evolved from his "roving center" device. Coach "Pop" Warner introduced it at Stanford with All-American results. Thereafter, the innovation became nationwide and developed into the position of linebacker. By then his scheduled beatings ended and so "did a hell of a good time."

The demise of Saturday football did not mark the end of Hallinan's athletic activity. He beat the Olympic Club and then joined it but at twenty-eight he abandoned football and switched to boxing, swimming, and rugby. Of the three he liked fighting best. Bill Leonard, a boxing coach, taught the scientific techniques to a Hallinan whose previous fights consisted mainly of sailing in with both fists to outpunch or outlast his opponent. He began sparring on even terms with the young champions the Olympic Club sent to the national amateur finals. Occasionally he boxed with one of them at smokers. The only thing he disliked about those exhibitions was the foulness of the air. He could not understand why tobacco smoking appealed to anyone.

Fighting was as natural to Hallinan when he was angry as laughing when he was amused. Particularly in the early days of his legal practice, verbal abuse often spilled over into physical violence. "I saw lawyers," he recalled, "pull their punches in court, even, in cross-examining a witness, for fear of being clobbered outside." Hallinan himself "settled out of court" with ease twenty-six times. The twenty-seventh was a split decision with a younger and bigger corporate lawyer, Paul C. Dana. Their acrimonious exchanges got out of hand while the jury was out deliberating. Hallinan surprised Dana with a wicked left hook which sent him sprawling on the floor. Hallinan assumed that the fight was over and, imprudently, dropped his hands. Dana, who, unknown to Hallinan, had fought professionally, got up with help from his associates and then drove a powerful right hand into Hallinan's left eye. "After that I saw three Danas in front of me. I figured that the real one was probably the one in the middle and I rushed it. Unfortunately, that middle figure could punch good enough without help from the twins." By the time the City Hall regulars broke it up, both attorneys were well bruised and bloodied.

The aura of physical primitivism never embarrassed Hallinan; he cultivated it. This was particularly true after rugby and football injuries permanently disfigured the left side of his face and his left hand. By the 1930s corridor beatings had become unfashionable and younger lawyers hardly knew how to protect themselves. As late as the 1970s, Hallinan hit young attorneys who had lost their composure and called him vulgar names.

Hallinan's more dangerous battles began inside the courthouse. Since the California gold rush days judges had relied upon professional jurors, mostly agreeable old men of some property who met the minimal legal requirements of "ordinary intelligence and not decrepit." Until World War I no one became terribly concerned that age and property made conservative juries. Then, when the old professionals convicted a labor radical of dynamiting a military prepared-ness parade on blatantly insufficient evidence, the public demanded jury reform. The change, from Hallinan's vantage point, turned an abuse into outright corruption.

In the name of reform the superior court judges created the office of court secretary and commissioner and cen-tralized in it the critical function of jury selection. Their unbelievable first appointee was a professional fight pro-moter and gambler, James Coffroth, who had bribed city supervisors.

On the side Coffroth conducted a gaming parlor that accepted bets on almost any contingent event, including court trials. So prominent was Coffroth that the newspapers habitually referred to him as the "Gambling Commissioner." If the judges had a free hand, there was no genuine reason to choose a man of his background for so important an appoint-ment. Hallinan's conclusion was that "a criminal plutocracy owned several of the judges and intimidated most of the others." Through Coffroth's office, an organized combina-tion of transportation and insurance corporations controlled the courts in which they were regularly sued for damages.

By the time Hallinan started trying major personal injury cases, Coffroth's understudy, Thomas S. Mulvey, had succeeded to the position of power. He, in turn, served suc-cessive one-year appointments from 1917 to his death on the job in 1946.

Hallinan understood Mulvey. He came up from the Irish Catholic working class of the preceding generation on only a public grammar-school education. "He fitted exactly the requirements of the situation. Outwardly he was quiet, courteous and diligent. Inwardly he was enormously suspi-cious and fearful of disclosure or betrayal." To protect him-self he stayed close to his work; he seldom took a vacation or a day off. At mid-career he brought in David F. Supple and William Lynch. Supple was a prominent Catholic layman and although he possessed only a high-school education, Mulvey put him in charge of the grand jury and gratuitously conferred upon him the title, "grand jury expert."

Lynch's job was more sensitive. He helped Mulvey select trial jurors. Throughout the years during which he performed this task, he remained a covert employee of the single most frequent defendant in the courts, the Market Street Railway. The traction company's man inside the commissioner's office, of course, accepted a salary from the City and County of San Francisco too.

This was the set-up Hallinan encountered when he entered the personal injury field. It was the only area in which a young lawyer without political or financial connections could earn substantial fees. But any hope he may have entertained about being on easy street quickly vanished.

Once his reputation for winning verdicts got around, his cases started being assigned regularly to one or the other of three particular judges. In six successive trials the juries returned verdicts in favor of his client, and in each of them, the judge granted the defendant a new trial on the asserted grounds of insufficient evidence to justify the award. Moreover, the jurors debated longer and returned verdicts for amounts smaller than those he had been getting for claimants with similar juries in previous trials. The three judges — Fitzpatrick, Griffin, and Deasy — always displayed to him a friendly, and even cordial, manner. Finally, however, the pattern became so obvious as to exclude his doubts.

In a case against Lynch's covert employer, the Market Street Railway, the panel of prospective jurors included the brother of the railway's chief counsel and the mother and sister of the lawyer who was actually going to argue the case against Hallinan. With something akin to shock, Hallinan concluded that he and his clients were marks in a confidence game. At that point Hallinan commenced his own investigation.

The county clerk's records revealed that for the previous ten years the Market Street Railway had been the defendant in 181 trials, of which 92 had been held before the same three judges. Of the 61 cases tried before the two most blatant judges, only five insignificant verdicts had been permitted to stand. All others had been overturned by orders granting new trials on the grounds of the insufficiency of the evidence.

Next, Hallinan employed an investigator to help him review jury selection. By checking the first ten names in each alphabetical subdivision of the year's jury roster, they discovered interesting facts. Over thirteen percent were directly employed by insurance companies. Of the women on the list, twenty-three percent were wives of insurance company employees. Most of the remainder owned their own businesses or were corporate executives. There were three laborers and seven artisans listed from a hundred thousand men so employed in San Francisco. Geographically, the sample was likewise skewed; twenty-three percent resided in the posh Nob Hill–Marina assembly district. A great majority of the city's population lived in the four districts south of Market Street "where nineteen times as many people were killed by motor vehicles . . . than in one wealthy district. . . ." Yet these constituted only six percent of the jury roster sample.

The leading damage lawyers in the city affirmed Hallinan's conclusions but none would openly cooperate in any effort to change the situation. One actually warned him not to expect help from any other lawyer, saying, "We're a bunch of cowards."

The night Vincent Hallinan unrolled his statistical tables before the San Francisco Bar Association marked the end of whatever legal innocence he ever had. The board of governors resembled the stacked jury panel. Insurance company lawyers controlled the meeting and established the atmosphere of cold contempt. They attacked Hallinan and in the end announced they would not "convict a yellow dog on the 'evidence' Hallinan presented. . . ."

Meanwhile Tom Mulvey moved into a fashionable downtown penthouse, and the corporate attorneys stepped all the more confidently before understanding juries and friendly courts.

Incapable of surrender, Hallinan went public by filing a motion to have the city's entire jury panel disqualified. The court made quick work of his motion, accused him of "attacking the courts," and cited him for contempt. Going public earned him a day in jail. Still, he could not quit.

Thereafter Hallinan trained his fire on each judge in his own courtroom and lined up as much publicity as the sensation-hungry press would provide. Each time his case was assigned to one of the three judges, he presented an affidavit citing partiality and demanded a hearing. To avoid the undesired publicity, the courts began to reassign Hallinan's cases. To keep him from kicking over the entire apple cart, they let him have his bite, which was a miscalculation.

Hallinan's lonely agitation began in a barely noticeable fashion then surged and ebbed sporadically over a decade and a half. Characteristically, he did not kill court corruption with a single blow; he just hung on and kept kicking.

In 1937 he forced a formal review by three outside judges and used it to dump his sixteen years of accumulated evidence into Mulvey's lap while the commissioner sat in the witness box. The judges exonerated Mulvey and rejected Hallinan's reform plan—popular election of the commissioner and juries selected from the voting register. Mulvey used the occasion of official approval to brand Hallinan as an opportunist who attacked him personally in order to advance his own legal practice.

Hallinan always liked publicity, and the notoriety associated with the long fight did indeed bring him prime cases. Hallinan's unprecedented string of successes prompted one insurance company attorney to demand why Hallinan "represented about one-third of the damage suits filed locally." "We save them up," Hallinan replied, "and file them in wholesale lots to hear you fellows squeal."

His unrelenting agitation paid off, even though his antagonists were never openly unmasked. Privately, the out-of-town judges said plenty to the superior court. Quietly and without formal announcement, juries came to be selected by the method Hallinan had long advocated. The judges he had held up to public scorn became solicitous of him and his clients in their courts—to the open-mouthed amazement of the insurance lawyers—and for the first time since the aging Pat Hallinan became a citizen, he received postcard greetings from Mulvey. Jury duty!

During the commissioner's twilight years, the curtailed system, which Mulvey and Supple still managed, lashed back. It began when Hallinan's associate, Emmet Burns, sued the Savage Transportation Company for one hundred thousand dollars on behalf of Elizabeth Bliss. Her husband had been killed in a collision with a company truck.

Two drifters presented themselves at the Hallinan-Burns offices and offered to testify as eye witnesses, but Burns doubted that they had actually seen the fatal event. They were vague on details and their need of money was obvious. Hallinan confirmed the suspicions with a few questions and pointed out how, under cross-examination, they would lose an otherwise promising case. He gave the men lunch money and told them to get lost. Their scheme could land them in jail.

That night the twosome, Curtis Cox and Robert Patterson, testified before the grand jury that they had been bribed by Hallinan and Burns to give false testimony. William Lynch manipulated their testimony and David Supple, by then Supreme Warden of the Knights of Columbus, let the Catholic members of the grand jury know that Hallinan was a renegade from the Church.

On the testimony of an unemployed ranch cook and his friend, the grand jury indicted both Hallinan and Burns for suborning perjury, even though Cox and Patterson never appeared as witnesses in any case and did not commit the offense that the attorneys were charged with inspiring.

Instead of merely sitting still, Hallinan made a serious error at this point. One of the men phoned him and claimed that they wanted to retract their grand jury testimony. If Hallinan would meet them in Oakland, they wanted to talk it over.

According to Hallinan, when he met them they had

changed their story once again. This time they said that if they retracted their testimony, they would be indicted for perjury. If Hallinan would give them some money, they would just disappear. For the better part of an hour Hallinan argued and cajoled, all the while standing at a doorway on the well-lit downtown corner. When he gave up in disgust and returned to his car, a binocular-laden San Francisco police detective, Frank Lucey, placed Hallinan under arrest. The whole thing was a set up and Luccy had been watching all the time.

Cox and Patterson gave the detective five twenty-dollar bills as evidence and told him that Hallinan gave them the money to leave town. Now Hallinan faced two trials: suborning perjury and bribing witnesses.

Hallinan knew Lucey by reputation as a loner on the force and a confidant of Jake Ehrlich, a flamboyant and well-published San Francisco attorney. Between books the short, dark, and dapper Ehrlich spent considerable time being associated in criminal defense cases in which Frank Luccy had been the arresting or investigating officer. Hallinan lost no time in retaining Ehrlich and paying his substantial fee. The value of his services was shortly demonstrated.

Hallinan assumed that the first charge, suborning perjury, would be tried first. From Ehrlich's police confidant, however, he learned that the prosecution intended to reverse the cases and try the stronger indictment first, bribing witnesses. The move was designed to lead with the stronger case and to catch unprepared Hallinan's actual trial attorneys.

The critical testimony came from Lucey, the arresting officer. He swore that he and his partner had watched Hallinan throughout his street-corner conversation with Cox and Patterson. "The binoculars," Lucey swore, "brought them up . . . within ten feet of us" and no money passed between them. On further cross-examination by John Taaffe, Hallinan's lead attorney, he admitted that the disreputable accusers had not been previously searched for money that could have been planted by insurance company agents before the meeting.

The jury quickly returned a verdict of not guilty. The

weaker case was then dropped and the rearguard action against Hallinan ended.

Thirty-two years after Mulvey's funeral cortege passed City Hall and delivered the commissioner to oblivion at Holy Cross Cemetery, Hallinan was still granting interviews. It was fifty-seven years after the first hint that something was wrong in the courts. When confronted with fixed judges, planted juries, and a corrupt system, he said, "I would do any damned thing I could, crookedness for crookedness, perjury for perjury, lie for lie to overcome the corruption of defrauding people."

Whether he resorted to the Jimmy Carroll defense in order to escape from his own first serious scrape with the legal system, only Hallinan knew for sure. "Of course I didn't split with the cop. And if I did, why should I tell history?" Ehrlich certainly would not, and neither would Lucey. They were dead.

From its inception, Hallinan's law practice brought in money in ever increasing amounts. At first he rented space in the reception room of another struggling attorney and installed in it his only furnishings, a desk and two chairs. He did his own typing. Shortly he moved across the hall to an office and reception room of his own where he even had a part-time secretary. Next, he leased a five-room suite in the prestigious, newly constructed Russ Building, added a couple of young lawyers just out of law school, and hired a secretary full time. The secretary was shy and delicate Margaret Sullivan, fresh out of the convent schools. She had consulted the nuns before going to work for a man who argued in public about God and the faith, but who paid well. Knowing that Margaret's mother badly needed the wages she would bring home, the good sisters gave a reluctant approval but they watched the rail at Sunday mass to check the fidelity of their best secretarial student.

While clicking away on the Remington typewriter, Margaret pretended not to notice the succession of stunning young women who arrived each Saturday at noon to accompany her boss and his old high-school friend, John Wilmans, to the football games and then to dinner and dancing. She knew that Hallinan and Wilmans occasionally weekended with the girls at Hallinan's new summer cabin, but the nuns never learned of it from the Sullivans. Hallinan later hired Margaret's outgoing younger sister, Catherine, and also assumed the family's tragically large medical bills.

Wilmans, Hallinan's closest friend, stood six feet, four inches tall, weighed 208 pounds, and had captured the national amateur heavyweight boxing championship. He and Vince worked out together two or three times a week, either at the Olympic Club or in a ring that Hallinan had constructed at his summer place. There, one Saturday afternoon, Wilmans gained and regretted the distinction of being the only man ever to put Hallinan away. In a sudden, heated exchange, he landed a terrific right cross which put his friend in the hospital not only with a broken jaw, but with traumatic pneumonia, which accompanied the injury. Blessed with chronic good health, it was the only significant medical problem ever to bother Hallinan and he recovered quickly. Soon enough the two were back in the ring and after the girls.

Wilmans did well in stocks and bonds while the market remained bullish. On his recommendation Hallinan invested a few hundred dollars now and then with unbelievable results. By early 1929 his friend calculated that on less than five thousand dollars in cash, Hallinan's paper exceeded one hundred thousand dollars in market value. Hardly interested in the matter before that, Hallinan thought it was crazy and started reading in economics and studying the operation of the stock market. His timely conclusion was, "It's a racket," and it was about to collapse. In the spring of 1929 Hallinan became a panic seller, all by himself, and received a check for $109,000.

The more money rolled in, the more he lavished it on the family. Annie needed a bit of coaxing to nudge her boyfriend into a proposal, so Vince offered them a small home, properly furnished, as a wedding present. Years later, when their children were growing, Vince provided a country home adjacent to his own at Emerald Lake, south of San Francisco.

For the other sisters he provided leisure, education, amusements, drama and music lessons, vacations, lavish wedding presents, investments, and trips abroad. For his younger brother, Jerry, who assumed their father's old drinking habits, he arranged employment in his office as an investigator and gave him a seven-room home near Twin Peaks. That was after Jerry stole his girl friend and married her. Vince provided for everyone who remained at home and, as they left, he sent them along as if he were their indulgent father.

By the time Hallinan arrived at the position where he could intervene in the lives of his family, only his sisters Emily and Patricia were still young enough to be receptive. Before developing any specific career plans for them, he decided to indulge himself for a change.

On top of his world at age thirty-three, Vince turned his law practice over to his associates, handed his mother a bank deposit book, and announced his intention to reside abroad indefinitely. The only flaw in his plan was that when he arrived in Europe, he hated it. The tough guy was homesick.

He had scarcely landed in Le Havre when he began to miss his family, his home, and his friends. Pushing this aside, he bought a small used car and drove on to Paris. There he met Dan Mahoney, an old acquaintance who had proclaimed himself back in high school by publishing an essay, "Perfume," in the *Ignatian*. Gay, cultured, and a long-time resident of the French capital, Mahoney introduced Hallinan to his friends and guided him around the city's grand sights. When a Parisian friend of the still-fragrant Ignatian started pushing extravagant gifts on Vince, he left for Germany.

As a cultural experience Hallinan's grand tour failed miserably. Historical sights, cathedral facades, and public buildings could not yet replace laughs, action, and beautiful girls.

Except for Elizabeth, who honored the Church more in word than in deed, the Hallinans were fervent in their devotion. As the years of frustration faded, Pat gladly exchanged toil and the bottle for gardening, poetry, and an increasing attentiveness to priests and religion. His devotionalism reached the point where he would withdraw to his room for hours of prayer and meditation, preparation for Holy Communion when, he believed, the Lord would enter into him with the sacred host.

While Vince was in Europe, Emily entered the Sisters of the Holy Cross over Elizabeth's opposition. Vince tried to have her return home but he failed. "It broke my heart. She was the first one I had a chance with, to get her over the limitations of an impoverished immigrant generation. I turned my back for a silly trip and the oldest, a good woman but the family's religious devotee, sees her off to a forfeited life. She threw away the only thing any of us will ever have."

Unable to change Emily's mind, Hallinan shifted field and tried to fortify her for what he considered an unrewarded life of sacrifice and superstition. Through the summers that followed he paid for her travel across the country, so she could be with their ailing mother, and later with her sister, Patricia. It was little enough, he thought, given his failure to assure better direction to her life.

When Vince was thirty, little Patricia was only ten. Vince, always gratifying her childish requests, was the joy of her youth. Over his protests she attended Presentation High School. Four years later he prevailed, redirecting her from a small Catholic college for women to Stanford University. With the aid of a federal judge who was a friend of the university president, Hallinan insured her matriculation. He bought her a car for weekend visits home and put her through the undergraduate program, medical school, and an internship. On her graduation from medical school and her marriage, her providing brother presented her with a charming house in the exclusive suburban community of Ross. Later he enlarged it to meet the needs of her growing family.

Of the eight Hallinan children, only the two boys slipped through the resolute hands and orthodox ways of Annie, the strong-willed eldest child. Jerry succumbed to the Irish curse, dying at 44, divorced and alcoholic. Because of his divorce and remarriage, the Catholic church refused to bury him in consecrated ground, a blow that compounded Pat's sense of profound loss. The old man wept bitterly as his youngest boy was lowered into his final resting place out beyond the pale. Vince watched, and as the tears streamed down the old man's swollen face, he hated the Catholic church all the more. "They told my father that his dead child was not worthy to be buried in their damn cemetery and, presumptively, to enter their paradise."

When Pat and Elizabeth's time came, their non-believing son laid them quietly to rest beside one another, inside Holy Cross Cemetery, according to the rites they had so painfully adhered to. As he had since the morning he drove his parents away from the old flat, Vincent met all expenses. He made the traditional offerings but despised the Church that had compounded Pat Hallinan's sense of personal failure; a father who was unable to lead either son to eternal happiness.

In the early years of his own apostasy, Hallinan, like most converts to or from a religion, publicly deprecated his prior convictions. He became a free thinker who sought rational, scientific explanations to the problems that perplexed man's world. Scripture, he told his former co-religionists, was the compilation of the sporadic writings of ancient, near-primitive people. To believe those stories was a reflection on the moderns, not the primitives. To accept miracles was ludicrous enough. To believe that a Supreme Being, who created a universe the magnitude of which man could not comprehend, selected earth as the residence of the apex of his creation, and made man in His image and likeness, was absolute folly.

The concept of redemption Hallinan saved for his most elementary ridicule and scorn. "Redeem from what? The act of some primitive who ate an apple? Ridiculous! Can you imagine this? Here is the universe as we are beginning to understand it. There is God the Father pointing out this wart, Earth, to God the Son. He tells His Son that a guy named Adam ate an apple he was told to let rot on the tree. So God the Father punished all those itty, bitty specks which He called people and made them swarm around in pain to earn bread by brow sweat. But later He decided to give them another chance, to come up and be happy with Him by sharing His presence and perceiving that they share His image and likeness. Crazy! But that's not the best part.

"If you were the Son, this would make interesting listening until your Father got to the punch line. 'I want you to go down to these specks, take their form, and let them crucify you. You can suffer and die to make up for the apple eaters.' "

With yards of blackboards filled with extensive diagrams of the universe and waste spaces loaded with astronomic calculations reckoned in light years, Hallinan's conclusion was always curt. "If this actually happened, the Son would say, 'Pop, you've gotten senile. If you want to forgive them, just do it. If you don't, just think them out of existence or whatever you want.' "

From every platform he could mount, he argued against the existence of heaven, hell, and purgatory. His message was unpopular enough but its offensive characterization was even harder on conservative Irish Americans who could identify with Hallinan on most matters except religion. "To accept Catholic beliefs and doctrines," he maintained, "is to accept an intellectual straightjacket. Nothing should be tried or abandoned in the name of church or God that would not be done had mankind never invented these entities.

"The answers which all institutions and systems provide are in essence and nature flawed, even self-serving. The closer you examine the answer machines the more you realize the foolishness of accepting what is no more than another's decision. You may call it consensus, faith, patriotism, or whatever you like. Ultimately every person must decide his own answer for he alone is responsible for his action to himself and his fellow man. That's all there is, my friends."

Rationalism and individualism brought Hallinan to atheism but he had personal reasons for his militant anti-Catholicism. Perhaps his father's early brutality at home, which gave way to religious enthusiasm, helped. His mother's lip service to the Church, her opposition to Emily's

entry into the convent, along with Vincent's strong attachment to her were also factors. A repressive Irish Catholic
prudishness, which he felt drained joy from the lives of his
family, also had its part. He tried but could not, and then
would not, repress his own sensual passions. Confessing his
first crude affair to a celibate became more than the young
Hallinan would bear. That Tom Mulvey was a believer and
David Supple was a celebrated Catholic layman were
unnecessary irritants after the fact.

"Religion and Catholicism are junk, impeding man's
personal development and his rational solutions for the problems of our times. Eternity? There's no such thing. We are
born, we suffer, and we die. Life is all we have, so live it for
what it's worth."

Reverend Raymond T. Feeley, S.J., was a close and
enduring critic of Hallinan's philosophical and theological
views. Feeley preceded Hallinan through St. Ignatius, taught
at the law school, and became a Jesuit, ending his days as a
professional anti-communist and vice president of the University of San Francisco. He considered Hallinan to have
been his most brilliant student. Feeley's studied conclusion
was that Hallinan left the Church because of "intellectual
pride." He would not subordinate his mind to any teacher,
any authority, or any institution. Hallinan, in his way,
agreed with his life-long priestly critic. "Of course, Ray
Feeley was right. His tragedy was that he accepted as sin
what should have been his goal for an independent intellectual life. He was a professor who accepted intellectual
subordination. The real tragedy was that he thought such
subordination was proper. . . . Intellectual pride or freedom,
whatever, must have been why I left the Church because it is
the only explanation of anything Ray Feeley and I ever
agreed on. . . .

"You know, he never did teach me."

In 1930, the end of the first phase of his professional
life, Hallinan had traveled a considerable distance from the
fidelity of his youth.

For they are the bringers of Christ-like peace,
Who plant the cross on every sod
Whose life-giving struggles never cease —
They are the soldiery of God.
The greatest laurels the Irish win —
And many our emerald banner grace —
Are the hard-won bays of our noblest men; —
The Catholic Priests of the Fighting Race!

— Vincent Hallinan
1916

"They've got you at last, Frank Egan. . . .
They've got you at last! My wife was one of
your victims. So am I, you — — —!"

— From The Mob
The Hall of Justice, June 8, 1932

5. Defending the Public Defender: The Egan Murder Case, 1932

A major case of national or regional significance punctuated each of the six most active decades of Hallinan's career as a California trial lawyer. For his various murder trials death, either on the gallows or (later) in the California gas chamber, would have claimed anyone whom Hallinan would have represented unsuccessfully. In the celebrated case of Harry Bridges the penalty would have been the loss of United States citizenship and deportation. Throughout this record career of active trial practice Hallinan lost no one to those ultimate punishments, not even Frank Egan, a public official whose guilt the press proclaimed well before the trial began.

Hallinan's client was San Francisco's public defender, a man elected in 1921 and regularly re-elected thereafter. He was a well-known, popular civic figure and had a good chance of becoming mayor of San Francisco if he chose to run. Once accused and detained, he had an acute need for a criminal defense far superior to any he himself could devise. As the deputy sheriffs prodded him from the county jail to the Hall of Justice, Egan tried hard to maintain his composure before a hostile mob. He knew Hallinan would be waiting for him inside the arraignment court.

74

Egan and Hallinan first met back in 1919, when Vince was a boy wonder, winning all those small police court cases. After Hallinan passed the bar and moved up to the superior court, Egan threw an occasional personal injury case his way and the considerate youngster usually split the fee. Now he regretted that he did not give Hallinan the claims Jessie Hughes had against the Southern Pacific Railroad for the death of her brother. When a coroner's jury found negligence on the part of the corporate giant, he kept the case for himself only to accept a miserable $572 in the end. That was when Hallinan was settling for record amounts. He was not sure, but maybe if he had given that one to Hallinan too, just possibly he would not be in this Hughes mess now.

Egan had been in hiding and, while evading the police and reporters, he developed an emotional dependence upon the younger attorney. Anticipating him now on the other side of the next door, Egan hoped his ebbing composure would last. The jammed corridors were pushing in at him. Outraged and curious people everywhere jostled for a glimpse of Frank Egan, as if he were some sort of sideshow fiend. He felt at a loss and over and over in his mind he repeated, "I can't express myself like I would if I were the Frank Egan that was Frank Egan."

Suddenly he was oriented again. The police had lost control, and the former husband of a deceased client sprang for his throat. Screaming and yelling, the outraged man drove Egan and the line of prisoners back into the squad of deputies behind them. No one was injured, certainly not Egan who landed against the soft paunch of an equally outraged officer.

Hallinan was already in place at the defense table inside. Minutes before, he had pushed his way through the crowds with an older and more experienced criminal attorney he retained to help in what he correctly believed would be the most desperate case of an already exciting career. Egan's physical safety did not worry him, at least for the moment, for whatever differences Hallinan had with the police, he knew that they had never surrendered a prisoner to a mob since the gold rush vigilante days. Besides, this was nothing like Hanford seven years earlier. These people were mad because they could not get in. They wanted to see Egan, not lynch him — at least not yet.

In this case the San Francisco Police Department's investigation seemed to be so efficient and effective that Hallinan had to abandon several lucrative personal injury suits and delay a choice divorce case just to stay abreast of the fast-breaking developments. The police had been everywhere on this one, and whatever they did not discover for themselves the reporters unearthed and spread across the front pages. Through the middle half of 1932 only the tragic discovery of the Lindbergh baby's shallow grave pushed Frank Egan from the headlines. And from the start Hallinan immersed himself in Egan's tangled affairs far more deeply than the public suspected.

To all outward appearances Egan deserved the respect which San Franciscans accorded him at every election since the office of public defender had been created. As a former patrolman who had been admitted to the practice of law and then captured city-wide public office, he was a successful and well-known political personality. His initiative and ambition were roundly respected and, whatever his limitations, certainly he suffered little in normal comparisons. From his success followed the natural assumption that he had ability.

An apparent hit-and-run fatality had taken place out in the new and moderately well-off Ingleside Terrace area of the city not far from the palatial home which the public defender shared with his family. On the night of April 29, a middle-aged couple, walking home from the nearby movie theater, watched a dark Lincoln drive past. It disappeared around the corner only to materialize minutes later at the top of the hill ahead of them. This time its lights were out. Warren Louw, a mechanic, recognized the make, model, and distinctive markings of the heavy machine, but as it accelerated toward them he was frankly concerned about personal safety, not about the mystery vehicle's license number. In their relief at not being struck or robbed, the Louws might easily have forgotten the over-sized sedan with its tightly drawn curtains but for what immediately followed.

As they crossed the deserted street their relief turned to curiosity and then to horror. Lying in the gutter they discovered the body of a fifty-nine-year-old widow who lived nearby. Her dress was torn. Her undergarments were showing. And her body was broken and cold.

Next morning Frank Egan appeared downtown at the coroner's office and identified the deceased as Mrs. Jessie Scott Johnson Hughes, his client and personal friend of long standing. She had been the young widow who, after the 1906 earthquake and fire, had encouraged him to join the police force and then to study law. He told the deputy coroner, Jane Walsh, that he was the woman's executor and the beneficiary of both her will and several insurance policies. It was too bad, he added, that she disregarded his frequent admonitions not to walk alone at night. As friend and executor, Egan said that he was familiar with all of her affairs and he promised to take care of everything. The coroner would not have to worry about anything.

Within the hour Egan phoned the carrier of Mrs. Hughes's life insurance policies, left the vital information, and asked that his call be returned. This coordination had become rather routine for him. It was not an official function of his office at all. It was, in fact, quite private. He had similarly dispatched the affairs of other women in whose estates he and his wife were financially interested. Deaths and dispositions of estates had not been strangers to the Egans.

The interest of Charles W. Dullea, captain of inspectors, who sought out Egan for a chat also seemed routine. In passing, the public defender nonetheless let Dullea know that on the fatal Friday night he had been at the fights with his physician-friend, Dr. Nathan S. Housman. He and the officer parted and everything seemed fine until that evening when

Egan returned to his split-level home and learned that Dullea's men had been talking to the servants and measuring the tires on his own light blue Lincoln.

By Monday the papers announced Dullea's conclusion. Jessie Hughes had not been the victim of a street accident. The crime was murder and Egan was the prime suspect. The certainty that the police and the district attorney shared about his guilt was not simply that required by law — beyond reasonable doubt. It was absolute. As sensational as the revelation was, Egan upstaged the police by dramatically disappearing.

He phoned Captain Dullea that he was being kidnaped, proclaiming before the line went dead, "Charlie, I'm innocent but they've got me."

Once the Public Defender became enmeshed with the police, he aroused Hallinan's hitherto unexpressed, possibly unfelt, sympathy and concern. Though people easily slid in and out of friendly association, when they were in trouble, Irish clannishness compelled an almost primitive solidarity. If you were on friendly terms, Hallinan would help, no matter what you had done, assuming you had not done it to him or his family.

When Mrs. Egan came to him for Frank, he immediately accepted the case and consulted with Egan in hiding, staying with him until he absorbed the whole story. He advised the public defender to remain secluded and try to collect his very shaky composure. No arrest warrant had been issued and he was only "wanted for questioning," which was a police-devised ruse without legal merit. Normal police practice was to examine a suspect without his attorney and in the process get him to incriminate himself. Then they would arrest him. That trap Hallinan intended to avoid.

Instead of improving with time, Egan got worse. With total breakdown as a distinct possibility, Egan simply could not be trusted to mind his own welfare, particularly if he came into police custody. Already they had seized the death car and rumor had it that Dullea's men were secretly working over an ex-convict, Albert Tinnin, attempting to extract a confession before bringing him in where Hallinan could intervene. Tinnin's record was a long one and included attempted murder. He had spent a decade in Folsom Prison even though none other than Frank Egan was his alibi witness back in 1922. Later, Egan had intervened for his parole.

Clearly police intent was to force Tinnin to confess and to name Egan and an accomplice, Verne L. Doran, who was still at large. Doran was another ex-offender similarly indebted to Egan for his freedom. The only part Hallinan could not fathom was how Dullea collected so many well-fitting pieces so quickly, when five other cases of outright murder languished for lack of a single clue. How did the police find the death car? What prompted their immediate interest in Egan? Why did they pick up Tinnin? Why were they after Doran when Tinnin obviously had not named him? The newspapers saturated the avid readership with a torrent of fast-breaking developments, but each revelation left Hallinan in a greater quandary. Dullea was too quick and too sure.

Sooner or later the police would close in on Egan's hideout, so Hallinan installed him in a sanitarium with the assistance of cooperative doctors. Then he took the initiative. A barber spruced Egan up and Hallinan invited in the press. He managed the conference by limiting it to pictures, the distribution of a statement he prepared for Egan, and a charade which he would incorporate as a major defense tactic. After the reporters read the statement Hallinan elaborated. The whole thing, he alleged, was a police conspiracy against Egan, who, as public defender, helped the otherwise defenseless poor to avoid police frame-ups. Dissatisfied with this blatant management of the press, the reporters bombarded Egan with all the questions Hallinan wanted left unanswered. But Hallinan wanted Egan to remain silent without bringing down further the wrath of the newspapers upon him.

As soon as Egan started to answer, Hallinan intervened. But Egan persisted, "Why Vince, I have no objection to answering that question; these boys are all friends of mine.

I'm willing to answer anything they ask me." According to plan, Hallinan then blew up and threatened Egan. If Egan wanted him to continue as his attorney, he had to do as he was told. Hallinan terminated the bedside conference by announcing that Egan would be back at work on Monday morning. The whole thing, he insisted, was a phony sensation without substance, as far as his client was concerned.

From Hallinan's point of view, two goals were achieved. He transferred press hostility from his client to himself. And Egan publicly surfaced without saying anything which the well-informed police might successfully contradict and use against him later. When Monday arrived, Hallinan announced a relapse and moved Egan to St. Mary's Hospital, adjacent to Golden Gate Park, thus instituting further delay.

Not wishing to have the Public Defender's image further tarnished by close legal association with previous offenders, Hallinan engaged separate counsel for Tinnin and Doran. He turned first to Nathan Coombs Coghlan, the most able California criminal lawyer of the early Prohibition era. His record for acquittals during the 1920s prompted the papers to call him "a one-man repeat of the capital punishment law." In his prime the whiskey-drinking, cigar-smoking Coghlan would not have come into the case behind Hallinan. But his best days were past, eclipsed for the moment by his struggle against the Irish weakness. Offering Coghlan possibly the last good chance to re-establish himself in his former luster, Hallinan brought the hero of his formative years into the case to represent Tinnin and provide the experience Hallinan lacked. At the same time he tried to convince Doran's mother that she needed Nate Coghlan to protect her son. When the woman failed to go along and the police apprehended the twenty-four year old, Hallinan slid in Walter J. McGovern. This move proved to be his only critical error in the case.

Hallinan did not know McGovern well, but the corpulent Hibernian had the reputation of being able to stand up to uncomfortable situations. Back when Hallinan was doing what he could to send money and guns to revolutionary Ireland, McGovern, at considerable risk to his legal career, held a press conference and denounced the most powerful corporate lawyer in the West, Garrett McEnerney, who had called local supporters of the Irish Republican Army "traitors to America." During the intervening fourteen years McGovern built a good reputation as a trial lawyer against the same packed courts as Hallinan. Vince thought he had the right spirit and proper integrity.

Meanwhile weeks passed and political pressures on Mayor Angelo J. Rossi mounted. The press and the public wanted him to remove Egan from office, regardless of the fact that the defender was an independently elected official, protected initially by the city charter and now by Hallinan's counterattack. Hallinan's response to the bad press Egan received was to broadcast that his client's troubles were politically inspired. According to him, the real objective of this sensation was the abolition of the public defender's office, an unpopular innovation in local government which ran counter to the conservative, law-and-order tradition. Egan's involvement was incidental. To maintain his counter-offensive momentum, Hallinan proclaimed Egan's recovery and returned him to work, but not until after he and Mrs. Egan had cleared out Frank's locked desk and private files.

The district attorney, Matthew Brady, made the next move. He served Egan with a subpoena for the first, long-delayed official encounter, the coroner's inquest. This was the spring of 1932, decades before court-instituted discovery procedures required prosecutors to share their evidence with defense counsel. In this case Brady and his chief deputy, Isadore M. Golden, were absolutely intent upon keeping Hallinan in the dark while at the same time they tried to extract self-incrimination from Egan. The coroner, Dr. T. B. W. Leland, cooperatively allowed Golden to manage the proceedings and to do the actual questioning of all witnesses.

Golden developed no evidence beyond what already was public knowledge. He exposed only the minimum necessary to demonstrate that, instead of being struck by a hit-and-run driver, Mrs. Hughes had been viciously murdered in her own garage. The autopsy surgeon revealed that the victim had been held in place, face up, by someone's foot while being crushed to death. The medical cause of death was a traumatized or ruptured liver. The lower portion of her rib cage was crushed, and marks on her head indicated that she may have been beaten into unconsciousness, before the crushing process commenced. Laboratory technicians completed the gruesome picture. Markings on Mrs. Hughes's clothing, the dimensions of her fatal injuries, and the tracks in her garage established that she had been run over, forward and in reverse, by a heavy automobile. The garage floor was then washed, the victim placed in the back seat of the murder vehicle which backed out of the garage and proceeded to the site where Mrs. Hughes was unceremoniously dumped from the moving car.

Under Golden's direct examination Oscar F. Postel, a fire department lieutenant, testified that earlier that same day he lent his 1925 blue Lincoln to Verne Doran, Frank Egan's chauffeur, who said he wanted it for Egan. Postel had acquired the machine from the estate of a slain mobster and held it under a fictitious registration. He was a friend of Egan and had business dealings with him. The vehicle's tire treads matched tracks in the Hughes's garage and hairs found in the back seat were identical to those found in the drain of the washed garage. They came from the head of the victim. To sum up the horror, various police investigators testified that the victim's body was cold when discovered, and was positioned so as to rule out being struck by a moving vehicle. There were no injuries to the limbs. San Francisco nights were cool, but Mrs. Hughes was wearing no hat or coat. Her purse and keys were not on her person but were found in a dining-room drawer. Furthermore, all doors were locked and all but one were bolted and chained. To gain entrance, the police had to climb a ladder and break a window. Presumably that too would have been the only way the victim herself could have re-entered her own home. She had not been out strolling when accidentally struck. Mrs. Hughes, Chief Deputy District Attorney Golden concluded, "was the victim of murder."

Throughout the proceedings Hallinan was aggressive and truculent. He objected to Golden conducting the questioning rather than the milder, less experienced coroner. He boldly and presumptuously assumed the right to cross-examine inquest witnesses and put the onus of uncooperative refusal upon Dr. Leland and Golden. When Hallinan persisted and the coroner called for the police to eject him, the obstreperous attorney feigned surprise and disappointment in Dr. Leland, stating for the benefit of the jury, "We expect your honor to protect us." As it was abundantly evident to him that the coroner intended to remain an agent of the prosecution, Hallinan quickly abandoned the fruitless posturing of an injured party and warned that if the doctor expelled him, he would take Egan out with him. Hallinan kept the small room electrified. He was menacing even though the authorities clearly were in control.

When Egan's turn to be sworn came, he and Hallinan replayed the bedside scene they performed for the reporters. A shaky Egan, rambling again in the third person, rose and blurted out, "I am here to testify. The jury wants to hear from Frank Egan. The whole case in the minds of everybody is Frank Egan."

Hallinan's response by now was automatic. He shut Egan up and then sat him down. This "has become the privileged inquiry of the police department," he roared so that the small jury room all but exploded from the noise.

If he could not question the police witnesses, he would not allow a representative of the district attorney's office to question Egan. All he wanted, he protested, was evenhanded treatment. So once more he presented Egan as cooperative and forthright then promptly moved in front of him. The press depicted him as a vicious obstructionist.

When Golden completed his argument to the jurors, Hallinan tried to argue too. He ignored the exasperated coroner and turned directly to the jurors, asking them if they "would like to hear us . . . refute these imputations." At the end of his patience, Dr. Leland told them to decide. And they did easily: "Mrs. Hughes was murdered."

Hallinan and Coghlan were exasperated too. From Golden's management of the coroner's inquest they learned nothing about the inevitable prosecution of their clients. One street-scene witness, for example, identified Doran as the driver of the death car but Coghlan was prevented from asking who else, if anyone, was also seen with Doran. The big puzzler remained—what attracted police interest to the fireman's car in the first place? Given his irregular registration and a dubious personal background, Postel would hardly invite police inquiries. It was clear to Hallinan that Dullea had begun investigating the public defender even before Egan talked too much on the morning he identified the body. But what sparked his interest remained unknown.

Two days later Hallinan's critical mistake overtook him and Coghlan. Walter McGovern announced Doran's confession. He killed the woman and he was prepared to testify against Egan and Tinnin in return for a separate deal. He named Tinnin as his accomplice and Egan as the mastermind. Tinnin, he said, held the woman in place while he drove twice over her body. Further, Doran claimed to have discussed burning the car with Egan and Dr. Housman but the police had seized it too quickly.

This devastating setback stunned Hallinan personally more than professionally. His reaction was identical to each of the other few times in his long, combative life when he was had. He ignored it! Never did he make public mention of what he thought of Walter McGovern and thereby draw attention to his own lapse into credulity. Privately, and after all the principals were dead, he reflected that, "Bringing in associates was a mistake. I should have kept all three men in my own hands and everything in my own head. On June the 5th, 1932, I learned an expensive lesson. Since that day I have tried, in similar cases, to represent all defendants myself. Now in cases like that the only attorneys I have complete confidence in are my sons. Coghlan was good and I was pleased to remain associated with him for years after. But in 1932 Frank Egan would have been better off if I were alone."

Clearly, Doran and Tinnin were prosecution expendables. Egan was the target. The nature of the crime along with Frank Egan's legal experience ruled out plea bargaining, pleading diminished capacity, pleading that he had acted in the heat of passion. Besides, Egan insisted that he was innocent, framed by a beleaguered, conviction-craving police department. For all these reasons Hallinan pleaded him not guilty, a legal defense to which Egan was entitled. Besides, there were no options.

Hallinan's thinking was interesting. The law afforded the not-guilty defense to everyone. To claim it and then not back it up was far worse than throwing a client upon the mercy of the court. This meant an aggressively active defense, not just passive and ineffectual denials against substantial evidence that a district attorney would use. "Every criminal lawyer," Hallinan felt, "has no concern whatever with the guilt or innocence of a client. He can't. The whole thing is a racket. The prosecution puts on its case not for justice but for conviction and you put on yours only to acquit. If you are unwilling or unable to do all that is possible to obtain your client's acquittal, you are allowing a vicious system to grind him up and you have no business on the defense side of the court. And you won't be there very long either."

In its application this philosophy made Doran a solitary killer. He borrowed the car. Surprised in mid-burglary the previous offender lost his head and killed. He confessed to the horrid act. To save himself he obligingly accepted police prompting by saying what they wanted to hear.

This was the essence of Hallinan's direct defense. Its vitality under a withering prosecution rested on many factors, thorough preparation being the one Hallinan counted on most.

Hallinan remained puzzled by Dullea's extraordinary investigative success. He was on the main track long before Doran crossed over and turned state's evidence. If the police appeared to be manufacturing the pieces which fitted so well, why not just say that? After committing "one of the most heinous crimes in the history of San Francisco, Doran would be allowed to escape with a sentence of manslaughter" as a reward for framing Frank Egan and Albert Tinnin.

Thus Hallinan blended a bungled burglary with a police conspiracy. That became the defense line.

Unknown to its creator, the San Francisco Police Department actually was guilty. Their conspiracy was not the active framing of an effective public defender, as Hallinan maintained. It was one far more insidious

One full year earlier the police ordered the office of Dr. Housman, Egan's friend, electronically bugged. Over the wires the police heard and recorded Egan planning the actual murder of Mrs. Hughes! Yet, they did not intervene. When the illegal tape became public knowledge—after the trial ended—San Francisco's most responsible daily editorialized on how the police 'framed,' not an innocent man into undeserved punishment but an innocent woman to her death and a guilty man into the culmination of his crime."

At the time Hallinan was charging that Egan had been framed, the police hoped he never would discover the truth of what he said, at least not until Egan was safely dispatched to the care of the San Quentin hangman.

Actual police complicity constituted only the first hidden dimension of the Egan case. There was a second and more deeply masked one.

Through the preceding two decades San Francisco had been governed by its most beloved and beflowered mayor, "Sunny" Jim Rolph. The irrepressible "Lord Mayor" loved parades and pageantry but loathed administration, which he graciously abandoned to a kitchen cabinet dominated by Theodore Roche. The power-conscious Roche served as president of the San Francisco police commissions and behind him stretched the long green line, the law-enforcing legal substructure of Irish urban control.

Precinct Captain Michael J. Riordan, a law graduate and one-time Hallinan partner, was the youthful police chief-in-waiting after the immediate heir apparent, Dullea, succeeded the incumbent, William Quinn. John J. O'Toole occupied the city attorney's office and Matthew Brady served as district attorney. With Egan in jail, another Irishman, Gerald Kenney, moved up to be the public defender.

Angelo Rossi sat behind the mayor's desk because Jimmy Rolph, for all his baby kissing, had managed to pass the crown to his personal political heir. Once enthroned, the Italian became a captive of the Irish system, which nevertheless tolerated his presence.

The murder of a woman, who may not have known the names of these notables, threatened their hierarchy all the same. It did so by acutely embarrassing the mayor by holding him publicly accountable for what he could not control. His police had not apprehended Egan. His city attorney had not removed Egan from office. His inaction appeared to be confirmed by Hallinan's political counteroffensive.

Hallinan realized that the defense he designed was a threat to establishment figures. He did not choose the defense for this reason, but, he said, "I didn't care what head rolled as long as it wasn't Egan's."

Police leaders had discussed Egan's planning of the murder of Jessie Hughes and had not intervened. Some officers simply discounted his plans with Dr. Housman as meaningless bravado induced by an equal mix of inferiority complex and the bootleg booze his underworld defendants kicked back in gratitude for free service. Others thought, let him sound off "like a raving 'kook' and a potential maniac. . . ." If the woman turned up dead, it would be one murder the department could solve and its solution would leave a good job vacant. The difference between these reactions was the difference between honest though faulty judgment and absolute callousness. After the killing, Egan no longer enjoyed mayor-in-waiting status, so protecting him fell to an even lower police priority than saving Mrs. Hughes had previously. In fact, the sooner the police could get Egan out of the way without exposing themselves, the safer they would be.

Chief Quinn was avid to learn what Egan and his attorney actually knew about the police, particularly after Hallinan threatened to "blow the lid off the department" if the police did not lay off Egan. No sooner did Egan finally surrender than the chief himself rushed out to the station house to confront him. Quinn insisted on knowing, "What dirt does Egan have on the department?"

The newspapers shared Hallinan's lack of knowledge about police involvement but stepped up the attack on the mayor anyway and predicted a scandal big enough to rock the nation. Pointed editorials asked, "What, Mr. Mayor, Are You Going to Do About [the] Police?" Among other wild charges, the papers suggested that the police had let Egan remain at large so he could commit suicide.

Outraged by the way Hallinan twice had intervened and prevented the police from apprehending Egan, Mayor Rossi phoned Hallinan and asked him to allow the police to serve Egan with a subpoena.

Amid the political uproar that followed, Rossi threatened to "clean house" in the police department. To do so, however, would be neither easy nor wise, given Roche's virtually independent leadership of the police. And to attack Roche in order to get at the department would jeopardize that sensitive ethno-political equilibrium which provided for the tranquil governing of San Francisco. Any move against Roche would signal the Irish to drift away from Rossi and to gather behind one of their own kind. Rossi knew that the long-term labor supervisor, Andrew Gallagher, for one, would welcome that political indiscretion with glee.

The Frank Egan case elevated Vincent Hallinan to a position of legal prominence from which he never retreated. Always a fighter, he liked to be well-prepared and to unload on the opposition. This time his uncertainty about the prosecution's secret source of information offered added incentive. First, he intended to prevent Golden from unloading on him.

Hallinan and Coghlan agreed that they knew more than Golden did. After all, Egan and Tinnin were their sources. How close they would stay in the running would depend, not on further preparation but on juror bias. The more experienced Coghlan told Hallinan, "We must let the jury know that they can return less than a hanging verdict without making them suspect that we will be satisfied." Hallinan fully accepted that objective.

Together in examining each juror they explained the different verdicts and pointedly asked, "If at the end of this trial you have some reasonable doubt, will you acquit or will you resort to some compromise verdict?"

Since personal integrity required "acquit," that was the answer each juror automatically mouthed. Hallinan considered the answer irrelevant. It was the question that was important. It offered a tempting moral compromise to any juror who did not want to execute a human even when there was no reasonable doubt. They aimed the question at jurors who doubted themselves, not the evidence.

Their objective then was a verdict just short of the death penalty. Any unexpected ground they might pick up during the trial could allow Hallinan and Coghlan to demand more in final arguments, but, first, prudence compelled them to seek only the lives of their clients. On that basis they entered the court.

When Judge Frank H. Dunne, a shrewd veteran of the California Superior Court, seated himself on the bench and looked down at Prosecutor Isadore Golden and his daytime shadow, Captain Dullea, he saw two law enforcers absolutely certain of the defendants' guilt. Dunne also saw two officials terribly mindful of their ghastly predicament. Their most conclusive evidence, improperly acquired, impaled them with their prey since a timely word could have prevented the killing of a woman the police were sworn to protect. Whether Judge Dunne was privy, at the time of the trial, to police foreknowledge is unknown. The jurist was seventy years of age and since his elevation to the bench in 1898, he regularly assumed the popular side of sensational cases and vehemently backed the prosecution. Perhaps he did so because he was correct, or because Hallinan was irritating, or because he was concurrently running for re-election. Each of these adequate explanations assumes, however, his blissful innocence of the police complicity.

To watch Hallinan deploy the Egan defense, as many as 2,000 hopefuls formed pre-dawn lines for a chance at 180 courtroom seats. On fogless mornings they gathered as early as 2:00 A.M. Those less hearty contented themselves with the frequent radio bulletins and well-photographed court scenes which the papers featured daily throughout the summer. In California and the West, the news coverage was monumental. In fact, the national interest in the case was one of the enticements Hallinan had offered Coghlan for his participation.

Prosecutor Golden plunged immediately into the morass of Egan's financial affairs in order to establish a motive for the crime. He called bankers, brokers, and a variety of business people to the stand to plow through a tangle of mortgage foreclosures, altered bank books, defaulted notes, and a web of personal indebtedness. He interspersed pitiful case histories of older women who had trusted their savings and property to the care of a respected public official, all with unprofitable and some with fatal results. Each irregularity, Golden maintained, brought Egan closer to the edge of discovery and disgrace. Through the evidence he constructed a picture of a hidden Egan who looted the next estate to cover his tracks across the last. Golden produced the Hughes insurance policies and developed the implications of Egan's double indemnity clauses in case of Jessie Hughes's accidental death.

Even though Egan earned a princely salary during the depression year, (eight thousand dollars), his financial affairs appeared hopeless. Other attorneys and businessmen who represented the interests of those whom Egan allegedly had fleeced had commenced action for forcible recovery. Right before her death Mrs. Hughes herself had resorted to hounding Egan at his office and creating scenes whenever she cornered him. Publicly and loudly she demanded her money back.

Golden concluded that Frank Egan's motive was strong. The woman's death would relieve him of her claims, and her insurance money and estate would add buoyancy to his sinking accounts. The prosecutor's only deficiency was his inability to produce the woman's will.

Thirty years later Hallinan advised beginning lawyers that, "It's well . . . to use reasonable refinements. But, in the last analysis the rule is: Get your hands on the Thing and bury it." His instruction appears to be the best explanation of the missing document. Before Hallinan entered the case Egan unwisely claimed to be the sole beneficiary. After he entered there was no evidence on the matter.

Establishing the motive was the prologue to the accusatory testimony of Golden's star witness, Verne Doran. This baby-faced offender swore that he followed a murder plan concocted by Egan because he depended upon him for his continued liberty and because he thought Egan was brilliant. He turned on his former benefactor and offered state's evidence only because he felt trapped when Egan failed to help him at the coroner's inquest.

Yes, he drove Postel's big Lincoln over the woman, while Tinnin held her under the wheel. The act was theirs. The plan was Egan's. For killing the woman, Egan gave him a new hat. That was all there was to it.

Almost every question which flowed from Golden's lips brought Hallinan to his feet with challenges and objections. The more often Judge Dunne ruled for the prosecution, the more aggressive Hallinan became. First Dunne ignored him. When Hallinan argued, Dunne told him, "That's enough."

"No, that's not enough!" Hallinan shot back again.

"You're not going to make a speech now," Dunne rebutted, only to have Hallinan take exception to Dunne's deprecatory remarks toward him in the presence of the jury. Typical exchanges ended with Hallinan asking Dunne to cite himself for judicial misconduct. That Dunne ignored contemptuously.

Each day the reporters tangled their metaphors, describing Hallinan as a prize fighter, who so far had evaded Dunne's knock-out punch, or a high-wire artist courting a fall. "How long will Hallinan last?" they wondered in print. He did not wonder. Instead, he used proper language, watched Dunne's tolerance, and calculated. His father, Pat, showed him a clipping from one of Father Yorke's old editorials in the Irish *Leader*. The militant priest had called

Dunne a "wretched little renegade" who "looks like the
'before taking' advertisement of a patent medicine." Vince
intended not to go that far, but he figured he had plenty of
room. He felt certain that Dunne would keep the trial moving
at least until his own safe re-election.

Hallinan's previous objections looked like innocent
inquiry compared with his cross-examination of Doran. Even
though Golden and Dunne gave the witness all the protection
they could, Hallinan used the slow-witted accuser as the
launching pad for the defense. Every question contained
Hallinan's slashing accusation that Doran acted alone in a
burglary gone wrong and now, to save his own neck, he gave
false testimony against former friends. To discredit Doran
and restrict to him alone the full responsibility for the
murder, Hallinan contorted his demeanor into a savage
mockery. Every question was a frontal assault delivered with
a sneer.

He bared Doran's powerlessness, his utter dependence
upon his captors. His probation was revoked by them and his
current term would be determined by them. Hallinan
brushed aside the shallow illusion that Doran had no "immunity," which Golden had tried to foist upon the jury.
Doran had turned state's evidence and surely would be
rewarded. Next Hallinan detailed Doran's preferential treatment in jail and lunches he, the confessed murderer, enjoyed
at the home of his mother. Hallinan intended to lead the jury
to conclude that Doran was the one who was getting away
with murder.

Demeaning Doran was a painless enough task but its
purpose was to prepare the ground for defense witnesses.
Since Hallinan would be unable to destroy Doran's testimony
with spectacular evidence of his own, he pinned him down
on the exact details of times, places, and people. That
allowed him to firm up the witnesses for the defense.

Next, Golden called Doran's sister to support his confession. She knew of his activities on the day of the killing because he took time out to use the death car to help her move.
This time Coghlan cross-examined. What he lacked of Hal-

linan's drama he gained in brutal directness. Coghlan's starting point was that Doran's family had previously prepared an alibi story for the boy; only his confession forced them to abandon it. Since Coghlan and Hallinan were ideally suited to know that, Coghlan's eye-to-eye confrontation with the young and frightened woman provoked telling results. She would not admit and would not deny what her crumbling appearance testified was true. She suffered an emotional breakdown in the witness chair.

She wanted to save her brother. If she had been prepared to save him through perjury for the defense, Coghlan observed, why should she not do the same for a more powerful prosecution? The implication reflecting upon defense counsels hardly flattered either of them, but neither entered the Egan case for appearances.

Attempting again to corroborate Doran's confession Golden produced neighbors of Mrs. Hughes, one of whom had seen a "big black automobile" backing out of the Hughes garage at the time Doran swore he and Tinnin were executing Egan's plan. Another neighbor swore she saw Egan himself as per Doran's confession, loitering near her home for forty minutes on the afternoon of the murder. Golden kept this witness, Elizabeth P. Thompson, a secret and sprung her on Hallinan as a complete surprise.

Again Hallinan was abusive and denigrating in cross-examination. Once more Judge Dunne warned him about "barking at the witness." Mrs. Thompson's reaction to Hallinan was to play the offended coquette. She playfully declined to state how long she had worn eyeglasses and she refused to reveal her age. This Hallinan seized as vanity which he quickly compounded with a desire for personal notoriety. Having used her in that limited way for the defense he dismissed her as a vain publicity seeker. More was needed though. Her testimony placed Egan near the scene of the crime and corroborated a part of the confession. Therefore she would have to be contradicted by the defense.

Vincent Hallinan transformed himself on August 23, the day the prosecution rested and the defense began its own case. No longer did he "bluster, shout, thrust forward that square chin of his! . . ." The new witnesses were his and he treated them with polite consideration.

His first move was to discredit the motivation Golden attributed to Egan. Dramatically he waved in the air a pack, four inches thick, of canceled checks Egan used to pay the widow's bills. He admitted that much of the money was her own but he claimed that much of it was Egan's too. Instead of Egan owing her money as Golden alleged, financial obligation ran the other way. To enter all the checks into evidence Hallinan called a parade of twenty-seven witnesses. His motivation was deeper though.

During free evenings he unraveled the labyrinthine world of Egan's financial affairs. After he sorted things out, he catalogued the numerous payments Egan made to trades-men to cover Mrs. Hughes's normal purchases. At the onset of the depression these merchants were happy for the patron-age and neither knew nor cared where the money originated. Next, Hallinan had his investigator, William Shaughnessy, compile a list of businessmen with whom the jurors traded. Then he paired up the lists and selected defense witnesses who appeared on both lists and were known to have friendly relations with the jurors. "When the prosecutor is capable and prepared, and the judge is with him, all you can do is to go to the jury. If the evidence you have is not the best, you need to offer them encouragement to forget the evidence." Each witness exchanged friendly greetings with Egan in the presence of the jury.

The heart of the defense was the attempted refutation of Doran's confession as it implicated Egan and Tinnin. For their main thrust Hallinan and Coghlan produced two wit-nesses, both convicts. One San Quentin prisoner testified that Doran had previously asked him "to prowl the old lady's joint" so they could sell whatever they found. The second, a narcotics offender from the county jail who shared a cell with Doran, swore that Doran told him, "He's just bumped off an ol' lady . . . an' the only way he can save his neck is to tie in Frank Egan. . . . An' he says he's gonna do it. . . ."

Hallinan's humiliation of Doran had been intended to

reduce Golden's star to the level of the two who now contradicted him. His success the jury would decide.

Next, Coghlan called Mrs. Burton Barton, who unabashedly proclaimed to the court that Albert Tinnin, a ladies' man, spent three hours with her in her hotel room while Jessie Hughes was being killed. She had recently been found not guilty of selling fraudulent oil stock. The public defender's office had represented her. Besides these suggestive facts Golden was able to shake nothing else from her in two hours of cross-examination. Her credentials may not have been the best, but that was her testimony.

Hallinan had never been sure, until Golden rested his case, that the deputy district attorney would not, without warning, call Lorraine Kipp Egan to the stand as a witness against Frank and thereby reveal another choice morsel in an already saturated case. California law did prevent a wife from being compelled to testify against her husband, but, to add another bizarre feature to the murder trial, Hallinan had no proof that Frank and Lorraine had ever been legally married and he would be unable to offer any. If Golden called Lorraine, he intended to object and, while unable to produce documentation, he had worked out a story that included a timely church fire which destroyed years of records. Knowing that Dunne would overrule this, he prepared Lorraine so that Golden would regret having called her. When he failed to summon her to the stand Hallinan decided to use her himself. He staged a scene in which Egan sprang to his feet, proclaimed his love for his wife, and pleaded that she not be subjected to the agony of the witness stand. After due display Hallinan prevailed, as usual, and a validated Mrs. Egan was sworn.

She and Egan had three attractive young children and, married or not, she loved her man and remained loyal always. Her daily court presence, on Hallinan's advice, was intended to erode newspaper-induced hostility to Egan. She testified that she went to her husband's office on the afternoon of the killing and stayed with him during the time Mrs. Thompson said he loitered in the Hughes neighborhood. Frank drove her home where they had dinner and he remained until they argued about him going out again to the fights. He left and had to hurry in order to join Dr. Housman. In effect then, Doran's confession was as false as Thompson's corroboration was erroneous. So testified Lorraine Kipp Egan.

When Golden waived cross-examination, Hallinan's respect for the prosecutor plummeted. Had his research been thorough, Golden could have demanded proof that Mrs. Egan was who she represented herself to be. He could have destroyed the witness, destroyed the testimony and destroyed Frank Egan. That evening Hallinan and Coghlan concluded that whatever the cause of the extraordinary prosecution knowledge, it was not hard work. With that cue in mind Hallinan informed Golden that he did not intend to have Egan appear as a witness in his own defense, a tactic entirely consistent with Hallinan's manner and conduct of the case. His intent was to lead Golden to believe that the preparation of a formal cross-examination would be so much unnecessary work.

When Hallinan called Egan to the stand Golden's surprise exceeded Hallinan's when Golden had called Mrs. Thompson. Besides surprise, Golden showed indignation. He made the mistake of believing Hallinan and was taken in by the attractiveness of having to do less work.

Egan's testimony added nothing new to the evidence but it did satisfy Hallinan's imperative. Person to person, Egan told the jurors that he was innocent. They might not credit him with innocence but they would consider silence as self-incrimination despite the law to the contrary. Egan denied all guilt, contradicted Doran, and corroborated the testimony of the alibi witnesses. Throughout, Hallinan carefully restricted Egan's direct testimony to events of the day Jessie Hughes died and the day before.

Golden had been caught so unprepared that he asked Judge Dunne for time to prepare a proper cross-examination. It was early in the day, so in order not to delay the trial Dunne required Golden to proceed as best he could, just as Hallinan anticipated.

The cross-examination was a failure because Golden had

not worked out in advance the means by which he could draw Egan into his web of incriminating financial motivation. Each time Golden went directly to the question of looted estates, Hallinan objected that cross-examination was proper only on matters included in the direct testimony, the events of April 28–29, 1932. Had Golden thought out his questions beforehand, he might have molded them into a form which Dunne could have allowed. By misleading the opposing counsel, Hallinan advanced the case of his client. That too he considered an appropriate part of a not-guilty plea.

At the trial's end Golden showed the effect of a legal battle with a powerhouse twenty years his junior. At age fifty-four, Golden was anticipating a death or retirement from the bench so he could obtain a judicial appointment. In the meantime, both he and Dullea were making plans for recuperative fall vacations so they could forget the Egan case. Not Hallinan. The daily court combat was fun. Besides, every evening he was joining his new girlfriend, an absolute beauty named Vivian Moore. Just being with her calmed him down and made him feel content, even happy. "For the first time I thought I understood why others resorted to drink or drugs to turn on. After raising hell with Golden and Dunne in court, just riding to dinner with Vivian gave me a physical sense of relief and satisfaction. We didn't even have to talk. Maybe that was it."

The pressure Hallinan put on Golden caused the prosecutor's ultimate loss of composure. In a final strategic ploy Hallinan moved that summary statements be waived on both sides and that the jury should decide upon the testimony already on record. His intent was, given the bulk of evidence and the mental confusion which always surrounds it, the jurors would favor the story they heard last—that is, his. Golden, who knew he had been had by Egan's testimony, refused to so stipulate and he began his own review of the evidence with a roar.

His tirade dripped with venom as he piled high the hideous details of the crime. Normally a dispassionate speaker, Golden clearly displayed his conviction that Egan was a wanton and vicious man, a monster fit only for the rope. Transfixed by the two-hour denunciation Egan's eyes radiated pure hate.

So complete was Golden's horrible word picture that Hallinan could not be content with partial exceptions, reinterpretations, or mitigating circumstances. He had to attack absolutely everything Golden said. When he finished the papers concluded that the two "pictures were so widely at variance, so separated by all that is good and bad, that it was difficult to figure how two able attorneys, skilled thinkers, as Golden and Hallinan could both be convinced they spoke the truth."

Hallinan had begun with a lie. He apologized for his lack of oratorical skill. "My worthy opponent was a seasoned veteran when I was in knee pants."

He loved Frank Egan, his friend, and he did not want him to be lost because of his attorney's inadequacies. That was why Hallinan wanted the evidence, not Golden's experience and polish, to determine the decision.

With that prologue, he unloaded on Golden and the police everything but Judge Dunne's gavel. He traveled down his mental check list: Egan's humble start, hard work, ambition, and merited respect, his love for his wife, the three innocent children, the despised of the city whom Egan defended, the enmity of the police and the district attorney. Egan was a brilliant attorney who, if he wanted Mrs. Hughes killed, would not have concocted such a muddled plan to be executed by a dim-witted boy. Doran gave a false confession to gratify the police and to save himself from just punishment for a stupid, burglary-related killing. Without Doran's self-serving testimony, there was no case. The whole prosecution, Hallinan said, "the State has manufactured from their scheming minds!"

Hallinan had been tipped off that there were two anti-Semites on the jury so he played that card too. Omitting Egan's marital irregularity and his uninterest in Hibernian affairs, Hallinan cast him as a persecuted Irish Catholic. The prosecutor was Golden, the Jew. Golden's God was not the Christian savior of mercy and justice. He was the God of vengeance and hate. He referred to Edward Gibbon's *Decline and Fall of the Roman Empire* and asserted that Jews hated the rest of mankind and got what they deserved when the Romans destroyed Jerusalem and dispersed its people to wander the earth. "Isadore Golden is a fanatic."

Golden's wife was prominent in San Francisco philanthropic circles which, given the ethnic peculiarities of San Francisco, was dominated by upper-class, civic-minded Jews. Frequently she brought her friends and occupied reserved seats just behind the prosecution table. Hallinan was piqued by the way Golden protected Dr. Housman throughout the trial and saved him from being arrested by Dullea. Hallinan was convinced that because "Housman's father was a Rabbi and a friend of Golden" the "combination of personal, social and religious motives rescued" the doctor. Still, Hallinan's anti-Semitic statements were the low point of his final initiative for Egan, all the more so because they sprang from calculation. "If casting myself as a religious bigot would save my client, that is what I would do."

Though procedurally excluded from participating in the prosecutor's final charge to the jury, Hallinan would not be silent. At each utterance by Golden he objected, argued, and took exceptions. Now the trial was all but over, mistrial was impossible and Judge Dunne was safely re-elected. With these restraints gone Dunne cited Hallinan for contempt of court, had him forcibly removed, and placed him in jail. It was the fourth contempt citation of his career but not his last.

Hallinan's reaction was, "So what?" The day in jail symbolized his extra effort for Egan. By depriving Hallinan's client of the counsel of his choice and by substituting in his place Egan's former deputy, a man who actually testified against Egan, Dunne added to the grounds for appeal.

The jurors' deliberation was longer than any of Hallinan's previous cases; they were locked up for three days. In the end the verdict was the compromise Coghlan had envisioned. Egan and Tinnin were found guilty of murder in the first degree, but the jury rejected Golden's demand for the death penalty. From the start no juror chose execution and two held out for acquittal through fifty hours of discussion.

Whether or not they were the pair Hallinan aimed at is mercifully lost to history.

Police foreknowledge was a secret which could not be kept indefinitely. A private operative, Ignatius H. McCarthy, planted the tap for the police. Gradually the canard made the rounds of the precinct locker rooms that cops who were assigned to visit Dr. Housman's office on other matters were overheard trying to interest him in side deals of their own. In any case, the police, anticipating the inevitability of public disclosure as well as Hallinan's appeal for a new trial, acted decisively. Captain Dullea revealed that the police knew the murder plan all the time!

A belated, incredible disclosure.

Hallinan responded by advising Egan to abandon his appeal for re-trial, because if he got it, according to California law he might exchange a life sentence for the gallows.

The new sensation reduced respect for the police to an unprecedented low; popular revulsion became widespread. Since the case had first broken, opinions of the police roller coastered from images of incompetent oafs who could not catch Hallinan's client, to master detectives who cracked a brutal murder, to co-conspirators who for their own unfathomed purposes snuffed a life they had sworn to protect. The end result, however, was nothing. Since the police authority contained the dubious mechanism for investigating its own misdeeds, the self-applied whitewash surprised no informed observers. No members of the police commission asked *the* question. Why did the department let Mrs. Hughes die? No official explanation of police motivation was therefore offered.

Undoubtedly the mayor, district attorney, city attorney, police chief, commissioners, and all the inspectors breathed sighs of relief. Egan was locked away in the state penitentiary. The task had not been as easy as they had hoped, but at last his attorney finally lost the handle which rattled the Hall of Justice and with it City Hall itself.

The traditional disposition of power in the city remained undisturbed, and comfortable routine, sanctioned by the status quo, settled in with the ease and comfort of the evening fog.

Needless to say, Hallinan's credibility with the police and the press hardly improved. For the moment, the papers attacked the police department and forgot Hallinan, but that about-face was as temporary as it was unnatural. After the police commission applied the wash, the press reverted soon enough to law-and-order traditionalism, once again casting the city's finest in the role of guardians of civic peace and personal safety. That left Hallinan, the proponent of police conspiracy, as a troublemaker at best, a suborner of perjury at worst. From his own ethnic subculture he continued as an outcast. Official misbehavior by the police was acceptable because of close Irish Catholic identification with authority at the personal and theoretical levels. Occasional abuse of power was expected. Hallinan's challenges and ridicule of authority were not occasional and, therefore, not acceptable.

To the Irish the behavior of their most promising son could be explained only one way. "He was depraved!" Those who were less politically aware found little in the newspapers to suggest that the Irish were wrong.

Subsequent Events

1934   Doran released from prison after serving two years for manslaughter. Isadore Golden appointed judge.

1939   Hallinan tried for bribing witnesses. Defended by Coghlan. Prosecuted by John R. Golden, son of Isadore Golden.

1940   Charles Dullea appointed chief of police.

1948   Michael Riordan appointed chief of police.

1957   Egan and Tinnin released from prison after twenty-five years. Lorraine Kipp Egan deceased. Hallinan hosts Egan at reception also marking his own reinstatement to legal practice.

1961   Egan dies at San Francisco General Hospital.

Patrick and Elizabeth Hallinan with son, Vincent, and his two older sisters (1897).

Vincent Hallinan, second from right, wearing mathematics medal; Saint Ignatius High School class at Golden Gate Park Lodge (1913).

Right: *Hallinan as Agnetian Club center (1923).*

Below: *Frank Egan (facing Hallinan), Hallinan, Nate Coghlan (partially obscured), Albert Tinnin (1932).*

Vivian Moore, Hallinan, Lorraine Kipp Egan (1932).

Isadore Golden, Walter Frame, Egan, Tinnin, Hallinan, Coghlan (1932).

Hallinan and Vivian Moore, off to Reno wedding (1932).

"Christ, if I believed in God, I'd have to admit
that He sent me Vivian."

— Vincent Hallinan
April 12, 1980

6. Settling Down for the Distance

Vivian Moore was unlike any of the other girls Vince had known. She liked danger and thrived on excitement, even at nineteen, when the successful attorney first met her. She was, Vince thought, "competitive, self-reliant, and a knockout. Even though I intended to stay a bachelor, she never gave me a chance. The little bastard picked me off just like I was nothing."

During the weeks when Frank Egan had been in hiding and Vince was making himself scarce too, the police barged into Vivian's apartment on the correct assumption that her boyfriend would call. Unknown to the plainclothesmen, Hallinan already had. Their surprise visit delayed Vivian's departure for a rendezvous with Hallinan at Egan's hideout. When Vivian denied being very well-acquainted with Hallinan, officer Mike Desmond smiled and sat down to wait.

At that, Vivian excused herself and promptly exited through the bathroom window. Her spirit and beauty created in Hallinan an admiration and enchantment from which he never recovered. Vivian Moore transformed him from a mama's boy the public never suspected him of being, into a fiercely loyal husband and a devoted, though highly unorthodox, father.

Fourteen years his junior, she was twenty-one by the time they married. He was thirty-five. For two years she had

102

toyed with the hot emotions of San Francisco's most noted attorney. She was as willful as he, every bit as designing, and considerably more charming—at least men thought so. What Vivian lacked in breadth of worldly exposure she possessed in intensity of personal resolve. So unpleasant were the recollections of her girlhood that at age sixty-eight she hoped, perhaps, that one line might suffice. "My childhood was what you would expect given the life I made and lived."

Unwanted and unloved by divorced parents, Vivian moved from home to home among her mother's extended family. In some she found abuse, in others, merely indifference. As she transferred from one school to the next, suspicion and rejection became her most frequent schoolyard companions. To compensate for her emptiness and insecurity, the lonely child embroidered what she later called her "great enterprise." When she grew up she would have children of her own, six in fact, and they would all be boys — intelligent, handsome, and courageous. Not until her teens did she fully realize that a husband would be required, one with characteristics suitable to her extraordinary expectations.

As a history student at the University of California, Berkeley, she could pick from among athletes and partygoers. Some were fun but none were right. One evening when a date's car broke down, his friend, Vincent Hallinan, called for her. "That night all those little boys walked into my dream. The biggest told me, 'Viv, this might be the guy.'"

Following the Egan verdict and before the sheriff arrested Vince to serve his time for contempt, they drove off to Reno and were married at St. Thomas Aquinas Cathedral on September 23, 1932. Religion meant nothing to Vivian, although her relatives were nominal Catholics. Despite her husband's hostility toward Catholicism, they married in the Church, he said years later, out of consideration to his parents. Whatever the reason, when they returned to San Francisco, Elizabeth objected to the union under any rite. Instead of celebrating the late marriage of her providing son, she accepted the condolences of older women who made no effort to mask their sympathy for Elizabeth at the loss of her prized possession. As the new bride stepped into the Hallinan home for the first time, one neighbor told Elizabeth, "Maybe she'll die young."

Vivian held her tongue as Vincent's mother stepped into the classic role of the deprived Old Country mother. Vivian was young and vulnerable but intended not to remain defenseless. That week she unfolded a plan she had already considered at length.

Hallinan's practice slackened considerably after the Egan trial. He still earned enough to keep his numerous dependents going but the dip in income made his bride aware of how uncertain an attorney's fees were. Factors as unpredictable as public opinion or even health were critical. She wanted her six sons but she also wanted security and independence for them regardless of their father's success or failure. A stronger propellant, however, moved her to action.

"I wanted to do something myself and I did not want him to dominate me or run my life. When his mother turned away from me in cold regret, I promised myself that her son never would. My subordination and dependence were therefore undesirable for both of us."

Hallinan held second mortgages on two apartment buildings when the depression hit and forced both owners to default. To retain his investment he assumed the bank payments on the first mortgages and met the monthly installments from his own reduced income. The buildings themselves earned nothing. The units were inadequately equipped, some even cannibalized to maintain the others, and more were vacant during the renter's market of the depression. Vincent's plan was to stop throwing good money after bad and let them go in default himself. The banks would not lend him any money for renovation and that sort of work did not interest him anyway. His bride's interest was so strong, though, that he gave her the structures and wished her luck.

She inspected the properties. ("They were even worse

than he said.") Then she talked with realtors and read all the books on property management in the public library. They told her everything she needed to know except how to convert the near-abandoned buildings into attractive, rentable units without money.

First she concentrated on the larger building, a five-story concrete structure containing twenty-four two-room apartments. "I went to the bank," Vivian wrote in her family history, *My Wild Irish Rogues*, "and stated the whole problem to the vice-president. . . . I wished to paint and furnish the building and wanted a moratorium on . . . payments for six months." He reviewed her plans and tendered the loan.

Next, she lined up furniture and appliance dealers, contractors, painters and en route she educated herself on interior design, fabrics, lighting, and rodent control. In these transactions she offered good business to eager merchants and tradesmen who were themselves beset by the depression. To close the deals, they had to shave their profit margins and accept installment payments ninety days after delivery.

Fortunately the building was centrally located and ideal for a distinct type of person which downtown San Francisco attracted, that is, one who did not own a car and liked to be near the action. At full occupancy Vivian could offer the units at low rates, still meet her payment schedules, and have a profit.

She had each unit painted and furnished in bright, cheerful colors and designs, with integrated carpets, drapes, and furniture coverings. She showed only two apartments to any one applicant so the emptiness of the building would be less apparent and in each unit she placed eye-catching vases with freshly cut flowers. The darker rooms she showed only in the daytime and made sure the shades were up. Within three months she had rented every apartment.

All her revenue went to satisfy the numerous outstanding accounts, and more than once she had to seek further extensions. The liberality of those she dealt with was, of course, a characteristic of depression era business life. She always phoned if she were unable to make a payment and they always were content to wait a bit longer. Vince attributed her success not to the shape of the national economy but to the shape of his wife. "She just charmed the pants off all those guys from the bank manager to the rag-bottle-sack man." Even when she was pregnant it seemed to help. Heavy in her eighth month she prepared herself to haggle at length with her favorite furniture dealer, but, mysteriously, he gave in without a fight. "She was so big! Babies are good. God sends them. I no want hers to land on my chesterfield."

The event that brought Vivian into property ownership and management for good was the announcement of one of President Franklin Roosevelt's depression-fighting tactics, the change of the price of gold at one point from twenty dollars to thirty-five dollars an ounce. Vivian was on the ground floor of what was to become a steady and then an accelerated inflationary spiral. She reasoned then that it was far better to encumber herself in debt by the old deflated standard, hold real property which would inflate with the economy, and pay off with less valuable, inflated dollars.

She did not foresee the runaway inflation of the next generation but by the 1980s she was on top of the soaring real estate market and riding higher with each surge. In 1935 she made her critical move.

A widening circle of bankers, realtors, and contractors knew her well. She was young but learned quickly and when she turned a profit so did they. One of these realtors brought her attention to a heavily mortgaged, thirty-nine unit apartment in downtown San Francisco. The owner was so hard pressed that he was willing to sell his equity for only $2,500, but he had to have the money by the very next day. Vivian was still stalling her creditors, and loans were impossible. What she did was gather the money from forty relatives and friends in small checks, even coins.

Four months later she purchased her fourth building. It contained thirty-two units. To make that deposit, she had to press for an advantageous division of rents from the very building she was trying to purchase. By then the first buildings Vince had given her were at full occupancy and helping to fund the others as well as meet their own payments. When she took stock Vivian realized that all of her transactions were completed on the investment of seven thousand dollars in cash, which represented about three percent of the market value of the properties. She was keeping her tenants happy, her creditors satisfied, and was learning all sorts of interesting business practices.

Through most of these years Hallinan's persisting battles against court corruption commanded his own professional attention. After 1939, when he turned the tide against Mulvey, he began winning record awards in damage suits. Hallinan's settlements marked the start of the California-led trend for larger and larger awards. In 1944 he won a $125,000 judgment against the Bank of America and four years later raised the California record to $195,000, that time against another corporate giant, the Bechtel Corporation. Given the opponents and the dates, both were stunning awards, which initiated a new era in American legal history.

Hallinan always encouraged his wife even though she seldom paid attention to his advice on matters outside his strictly legal domain. Occasionally when a strike prevented the delivery of furniture she had promised to snooty tenants, Vince happily transported tables and chairs across town and up the service elevators. "One lady even tipped me. A nickel! Of course I took it. When it comes to money, I'm hard to insult."

When it came to smoking rats out of sewer pipes, Vivian put the famous attorney on the smudge-pot end and wielded the bat herself. Baseball was a sport Vince had never played, and the first time he swung at a brown Norway rat, he hit the rusty pipe so hard he broke it. What Vivian had saved on the exterminator she more than lost on the plumber.

Hallinan was fortunate indeed to be pried away from a possessive mother by a youngster with good looks, good sense, and abundant nerve. She gave him personal stability, fortification in adversity, and six children—all sons.

Vivian planned her family so that one child arrived every other year through the first five: Patrick Sarsfield (Butch),

Terence Tyrone (Kayo), Michael de Valera (Tuffy), Matthew
Brennis (Dynamite), and Conn Malachy (Flash). Thereafter
she suffered three miscarriages; all would have been boys.
Daniel Barry, the youngest, arrived after sixteen years of
marriage but his nickname, Dangerous, never seemed to
stick. What was to become California's most uproariously
active family owed its strength in numbers to a half-Genoese
and half-Irish mother.

The poverty of Hallinan's youth stripped Vince of any
illusions about the joys of large families. "I never wanted the
kids, none of them. She wanted them so much that I couldn't
deprive her of them. Vivian was right though. She educated,
she changed me."

Pride in family was one Hallinan characteristic Vivian
counted on. As her fantasies started materializing she captured Vince's full commitment by drawing him gradually
into the pleasant aspects of infant care. Then, during an idle
evening at home, she suggested he read the standard, pre-
Benjamin Spock baby book of the 1930s. He devoured it
enthusiastically and then repeated his normal method of
acquainting himself with any new field of interest. He
checked out as many books on child care as the librarian
would allow.

Rather than examining reviews or consulting experts he
preferred to read everything and decide for himself the disputed points. In this case he adopted his historic approach.
He chose the two most recent volumes by major publishers,
another a decade old, a view of children written in the late
nineteenth century, and a copy of Rousseau's thoughts on
child rearing. Out of all these and his personal experience
Hallinan arrived at a simple conclusion. "Treat kids well,
enrich their environment as best you can, take a genuine
interest in them and share in their activities. Be rational. Junk
superstition. Don't pamper them and get them ready for a
rotten world where there is plenty of room for them to do
interesting and useful things."

The regular arrival of sons was interspersed with more
apartment houses. Each time inflation improved Vivian's

equity, she confronted the dilemma of playing it safe or growing. The bankers and brokers who worked with her had an abundance of property dragging on the market and naturally encouraged her boldness. If she was too inexperienced to realize the magnitude of the depression and that businessmen were committing suicide in despondency, she did know how to strike bargains. That was why the opportunities sought her out.

A major escalation in her holdings took place at the behest of one of these men. His bank had obtained through foreclosure proceedings a ten-story, earthquake-proof building with sixty-three two-room apartments and four street-level stores. Vivian held mortgages and loans on five other buildings, which she also managed. Certainly she could have done without another, but this one was a beauty. The bank would accept a small down payment if she would give a mortgage on all her other properties which, over the years, she had been lifting out of debt.

Charmed by the building, she marshalled all her liquid assets, shook down her husband and the same old friends but still was $1,500 short. Depressed by her inability to close the deal, she returned home to discover that they had been burglarized. Her fur coat, the silver, jewelry, camera; everything was gone. Heartsick from her double loss, she could hardly tell Vince when he phoned.

"Viv! Why do you sound so depressed?" he asked. "I have the money you need. I hocked all that junk we've accumulated lately."

From then on the apartments became a big business. Vivian incorporated, gave herself the title of general manager, employed a platoon of workers and building managers, conducted monthly meetings, offered cash prizes as incentives, and wrote her own handbook for the superintendents and janitors. When the average occupancy rate for San Francisco was sixty-five percent, hers was ninety-three. She hid behind her self-proclaimed title to fend off tenant requests for expensive improvements. When one older resident wondered why she had such a big job at her age, Vivian had

an answer. "I'm related to the president of the corporation."
Tenants also assumed that was why she could bring her kids
with her to work during the war when domestic help was
hard to get.

Vivian's most stunning property acquisition came at a
time when she was consolidating her holdings and contem-
plating selling off smaller buildings to end the reality of debt
and the specter of foreclosures. The building she was unable
to resist was the Clay Jones, perched high atop Nob Hill. It
rose twenty stories from a ninety- by sixty-foot lot. Constructed like a fortress, it had a two-level garage and an eight-
room penthouse which constituted the highest point in the
city. In between were forty-seven luxury apartments.

San Francisco, by common agreement, commanded the
most spectacular urban view in America, possibly the world.
This building commanded San Francisco: the waterfront,
Fisherman's Wharf, both bridges, the full Bay and all its
islands and estuaries, the total expanse of the city itself, the
Ocean Beach and the Farallons out beyond the mouth of the
Golden Gate, the wooded southern counties down on the
Peninsula. What Satan offered Christ from the pinnacle of
the Temple was markedly inferior to the Clay Jones
temptation.

A small, dissension-racked corporation owned the
heavily encumbered property, and a holder of a third of the
stock wished to get out. His broker, also Vivian's, proposed
that she trade one of her smaller buildings for his shares.

Vince thought the move was an unnecessary risk and
therefore opposed it. He pointed out that she specialized in
small, low rent units which she could usually fill on the day
a previous tenant left. If she was unable to do so, the loss of
revenue was not great enough to threaten the financial
stability of her larger operation. The Clay Jones was different. It consisted of high rent, luxury units in which one
extended vacancy could be a disaster. Vince was firm.

In scrutinizing the financial posture of the Clay Jones
Corporation, Vivian immediately noticed that the gross
income was quite high but it was being siphoned off into

questionable expenditures and salaries for the officers. Therefore, as a minority stockholder, she would be getting herself
into what the seller was trying to escape. Unknown to her
husband, she made a counter offer. If the seller would
acquire a controlling interest of fifty-one percent, she would
make the trade.

He was willing but not able. Like so many others after
the crash, he had exhausted his liquid assets trying to retain
his better investments. Rather than back away, Vivian proposed to deepen the mortgage on the building she would
trade, have the new purchaser assume that too, and use the
money to obtain the majority of Clay Jones stock, which
would become hers.

He accepted. The net result for Vivian was that she had
successfully parlayed her $2,500 earlier investment in the
thirty-nine-unit building she traded into control of the most
commanding private residential structure in San Francisco,
perhaps in the world. By 1948 she owned and managed 435
rental units.

Part of Vivian's program for successful building management included dragging Vince and the growing number
of sons from one apartment residence to the next. They lived
in each one so she could identify and solve problems that
daytime inspection tours might not reveal. As the older boys
became active, the man who never desired children became
obsessed by the possibility that one of them might fall from
a window or the back porch to the pavement several stories
below. When gates and bars became ineffective against the
childhood acrobatics he himself encouraged, they purchased
an expanse of land and built a ten-room ranch-style home
south of the city limits. Gasoline rationing during World
War II brought them back to San Francisco, but as soon as
victory appeared likely they invested in a palatial estate at
Ross, seventeen miles north of the Golden Gate in Marin
County.

The Mediterranean-style villa had seen better days but
the surrounding acres were ideal for the growing boys. A
driveway hugged the north boundary along the wooded

creek bank, passed the expansive veranda, disappeared beyond a tree-circled lake, and meandered out of sight toward the back exit. The property fronted on the intersection of two sleepy country lanes and remained secluded behind handsome stone walls and massive iron gates. At the time when the California economy ranked sixth among the nations of the world, Marin County was first in the state for income per capita and Ross set the tone for Marin.

While Vivian redecorated and restored the twenty-room Spanish-tiled edifice to its former grandeur, Vince established a football field of St. Augustine grass, constructed an olympic swimming pool, and contracted for a regulation-sized gymnasium complete with a large "H" painted into the hardwoods at the half-court jump circle. By now he was his own authority on the rearing of sons and was immersed in the most active and happy phase of his long life, the only part he ever recalled with fondness and sentimentality.

Summers belonged to the children. Each spring Vincent trimmed back his case load, and Vivian completed all but routine apartment activities she could leave safely in the care of the resident managers. On the day school ended, they would abandon Ross for roughing it in the high Sierra at Camp Mather. Located between the forks of the Tuolumne River not far from Yosemite National Park, it was a mecca for kids. The camp featured hiking and riding trails, cool, clear lakes for swimming and fishing, and an abundance of wildlife which prompted nature studies.

Accommodations there harmonized with Vince's least-common-denominator approach to food, clothes, and equipage. For their second summer, they bought a small cabin stocked with a row of cots and lumpy mattresses. It was complete: no frills, no closets, and no electricity. Everyone shared the outdoor facilities and ate in the cafeteria. Once Vivian accommodated herself to the spiders, bats, snakes, and bears, she had a grand time too. Vince anticipated the yearly abandonment of Ross and welcomed exchanging briefs and depositions for nature and adventure stories. The only unrelenting pressure on him in the mountains was to maintain an inexhaustible supply of stories to bribe the small fry into going to bed.

The ritual was the same every night. After dinner it got dark quickly. Everyone jumped in between the sheets and yelled for a story, the longer the better. Vince would embellish and update classic tales with vivid scenes and colorful characters, all from memory, since he could not read in the dark. No matter how many adventures he related, the boys would all yell for another. His complete recall and captivating expression made it fun for eavesdroppers as well.

Not until several summers passed did Vivian learn that neighbors from the surrounding cabins would quietly sneak up after dark, sit their own children at the edge of the Hallinan porch, and listen. One woman, unable to contain herself, marveled that any man could memorize so much. Since the flow of the story remained undisturbed by any pauses, digressions, or mistakes, she assumed that he laboriously memorized each episode from books, which the darkness made unreadable.

Swimming came with difficulty to Hallinan. He learned through sheer force of will on his first lesson at the Olympic Club. He mastered the basic strokes but not to the point of enjoyment. To swim, particularly in fresh water, was always work. Vivian, on the other hand, had learned as a child and could skim over the water with effortless grace. That was what Vince wanted for the boys, the sooner the better.

In the 1930s the Red Cross was the ultimate authority on the subject and no local teacher doubted its dictum that seven was the earliest that lessons might safely and profitably be given to a child. Since Vince had encountered cases of drownings before that magic age was ever reached, he fell naturally into his own familiar mode; he junked authority and plunged ahead himself. That meant reading the latest as well as the historically curious treatments on swimming.

At home he showed the boys how to hold their breaths in a warm tub. During the spring rains he led the little tribe in the nude, splashing through the large mud puddles and shallow lake, whooping all the while. Though secluded by the privacy of the estate, the childhood of the Hallinan youngsters did appear rather uninhibited and unorthodox to those who ventured in behind the stone walls.

Vince improved his teaching techniques with each son, so that by the time the younger boys came along, they learned to swim earlier and easier. When Vince finally ran out of sons he turned to relatives, friends, and the black ghetto youngsters Vivian brought on picnics to Ross. Some were severely handicapped and deformed, yet they learned, too, fortified beforehand with more than the usual psychological buildup.

"Sure, people will stare at you," Hallinan would say. "The hell with them. When they see you swimming, they'll be on your side. They're going to be your friends. You can do it. I know you will. I made cookies, and ice cream is ready. Just as soon as we do our swimming, we're going to have a real party. We'll invite everyone."

Besides aquatic sports, riding and boxing became Hallinan mainstays. Here again Vince read all the manuals on horses, tried it for himself, all but sacrificed Vivian on an unruly mount, and brought on the kids. When they were hardly big enough to stay in the saddle he was shooting movies as they circled past his tripod. When color film hit the market he constructed his own darkroom and mastered that process too.

Hallinan's craving for excitement prompted him to encourage the same thrill-seeking in his sons. By reading and practicing on himself and Vivian he tried to protect the boys. But what he refused to do was wait until they were older or abandon a thrilling enterprise simply because it was dangerous. He would not sacrifice fun and excitement to caution and restraint. And of course anything he and Vivian did, Butch, Kayo, and Tuffy tried next. Then the little guys would not tolerate being left out. Before their legs reached the stirrups they learned to hold the reins and pommel together, and an occasional nudge from an older brother kept them straight in the saddle. Everyone earned his own bumps and bruises. Tragedy came close, but the Hallinans stuck together and saw each other through.

Vince's oldest sister, Annie, had two spirited but delicate little girls. The first time Vince and Vivian took them to Camp Mather, Antoinette spent a complete week in bed with asthma. The second day that she was able to eat at the cafeteria, Vince noticed a tough little boy outside the entranceway. Each time a girl passed him he would throw a small handful of dirt into the child's face, look away, and pretend innocence. "I told Vivian, 'Watch this.' No sooner did he throw it at Antoinette, than she belted him and sent him running for his mother." In three weeks, she swam to the raft, and then around the whole lake, while Vince rowed along behind her.

Annie had been denied all these things as a child just like Vince. She never made much of it though as she settled heavily into her matronly ways. After her daughter developed a healthy tan, Vince's enthusiasm got the better of him. He gave her a few riding lessons around the corral, disregarded Vivian's cautions, and took the child out on the trail with the boys.

Coming through a pass the spirited girl kicked at the lumbering beast to no effect. Frustrated, she grabbed an overhanging branch with the intention of breaking it off to use as a whip. Instead of breaking, the branch swung her light little body partially out of the saddle; one foot was free, the other firmly twisted into the stirrup. The horse bolted at the abrupt shift and the next Vince saw was Antoinette dangling, head downward, from the side of her horse. It was galloping toward him.

He quickly dismounted and slapped his horse out of the way. Waving and cajoling proved futile, so he dug in. He hit the horse across the breast with his shoulder and was knocked sprawling. It slowed the animal enough, though, to let Vince get to his knees and pull the helpless child's foot out of her tightly ensnared shoe. He was bruised and he ached for a few days, but Antoinette was fine.

The next time tragedy closed in, physical courage was useless. Kayo was twelve and Butch was fourteen. Vivian and Vince approved one more pack trip twenty-six miles into the high country beyond Mather. A few cowboys and a professional guide were managing the trip, the last of the season. It was to be the final outing before the boys returned to school in the fall.

Near almost inaccessible Benson Lake, Kayo was thrown from his horse. His skull fractured at the base and, as the wet and chilling Sierra nights passed, he developed bronchitis. Besides his sleeping bag, he had little protection other than the campfire and his brother's clothes. The first news his parents received was a phone call telling them that he was in a coma.

Vivian and Vince rode in with Yosemite Park Rangers who had already organized teams of litter bearers for an expected five-day evacuation ordeal. Butch met them on the descent into the small valley and guided them to his brother. It was the same dismal location where a girl had fallen from a horse and drowned several years before.

When Vivian reached Kayo, he was lying unconscious on the ground under a stretch of canvas which kept most of the rain off of him. He looked like death. The doctor who had ridden in from Yosemite Valley did what little he could. He told Vivian that if Kayo were hospitalized, he would recover. But the boy could not ride out and five days' travel by litter could be fatal. The young, roughly clad doctor advised Vivian to be with her son whenever he should regain consciousness and talk to him. It was an unnecessary reminder that personal presence was the best form of moral support.

Spasmodically twitching muscles were the most alarming symptoms. When she touched Kayo's hand under the bulk of coverings it was cold. Vivian knew that she could do nothing but wait. As the hours and then nights passed the blood behind his eardrums became absorbed and the vessels in his eyes shrank back to their normal size.

The California newspapers had by then picked up and sensationalized the story until it reached the magnitude of the famous 1925 underground entrapment of Floyd Collins near Mammoth Cave, Kentucky. In the Collins sensation reporters slithered 125 feet underground to interview the entombed man. In the Hallinan case reporters who had never seen horses except in movies endured the punishing ride into Benson Lake for pictures and exclusives. By pursuing the story, these journalists set into motion events that culminated in the rescue.

This was 1948. World War II had ended and the Korean War had not yet begun. To the general public the helicopter was still considered an exotic toy, certainly little beyond its experimental stage. Yet, it offered the first hope of saving the boy's life, hope which quickly evaporated in the thin mountain air.

A volunteer pilot had such difficulty raising his strange new craft off the Yosemite Valley floor that he abandoned the attempt and trucked it back to crop dusting around Fresno. The mountain altitude, and therefore the thinness of the air, strained the machine beyond its capabilities. The aborted rescue attempt deepened the gloom by the edge of Benson Lake.

The publicity which surrounded the unsuccessful rescue mission attracted the professional and humanitarian interest of the Heller Helicopter Company. The firm decided to send in Jay Demming, its swashbuckling test pilot, at the controls of its most advanced craft. He looked the part of the gallant aviator but at heart Demming was prudence itself. He scheduled his takeoff from the Yosemite floor for 4:15 A.M. when the mountain air was cool and therefore dense. Over the Ranger's radio he instructed Hallinan and the cowboys to set signal fires and to clear a 250 foot runway just in case a horizontal takeoff would be necessary.

At first light Hallinan and the others heard the pop-pop-pop of the rotary-winged aircraft before seeing its green and red running lights. Minutes later all the medical technology of the modern world awaited the injured boy. Demming jettisoned all but the minimum fuel for the return trip, he abandoned his battery, and ignored the airstrip Vince and the others had cleared through a night of ceaseless toil. With Kayo safely evacuated, Hallinan joked about his blood blisters. Everyone felt great and ate heartily. Vivian, Vince, and Butch struck camp and rode out with the firm intention never again to visit Benson Lake.

Vivian had not embarked upon marriage as an outdoor,

athletic woman. As her sons arrived and her husband threw himself into family life with the same enthusiasm he once reserved for football, she responded in her normal way; she toughened herself up and went along as an equal. By sharing so fully in the childhoods of six active and unpredictable sons, she encountered far more delight and pain than her great fantasy had promised. Vince, by devoting what remained of his middle years to their sons, recast and replayed the youth he never had. He and Vivian became the private Hallinans that the public never knew about until they started wondering what sort of parents stood behind those six young men.

Even by devoting his private life so fully to his wife and children, Hallinan still did not recapture his own lost youth. Neither did he fully escape from its limitations. "When I was a kid if you did not know how to fight, you stayed in the house. Perhaps I went a bit overboard with the boys, but I doubt it."

The six Hallinans matured in a world considerably removed from that of their father's youth. Yet, he brought them up to defend themselves and the unpopular, progressive views they freely absorbed at home. What began as boxing lessons, so the oldest could complete his convalescence from polio and a broken leg and then re-establish his former peer dominance, continued for a decade. Vince installed an Everlast Boxing Ring in the estate gym, taught what he knew, and engaged a succession of former professional fighters to finish off the fine points.

In high school the boys developed into husky young men with a father who was their chief sparring partner and rooter. When they played football, Hallinan was incapable of remaining in the stands but preferred yelling his personal encouragement from the sideline, particularly when their opponent was Marin Catholic High.

During their teen years the Hallinan boys reflected their parents' advanced and unorthodox notions on politics, religion, economics, and sex. They were uninhibited by any restrictions at home on their freedom of expression and were always encouraged to speak their minds. The outside chance of an adult reprimand or a youthful beating meant nothing. If one Hallinan found himself in difficulty, there were always five loyalists right at hand.

All of them were disrespectful of the bigotries of others and occasionally became more than inconsiderate of accepted adult prerogatives and sensitivities. Their composite reputation expanded with their father's career. They brawled with servicemen, broke jaws in street fights, and continued pounding the line for the suburban high schools. While their father was in jail, Vivian received an extortion attempt under the threat of undefined violence to the children. Thereafter, with publicity feeding on publicity, two men invaded the Ross home while she was alone, assaulted her and unsuccessfully attempted rape.

Vivian was recovering from an operation for cancer, which she convinced her assailants was a communicable disease. The police arrested the pair before they learned otherwise and before the eldest sons found them first.

One by one as the young men matriculated at Berkeley, an awesome reputation for physical violence preceded them. The graduate teaching assistants, most of whom were scarcely older than they but considerably more apprehensive, frequently became unnerved when a Hallinan name appeared on their discussion section roster. Each of the oldest four won university middleweight boxing titles. One captured the National Collegiate Athletic Association regional crown with a total of thirty-five victories. Another was a national semifinalist.

No Hallinan ever had to climb into the ring without another being there to spread the ropes. And at the big fights the loudest supporter at ringside was an older man with a deformed left hand and a twisted smile.

Like Pat and Black Mick before him, Vince was proud of his family and no one ever accused him of being quiet about it.

> "So much of this is confidential, the client-
> attorney relationship. . . .
> "What do you want?"
>
> — Vincent Hallinan
> June 5, 1978

7. Creating a Defense: The Mansfeldt Killing, 1945

Annie Irene Mansfeldt was the middle-aged wife of Dr. John H. Mansfeldt, a well-to-do general practitioner with down-town offices in the fashionable 450 Sutter Building. Married for twenty years, they had one dog, two cars, three children and an eighty-five foot yacht. Splendidly housed in a multi-level Pacific Heights home, they overlooked the Golden Gate Bridge, Alcatraz Island, and the panorama of San Francisco Bay. As far as the neighbors could tell, all was well within the Mansfeldt household. A few undoubtedly had wondered about the doctor's premature return to civilian life from the Army Medical Corps while the Pacific build-up against Japan was yet in progress, but no residents of tree-lined Vallejo Street inquired. No one in this exclusive district would assume that volunteer physicians should be subject to the same regulations as draftee privates.

The Mansfeldt children appeared to be exceptional. They were attractive, studious, and artistically gifted young-sters who added obvious joy to their mother's life. The youngest, Terry, was studying for a musical career under

120

her mother's special direction and accompaniment, their days together being consumed in violin practice. The teenagers, Irene and John, attended the best private and public schools available in the city.

Since the Mansfeldts had no close friends, or even regular social contacts, no one really knew or even wondered about their lives together behind that lovely facade. The occasional passerby detected no signs of tension, no displays of restiveness, and certainly no indications that the reclusive Mansfeldts were shortly to catapult themselves from upper-class obscurity to life-shattering fame.

The ill-fated morning of Thursday, October 4, 1945, began ominously. John had been sleeping irregularly and losing weight. His avid responses to so many odd-hour calls prompted Irene to wonder if his genuine concern for the sick had become a convenient excuse to absent himself from the demands of family life. Too often he dined hurriedly and alone, washing down his modest caloric intake with milk which invariably dribbled its way onto his neatly tailored vest. Even as a St. Ignatius classmate of Hallinan back in 1913, he had been timid and self-effacing. Now no one beyond the family guessed why the doctor had left military service. No one but his wife knew that he had been discharged on psychiatric grounds. Laboring under this additional burden, he persisted at the profession of his father, the career Irene had insisted he follow as a condition of their marriage.

His wife remained hard-working, vivacious, and attractive. Nonetheless, she carried her own emotional history, which pre-dated John's. During her critical years of dawning adolescence she had her first breakdown. Thereafter, sex became a compartment of life that was fraught with anxiety. Her own marriage at age twenty-five was arranged by her music teacher and patron, Eva Mansfeldt. "As a favor for Eva's musical favors," Irene consented to wed Eva's son. By virtue of the solemnity of marriage, Irene the protege became Irene the daughter-in-law. Both generations continued, however, to live in the same family home.

In time Irene's hunch-backed father-in-law, Dr. Oscar Mansfeldt, died and his domineering wife, Eva, lost her mind. On their own at last, the young doctor and his family moved to the Spanish-tiled home to start life anew. Their lovely children enjoyed private rooms, physical security, and rich intellectual and cultural stimulation from two psychologically intense parents.

On that fall morning, after seeing the family members off to their appointed work places, Mrs. Mansfeldt drove through downtown traffic to keep an appointment she had made with a hospital nurse, Vada Martin. She spoke briefly with Mrs. Martin in the front seat of the family sedan. In the midst of the conversation Irene Mansfeldt drew her father's old .32 caliber revolver from her purse and shot the nurse through the heart, then pistol-whipped her as she died. With the expiring woman slumped against the passenger door, she drove directly to Central Emergency Hospital and announced to a startled clerk, "There's a dying woman in my car. I shot her." Irene slid the nickel-plated revolver, still loaded, across the receiving desk, swayed slightly, and collapsed.

The sensation was immediate. News-hungry reporters fled the City Hall court corridors, hurriedly crossed Grove Street, and reached the automobile—questioning and scribbling, but mostly picture taking—right alongside of the hospital stewards. In fact, the crime photographers took a series of pictures before the medical personnel were able to bring the victim's body into the hospital.

Before noon the stylishly dressed Dr. Mansfeldt arrived, hastily identified the unconscious form of his wife, ignored the corpse, then just as quickly faded into the approaching lunch-time crowds. The doctor made no statement, volunteered nothing to the police, and for the moment became as great a mystery as the two women he left behind. He walked off and vanished.

His absence hardly concerned the authorities. Both Police Inspector Alvin Corrasa and Assistant District Attorney Hardin McGuire knew their jobs well enough to realize that this crime offered no professional challenge. The basic mystery was not the usual, "Who done it?" but rather, "Why did she?" So certain was this case that anything short of conviction, even execution, would reflect unfavorably upon themselves and their departments. Methodically then, they commenced their investigation.

The contents of the victim's purse told Corrasa that Vada Martin was a thirty-six year old registered nurse. Normally she worked the early night shift at Sutter Hospital, then located not too far from Dr. Mansfeldt's office. She was a married woman who had been maintaining herself in a quiet and respectable manner while her husband, Navy Warrant Officer Wilbur Martin, served in the Pacific. Earlier in the war she traveled west with him from their home town near Baltimore and remained with him until the night before he shipped out for the war zone. She wanted to have a child but their war-induced anxieties got the better of them once again. Instead, she took the ever-present nursing job to wait out the war and her husband's return.

Corrasa and McGuire began interrogating Mrs. Mansfeldt as soon as she started gathering her composure. They persisted through a cross-town drive to the scene of the killing and finished at the old Hall of Justice, which housed police headquarters, the superior courts, and the adjacent city prison. Their stenographer accompanied them throughout, noted and transcribed everything, but not quite fast enough. When they arrived at police headquarters, they met Vincent Hallinan, who saw to it that Mrs. Mansfeldt did not sign her statement. Nonetheless, the two investigators were rightly pleased, since their work produced admissible evidence even without the signature.

In addition to this facet of her self-incrimination, Mrs. Mansfeldt had completely unburdened herself to the press. The reporters and photographers had reached her car before the police and bombarded the disoriented woman with their questions. The result was so vivid a public disclosure that anyone who cared to could read details of how she killed a defenseless human being.

Irene Mansfeldt told everyone who would listen a not uncommon story. Victim and killer met but once before, a brief encounter during the small hours of the morning one week earlier. Thereafter, Irene went through the emotional torment that culminated in the shooting of Vada Martin. This destructive climax to a year of uncertainty, discontent, and psychological turmoil had begun naturally enough. That night Irene had been in bed reading when Dr. Mansfeldt's answering service phoned concerning the impending delivery of one of his maternity patients. Just before eleven he returned home from house calls. Irene relayed the message and he left immediately. She drifted off to sleep only to be awakened three hours later by a call from the French Hospital. It was 2:00 A.M., and delivery was anticipated momentarily, yet the doctor was nowhere to be found. Worried about his precarious physical and mental health, Irene quickly slipped a coat over her nightgown and descended to the garage three flights below. As she drove over the crest of Pacific Heights and out through the mixed middle- and working-class Richmond District, she agonized over what could have happened to her husband. Neglect of professional responsibilities was not among his lamentable deficiencies.

She sighted his car right in front of the hospital on Geary Boulevard but her immediate relief evaporated once she edged close enough to detect the female form seated alone in his front seat. Parking her own vehicle Irene approached the stranger and inquired if indeed that was Dr. Mansfeldt's automobile. She identified herself, yanked the car door open, and pointedly asked the woman in white, "If you are his nurse, why are you not in there taking care of the patient?"

At that Vada Martin darted into the lobby leaving the doctor's wife in possession of both cars. When Mansfeldt himself descended the hospital steps shortly thereafter, he was unaccompanied. His explanation? First, he admitted that the nurse was from the Sutter Hospital near his cross-town office but that there was nothing between them. He was merely driving her home. Later, back at their home, he also admitted meeting Mrs. Martin after her shift and taking her on his late calls. Since Irene decided to terminate her long-established practice of accompanying him on these house calls he had become ill at ease in his loneliness. And since Vada Martin's husband still was out in the Pacific, she was lonely too. Their mutual needs for companionship drew them together. That was all. There was, he said, no more to it.

Throughout the past year the doctor had not bestowed upon his wife the normal and expected marital affections. Until she encountered Vada Martin, Irene assumed that John had become impotent. But now that assumption became highly questionable. The week between discovery and violence represented an eternity of unmitigated trauma for Irene. Unable to sleep, twice she ordered her husband from the house and twice consented to his return. At his office she removed the family portrait from his bookcase and smashed it into pieces. "In one devastating moment of . . . clarity, I saw," she recalled, "the past twenty years in their utter futility." She forced John to place their joint assets in her name and on her way home informed her psychiatrist that she was "going to shoot someone." At the end of seven days and seven nights of adrenaline-fed hypertension, exacerbated by her need for pretense in front of the children, she accepted tranquilizing drugs from the doctor-husband she so distrusted. Oblivion engulfed her and what followed in the morning constituted the subject matter of San Francisco's most spectacular and dramatic murder trial yet.

Hallinan immediately knew that this case would rival, even surpass, the Frank Egan trial of 1932. The crime's startling and shocking nature, and the fact that a woman, cultured and refined at that, had committed it maximized public attention. Unfortunately for Irene, and for her counsel too, her initial defense posture was deplorable. The act had been committed without the intent of avoiding detection or evading punishment. The case against her appeared so strong that any charge less than first-degree murder would be inappropriate and certainly unwise politically for the new

District Attorney, Edmund G. Brown, Sr. The newspapers, in fact, were into it sooner and deeper than Hallinan was, a fact he intended to rectify once he located his former school chum John Mansfeldt.

While Irene calmed down at the city prison with the help of an occasional visit to San Francisco General Hospital for sedation, Hallinan began hammering out a defense. First he wondered whether Irene had been wrong. What if the sensitive and withdrawn husband turned out to be an innocent neurotic who needed the psychological prop of human companionship—any companion—during his nightly rounds, and he simply was incapable of intimate sexual activity with anyone, Vada Martin as well as his wife? A successful defense depended upon one contingency. John Mansfeldt had to accept and sustain whatever Hallinan created.

For the moment only Irene was certain about John. In jail she claimed some sort of an extrasensory experience and over and over again rattled that her husband, just like Vada Martin was dead. Being the consummate rationalist he was, Hallinan listened, exercised a calming effect on Irene, and privately dismissed her vision as an aberration. While she sobbed her anguished story, Vincent could not help but think back to her wedding twenty years before. It took place on New Year's Eve in Chinatown's Old St. Mary's Church. He was John Mansfeldt's boyhood friend, maybe his only one, so John turned to him as he had done so often during schooldays, this time to be his best man. What Hallinan remembered most vividly was how Irene wept throughout that ceremony too, and all the way back to the Mansfeldt home. In prison she was still crying, but now her appearance was anything but beautiful. Her hair was tangled. Her own weight loss was noticeable. And her once bright and playful eyes seemed to have receded deeply into their sockets. Back at his office he made another round of phone calls seeking leads but still there was no sign of her husband. He could not be dead, Hallinan concluded, because if he were, he would not be so difficult to find.

He hung the receiver back on the hook and moved the

telephone over to the corner of his desk to make room for the backlog of newspapers, three days worth. An avid reader, he subscribed to all four San Francisco dailies and bought the eastern papers downtown. During the pre-trial phase of all his newsworthy cases, he concentrated first on the two morning editions since they usually broke what was hot. Once trials began he gave prime attention to the afternoon papers which were first on the street with the day's court action. He already knew the facts of the case so he read mostly to gauge the dispositions of the writers vis-a-vis his client.

As he sorted out the articles, the preponderance of experienced women journalists on special assignment to the case became striking. Their uniform task was to capture and record the behind-the-scenes drama of a woman on trial for her life. That was encouraging enough, so he read on with hope. The articles were severely damaging but not bitterly hostile. Nowhere, for example, was Irene referred to as a "murderess." She was not even called "killer." The papers labeled her "socialite," though not in a deprecating sense, then "wife," but mostly, "mother of three."

As he read, Hallinan assessed his own strategy of bringing the writers into the defense camp and thereby using the papers to present to the jury the facts, arguments, and stratagems which otherwise would be inadmissible in a court of law. Already the reporters were besieging his office. Why not use them to bring such extra-legal maneuvers to the attention of the jurors? He knew jurors read about the events they themselves would settle, despite the judicial admonitions against reading or discussing the case outside the jury room. Besides, in the papers he could make his points unencumbered by the mass of eminently forgettable official testimony.

Irene Mansfeldt provided her counselor with one advantage of strategic value. She was a "sympathetic defendant," which for Hallinan meant that detached onlookers viewed her with sympathy, not as some mad murderess who, if let free, would menace society. Thirty-three years later, this image remained even with her prosecutor. "If any one of the

thousands of independent variables were missing," he recalled, "she would never have killed anyone." Inspector
Corrasa fully agreed. He remembered her as "just a swell
woman." Beyond that, she was a reporter's dream: outgoing,
nervous, and a non-stop talker.

Hallinan spent almost a full day reviewing the press
coverage. As he placed the last article by Carolyn Anspacher
of the *Chronicle* into his clipping file and shoved the residue
off the far end of his desk into the wastebasket, Eleanor
Meherin appeared for her first scheduled interview. The
veteran reporter, assigned full-time to the case by a Hearst
newspaper chain, received Hallinan's warm greeting.

"Miss Meherin, we have a very fine mutual friend. Your
son, Terry, I know him from Camp Mather. He's been so
good to my kids. They love him."

Not wishing to call attention to Meherin's age, Hallinan
discreetly omitted that her son already was a young adult
employed at Mather where his brood had vacationed as care-
free children.

Eleanor Meherin was sympathetic by nature, and the
warmth of Hallinan's civility and charm did not hurt his
cause either. Thereafter, her favorable articles became integrated into the public mind. Hallinan rewarded her with
behind-the-scene information, which enabled her to color
and dramatize her daily stories. In time this *entente cordiale*
deepened to the extent that in court Meherin seated herself
next to the prosecutor's table and turned up the reception on
her hearing aid in order to eavesdrop on his conversations.
She reported what she heard to Hallinan.

Each of the other reporters and wire service representatives fell in line when they saw the benefits Meherin received for her cooperation—the inside stories, exclusives,
and the shared excitement.

The evening *Call-Bulletin*'s Jane Ishleman Conant put
Hallinan's cooperative resolve to the test when she asked him
for a prison interview with Irene. Since the initial poverty of
Irene's defense resulted in no small part from her having
talked too much already, Hallinan at first demurred. Conant

assured Hallinan of her belief that Irene had been mentally ill at the moment she committed the offense and that would be her story line. Through further procrastination Hallinan extracted her promise not to allow any re-write editor to "change your article and stick in some poison."

Coordinated separately by Hallinan, Conant and Meherin established the interpretive thrust that the others followed. By blending family contacts, agreeable personal relations, and the subtle reality of mutual self-interest, Hallinan wedded the fourth estate to his defense creation. Throughout the trial of Annie Irene Mansfeldt, not one news article referred to her attorney or his defense in an unfriendly manner. Usually they were laudatory. Once, near the trial's end, his rapport with the press allowed the planting of an article which was vital. Throughout all those months standard anti-Hallinan hostility ebbed to the editorial pages, a domain beyond the reach of the working journalists.

Meanwhile, in between his first interviews with the media people, his initial visits to his client in the city prison, and his searching for her missing husband, Hallinan suffered through his own private hell. A tragedy other than that which involved Mrs. Mansfeldt had abruptly and without warning engulfed his own family. In the midst of his frenetic activities two sons, Patrick who was nine and Michael who was five, were stricken with poliomyelitis. This was before Jonas Salk developed his vaccine, and no known remedy existed for the dreaded crippler of young children. The mortality rate from the variety which afflicted the older boy ran as high as eighty-five percent.

Vivian, pregnant and avid for her sixth child, started to miscarry, a condition not at all aided by the unavailability of the doctor who had delivered all five of her sons. He was the missing John Mansfeldt. Confining herself to bed in order to save her pregnancy, she agonized all the more over the fate that threatened two she already had. Her husband's research on the disease offered such little hope that he tried to keep it to himself but Vivian knew his nature would not allow the medical texts in his office to remain unconsulted.

"Strong, healthy children," he found, "survive the disease; weak, unhealthy children generally succumb to it. Death usually occurs within five days after the appearance of the symptoms; prognosis is good for patients who survive that period."

Every minute he could spare from case preparation Hallinan spent prowling the corridors of Children's Hospital where the boys were confined. Because polio was so infectious, even for adults, he could not enter their rooms but peered through the little windows of the doors perhaps to detect a movement which he could relate to Vivian thereby infusing her thoughts with a modicum of hope.

Between press interviews, when he found himself alone and sentimental, he squeezed back tears that would have surprised the rough and appraising world outside. The man who had intended never to marry and never to have a family was transformed by the love Vivian had brought into his life. He wanted those sons not only to survive, but to do so in a condition which would enable them to play sports as he had. If they lived, their time would come when they would have to stand up as men. He drove from his mind the thought of his children confined forever in apparatus similar to that in which Franklin Roosevelt dragged through his adult life. An unrestrained life of physical freedom certainly transcended a sedentary one, he thought, even in the White House.

He apologized to the nurses and hospital attendants for his repetitive inquiries and conveyed false assurances to Vivian who read the truth in his face and manner. All they could do was to wait while the days passed as an eternity. Despite her precautions, Vivian miscarried and then insisted on joining the hospital vigil. On the fifth day the hardy Hallinan boys stirred in bed demonstrating the validity of the general prognosis. Hope rose, then happiness soared. They had made it. Convalescence might take time, but they would live, their survival a validation of their father's vigorous rearing practices. He turned then with renewed vigor to the impending trial.

California criminal law provided for a two-part trial

when the accused entered a dual plea of not guilty and also not guilty by reason of insanity. Irene Mansfeldt tried repeatedly to enter a straight plea of guilty because, she insisted, she had done the killing. In Hallinan's absence during the arraignment, his associate, James Martin Mac-Innis, prevailed upon the compliant court and an understanding prosecutor to allow him to coerce Irene to change her plea. Accordingly, the first phase of a bifurcated trial was to proceed without any reference to Irene's sanity. Then, if she were found guilty, the same jury would hear a second phase and decide on her sanity at that time. Before 1927 the defendant's sanity and guilt were considered in one trial. The revised code allowed district attorneys to obtain convictions even though the guilty became institutionalized in facilities for the insane rather than executed or jailed as felons. Likewise, it offered Hallinan two chances to cheat the gas chamber, not just one.

Hallinan continued to assess his defense options but delayed the basic decisions as long as Dr. Mansfeldt remained unaccounted for. If he turned out to be uncooperative in his wife's defense by denying an affair, Hallinan could hardly employ the unwritten law of ultimate preservation of the home, even indirectly. And since Hallinan had not been in close or regular contact with John since Vivian's last full-term pregnancy, he had no idea of John's current feelings for Irene. Certainly this was an opportunity for any withdrawn husband to rid his life of a dominating wife. It would require no more than the little nerve that even John might muster. Hallinan had witnessed stranger events during his criminal practice. Anything was possible. While he continued to reposition in his own mind the few pieces of the puzzle which he commanded, Dr. Mansfeldt suddenly and unalterably intervened in such a way as to free Hallinan's hands completely, thus allowing him to employ whatever defense he felt would serve best.

John Mansfeldt killed himself.

Immediately after identifying his wife at Central Emergency Hospital the doctor drove to the seashore just south of

San Francisco where he ingested a lethal dose of barbituates with eight ounces of one hundred proof whiskey as a chaser. The subsequent autopsy revealed no signs of any established drug abuse.

Throughout his twenty years of marriage the troubled doctor had coped with difficult situations by performing what he called his "hat trick." He would ask for his wide-brimmed fedora and go for a stroll. Given his psychological limitations, this evasion of responsibility may have been wise for normally encountered unpleasantries. But his wife's shooting of Vada Martin prompted him to walk away permanently. Four days passed before a coastline resort owner, investigating what appeared to be an abandoned automobile, discovered the bloated, deformed body. Decomposition had advanced so rapidly in the warm and confined atmosphere of the car that even Mansfeldt's brother-in-law failed to give a firm identification. Hallinan did though. He was positive. His schoolboy friend, the bashful lad whose dominating mother encouraged young Vincent to provide a manly example and fend off neighborhood bullies, was distorted and dead. He took final leave from an always threatening world. No longer would he need protection and no longer would he suffer domination.

Hallinan's sorrow was so deep that over a generation later he loyally defended his friend's memory by suggesting that Mansfeldt's self-inflicted death might not have been suicide at all. "All he probably wanted was time to collect himself and think things out." Trying to convince himself, Hallinan added, "the overdose could have been accidental." Yes, even on the part of an experienced, drug-prescribing doctor.

Mansfeldt's act of self-destruction fixed Hallinan's conclusion that suicide should be accepted by American society as a legitimate option available to anyone who decides that life is not worth the agony. "Anyone should be allowed to step quietly out that door who so wishes, at any time."

On the practical and immediate level, John's death constituted a very generous, though hardly intended bequest. It allowed Hallinan to discard his weaker defense strategies and fix upon the most efficacious. By taking his own troubled life, Mansfeldt became anything Irene's defense required him to be, anything defense counsel was capable of creating. Veteran trial lawyers have a cynical axiom: nothing is so valuable as a dead partner. And Hallinan began implementing it immediately, despite his genuine sorrow at the death of his friend. Unencumbered by the doctor, Hallinan devised an escape hatch for his client. He knew that if the blame for her act could be imposed on her dead husband, she could be saved. "That must not be hindered by any sentimental concern with the memory of one who could no longer be harmed or offended by anything we say about him."

He did not articulate this to the press, at least not in those words. But he saw to it that the tragedy became "the fault of the deceased husband" and yes, "it was the victim's fault too." En route he seeded the press with the phrase "widowed mother of three" as a welcome substitute for the time-worn "socialite wife of prominent physician."

Obliquely at first, as in his autobiography, then bluntly as the years passed, Hallinan freely admitted during interviews that he was the expert at constructing defense stories. Clients who lied or concealed the truth from him, as damaging or disgraceful as that truth might be, constituted his most serious courtroom threat. He had to know everything in order to create a plausible and legal defense which he could sustain against skilled prosecutors intent upon convictions. In this regard, his autobiography tellingly omitted the name of Irene Mansfeldt, undoubtedly because her case illustrated only too well the correctness of his admission.

The basic defense line that Hallinan created for Irene centered on his assertion that she was not conscious when she killed Vada Martn and therefore could not be legally guilty of murder. This deficiency of consciousness was brought about by a mixture of jealous passion, involuntarily ingested drugs, and insanity. In order to present this mixture with each of its vital ingredients to the jury, Hallinan had to overcome the legal prohibition against the admissibility of sanity-related evidence in the first phase of the trial. His strategy was to blend together his evidence of insanity and temporary mental blackout, matters which legally were quite distinct, and use them along with everything else he had all in one huge dose. This case was so weak that if he separated and reserved that which pertained to Irene's sanity for the second phase of the trial, the defense would be so thin in both phases that she would be found guilty of murder first and sane besides. Only by non-selectively dosing the jury with everything he had did he hope to extract a favorable verdict and for that he had two chances. On the weight of evidence neither looked promising.

Since the late 1930s Vincent Hallinan had been experimenting with an unusual legal technique, the extended opening statement. Standard American practice had been to build a defense on the prosecution's presentation which came first. An advance commitment by the defense to any specific position and strategy was considered unwise since unexpected evidence could force embarrassing mid-trial reassessments. Necessarily then, an opening statement by the defense had to wait until the prosecution rested its case.

Outside the courtroom, defense attorneys maintained a parallel reticence. "No comment," or "It would be improper to discuss the case while it is pending in the court," were the accepted formulae used to fend off the reporters.

To Hallinan the transparency of the case and his personal familiarity with the Mansfeldts, not the discovery procedures mandated years later by the Supreme Court, made the traditional, conservative approach a liability rather than an asset to his client. The traditional reserve had always doubled the burdens imposed on the defense. The jurors came from the mass of newspaper readers and radio listeners. Undoubtedly they had heard of the case and even formed an opinion concerning it. "No comment," by Hallinan would convey to them a suspicion of culpability. Once seated in the jury box, they would hear the assistant district attorney list the charges and outline the evidence he would produce

to sustain them. In addition, the prosecutor was the representative of the government, and the jurors assumed that he
would not make these charges if he did not believe them
himself.

Everything stated by the prosecutor would be affirmed
by a succession of witnesses until even the thought of acquit-
ting the defendant seemed preposterous. After all this, the
defense counsel would be invited to respond as best he could.
Hallinan had not been long at the bar when he concluded
that it was at this point that the jurors arrived at a belief in
the defendant's guilt. His task, then, must be to push out of
their minds a well-fixed conviction.

> Unless you've been downright negligent you know all about
> the case—both sides—before you step into court for the trial.
> If you don't have a defense, you should have gotten rid of the
> case by a plea bargain. You've built up that defense and ham-
> mered it into shape so it will stand up. Do this before the trial.
> Tell it to the doubters and scoffers above all. Listen to their
> criticisms and ironies. Then do a little more hammering until
> those deficiencies are met. In this way [Hallinan felt] you'll
> learn how persuasive your defense is going to be and it's a
> damn sight better to do your adjusting before the trial starts
> instead of trying to patch it up in the presence of the jury.

Hallinan perfected the extended opening statement during ten years worth of minor civil and criminal cases and
decided to use it for the first time in a celebrated prosecution
because the situation was so appropriate. Even though the
prosecution was not required to disclose its evidence, Hallinan knew everything they did about the Mansfeldts and the
killing—even more. Besides, he enjoyed being an innovator.

By trial time Edmund Brown had removed himself by
degrees from active participation until he became little more
than chief spectator behind his able assistant, Norman
Elkington. The careful and methodical Elkington had recently abandoned his own defense practice, where he had
been working himself into an early grave. His problem was a
professional inability to handle any case without exhaustive

pretrial preparation, but to earn a living, he had to accept too many cases.

The contrast between the opening statements was stark. Elkington simply called the official attention to the facts, which by now appeared all but self-evident. He stated his intention to prove that the killing "was a planned, premeditated, deliberate crime and without any excuse." Armed with the self-incriminating statement of Hallinan's client, reports from his own investigator and the police, and a battery of disinterested witnesses which included the newspaper photographers, Elkington was prepared to do just that. He had well in hand a rigorous if unimaginative prosecution which reflected what other attorneys considered to be in the best interests of the people and ultimate justice. It also met Hallinan's full expectations of the traditional presentation. Elkington was forthright and brief. In precisely two minutes he stated the essence of his case after which he took his seat.

Hallinan followed immediately with his calculated legal innovation and held the floor for three hours during which he developed his detailed concept of the case. Since the Egan trial in 1932 which had established Hallinan's reputation for courtroom excellence the reporter, the public, and the individual jurors looked forward to his appearances, even in ordinary cases in the lower courts. This was an advantage and rather than cast it away in mundane, repetitive questioning of veniremen, Hallinan reserved himself for opening day. When MacInnis faded back into the defense staff and Hallinan stepped before the jury, the skirmishing ended and direct assault began. Hallinan's version of the case rolled easily but earnestly from his tongue and though it was extensive, the afternoon passed as if he were dramatically reciting from an engaging and thrilling Hollywood script. He lunged into the insanity history of the Mansfeldt family's Polish background, weaving it into the larger pattern of immigrant America: hard work, sacrifice, talent, and ultimate achievement. He cited the doctor's wartime discharge on psychiatric grounds, Irene's previous breakdown, and her suicide attempts. She brooded over the specter of her own impending insanity, he told the jurors, and in a state of depression she had tried to take her own life before the anticipated madness overcame her.

The first-hand knowledge Hallinan had of the Mansfeldt family helped his presentation, but he had also researched its history specifically for this moment. The notes remained in his briefcase though, since his practice was always to appear convinced and compellingly spontaneous. "If you have to read it, or even consult an outline, you tell the jury, 'Listen, I don't even know what I am telling you so how can I believe it?'" Throughout the afternoon he maintained eye contact with the jurors and the judge, studiously ignoring the prosecutor.

From family history he zoomed in on the week leading up to the killing. He stressed an actual affair between doctor and nurse as Mrs. Mansfeldt perceived it: discovery, jealousy, outraged honor, separation, reconciliation, sleepless nights, hysteria, fear for the children, pretense, drugs, and oblivion. On the night before the killing, Dr. Mansfeldt induced her to take unknown drugs when she was hysterical and exhausted. "This produced," Hallinan said, "a profound, unwelcome sleep for Mrs. Mansfeldt—a sleep so abnormal it tore loose the structure of her subconscious mind, which like Pandora's box, had been storing away the terror and horror and fears of countless years. When she awakened in the morning, she was suffering from a condition recognized both by law and medicine—the condition known as somnolentia in which she gave the aspects of consciousness but actually was only semi-conscious. In this state, her subconscious mind controlled her personality."

Somnolentia then, the basic defense, was caused by a long-established, growing instability, by jealousy and hysteria, and finally by drugs involuntarily taken. All of these, he maintained, brought about her flight from reality. "Somnolentia" was a big word, undoubtedly a strange word for the jurors, so Hallinan pronounced it clearly and blandly as if it were a common term in everyone's active vocabulary. As his main defense, it had to be introduced as sincerely as possible in order to overcome the normal, anticipated skepticism. "It actually occurs," Hallinan assured his listeners, "and this poor distraught woman you see here had it." He delivered the line just as he had recited it to his office mirror and to his most merciless critic, Vivian. He had rehearsed it again the night before, mostly to keep Vivian's mind off the improved, though still serious conditions of young Patrick and Michael.

In his attempt to add greater credibility to his dubious assertion, Hallinan disclaimed any intention to plea surreptitiously the unwritten law—justifiability of action deemed necessary for the protection of home and family. And with this disclaimer he intentionally advanced the very idea as an auxiliary defense.

"We will not sit in judgment on Mrs. Martin or on Dr. Mansfeldt." Yet, "the time must come . . . when we must ask why, if John Mansfeldt had no interest in Vada Martin beyond friendship, did he leave a loaded revolver in a house inhabited by his neurotic, jealous wife who had already shown a predilection to suicide, and why, when instead of killing herself she killed Vada Martin, did he go out and kill himself within the hour."

When Judge Edward P. Murphy adjourned the superior court, spectators and jurors alike reflected a state of high dramatic stimulation. Hallinan had once more provided engaging copy for Meherin, Conant, Anspacher, and the assembled press corps. Somnolentia became the new additive that rescued the case from impending over-exposure and guaranteed continuing front page coverage. For somnolentia to get into the jury box, Hallinan did not need the press since he dexterously slid it past Judge Murphy over Elkington's objections. He had other plans for the press anyway, so he saved the unspoken gratitude.

Drama aside, the opener pleased Hallinan because it foreshadowed a favorable disposition of the court. Under the cover of Irene's transitory mental condition at the moment of the killing, which was admissible, he brought before the jury information directly bearing on insanity, which, according to California law, the judge could strictly have reserved for a second phase of the trial.

The opening statement also allowed Hallinan "to break the ice so that when witnesses took the stand their testimony would appear far less novel to a more receptive jury. The witnesses would seem merely to be corroborating facts already admitted rather than asserting them for the first time on their own veracity."

The start was good but in the morning Elkington would begin his own well-designed demolition and now he fully understood in advance the defense against which he contended.

He began with a traditional, comprehensive predictability equal to his opening statement. To prove each of those initial assertions, Elkington brought forward just eight major witnesses. All but three were employees of the City and County of San Francisco who had simple and objective facts to relate. The hospital steward explained Mrs. Mansfeldt's bizarre arrival at Central Emergency, discarding the revolver and telling him, "I killed her." Inspector Corrasa reiterated Irene's full account of the killing, the immediate background, and he submitted her statement into evidence. Corrasa added, under direct examination, that the accused had asked him if the woman she shot were dead. In response to his affirmative reply the defendant said, "She deserved it." All this, he said, immediately followed the crime.

The autopsy surgeon, Dr. Jesse L. Carr, placed on record the obvious. Yes, the shot fired from the Mansfeldt revolver had indeed caused the death of Mrs. Martin. And yes, the deceased did have a bruised face presumably caused by being pistol-whipped with the gun butt.

In light of Hallinan's somnolentia defense, Elkington called his remaining witnesses to show that no affair took place between the doctor and nurse and, most important of all, the accused was neither insane nor disoriented at the time of the shooting. He began with Dr. Milton Lennon, the Mansfeldt family's psychiatrist and Irene's long-time personal friend.

The elderly gentleman told the jury that Irene had come to the private door of his office on the morning after her first encounter with Mrs. Martin outside the French Hospital. Excitedly Irene told him, "I am going to shoot someone." Three days later, she was calm, he maintained, and intended to shoot no one. As a witness for the prosecution Dr. Lennon swore, "I thought I had made a gain and I had been a good influence." In conclusion he testified that Irene was not insane.

Elkington consolidated this advance against the defendant by calling his next most damaging witness, Warrant Officer Wilbur Martin. The serviceman produced letters of endearment which his wife had posted to him so recently that they arrived only after her death. He swore she loved him just as the documents attested. The dead woman's letters spelled out her plans to return east with her husband upon his impending demobilization. She had given the required notice at the hospital, prepared his wardrobe for the Maryland winter and even purchased a bottle of wine so they might celebrate his return. Besides Martin's testimony, his uniformed presence throughout the trial seriously detracted from the sympathetic mood Hallinan wished to sustain around his client.

When Norman Elkington rested his case he had adequate reason for professional satisfaction. In a highly competent, undramatic manner he supported the basic contentions of his opening statement with traditional, reliable, and rather persuasive witnesses. But for Martin and Lennon, they were disinterested parties with objective facts to relate. When he finished, it appeared that Irene Mansfeldt did indeed shoot and kill the victim. If she had been motivated by marital jealousy, such provocation was both unfounded in fact and unacceptable in law. Perhaps the defendant was neurotic but she was not insane. She had displayed both mental competence and appropriate orientation to reality by explaining in detail what she had done and why she had done it. The prosecution covered all significant points, made no mistakes, and left no loose ends for Hallinan to start unraveling.

Since the basic facts of the case were common knowledge and irrefutable besides, Hallinan hardly wanted to deplete his credibility by trying to deny them. In his assessment of Elkington's case, only the testimony of Martin and Lennon inflicted damage beyond that which he and MacInnis were willing to absorb. If no love affair could have occurred and Irene had been in control of herself at the time of the killing, then the somnolentia defense would collapse and prompt a conviction, probably murder in the first degree, followed by an execution.

Both husband and the psychiatrist were sympathetic witnesses in Hallinan's sense of the term. Martin served the nation in war, still wore his uniform and returned to a ruined private life. Dr. Lennon was a kindly, maybe slightly out-of-date, psychiatrist who helped the Mansfeldts with their personal and domestic problems since they were young adults, well before their marriage. Hallinan knew he could not break either witness down and force a change of testimony but he had to reduce the impact of their accounts. That meant trying to change the jury's sympathetic perceptions of the men themselves. From Martin he tried to extract a statement of hostile desire for revenge against the widowed mother, but the naval officer skillfully slid around the attempt. Privately he disparaged the "mommy defense" Hallinan advanced for the woman who killed his wife but under cross-examination he responded with caution; the courts, not a vengeful spouse, would determine where justice resided.

Since the trial would be a long one and since Hallinan was simultaneously developing his own witnesses, which he anticipated would overwhelm Martin and capture total court sympathy, he decided to cut his loss. Hallinan excused Martin before he inflicted even greater damage on the defense and before his own designs rendered him repugnant to the jury, thereby adding to the impact of a bereaved husband's testimony. It was clear as Martin stepped down that he had advanced Elkington's case.

Lennon was different. Early in his career the doctor briefly directed the Saint Ignatius College pre-medical program. That was back in 1912. His younger brother attended school with Hallinan and another became a priest. Much older now, Lennon was more vulnerable himself than the content of his testimony, so Hallinan turned on him with devastating directness, prodded rather than restrained by the old school connection. He portrayed Lennon as a dated practitioner who had to testify that Irene was in control of herself if for no reason other than to excuse his own failure of psychiatric perception. Hallinan foreclosed all but one of his alternatives for not intervening when Irene threatened to shoot her rival, default of moral courage. A doctor "had the opportunity to prevent this entire tragedy and didn't," Hallinan concluded. Instead he came to court and swore that Irene was not insane "to preserve himself professionally."

In spite of the fact that her psychiatrist had damaged her case by testifying for the prosecution, Irene retained a strong and positive attachment to him. She genuinely enjoyed hearing the kindly father figure say that she was not insane regardless of its impact upon her defense. Hallinan, on the other hand, did not care if Lennon was her security blanket. He viewed the doctor as a hostile witness contributing to his client's conviction and treated him accordingly. By doing so he reinforced Irene's positive orientation to the psychiatrist. At the same time, by denigrating Dr. Lennon before the court, Hallinan antagonized Irene. In fact, she became irate.

That Dr. Mansfeldt ever had an affair with Vada Martin never became established beyond reasonable doubt. Relentlessly Elkington resisted every Hallinan move to confirm such a relationship as fact, but in the long run Hallinan used the prosecutor's predictable attention to detail against him. In order to shore up a minor weakness in his case, Elkington called Charles Kispert to the stand. That he was a friend of the deceased lent even greater credibility to testimony intended by the prosecution to render its case airtight. Unbeknownst to Elkington, Hallinan and Mrs. Mansfeldt had already argued over Kispert as a defense witness. Irene wanted him to testify on her behalf but Hallinan put her off with the assertion that Kispert would be more effective for the defense if the prosecution called him as a hostile witness. In time Elkington did just that and with Kispert he tidied up his case. In doing so the prosecution attested to the character and truthfulness of the witness, whom Hallinan promptly commandeered. With Kispert, Hallinan pushed in the roof.

Kispert responded to Hallinan's cross-examination that yes, the doctor did have an affair with the nurse. He knew it because John Mansfeldt had told him so! The suburban businessman had previously identified himself as one of the only two friends Mansfeldt had. The other, he said in establishing his credentials as a witness for the prosecution, was Vincent Hallinan. In a surprisingly swift counterstroke Hallinan all but established the affair's reality and did so with a witness whose veracity the opposition had certified. In redirected testimony, Judge Murphy intervened to prevent Elkington from impeaching his own witness.

Next Hallinan returned to the testimony of Dorothea Sonnenberg. She was John Mansfeldt's sister whom Hallinan also knew since high-school days. She had been maid of honor for John and Irene back on New Year's Eve, 1924. As Hallinan's lead witness, she had testified that during the week between Irene's early hour encounter with the nurse and the subsequent killing she had advised her brother to stop seeing Mrs. Martin, but he insisted to her that there had been nothing between them. From the witness stand she conveyed the impression that she believed him. There was no romance, she thought, and Hallinan had been unable to dissuade her.

On the critical point of Irene's sanity Mrs. Sonnenberg was inconsistent. First she testified only that Irene "was completely distraught. I don't know how to use the word 'insane' exactly." Then, under intense questioning the defense brought her around to what Hallinan needed. The only explanation she had of why her sister-in-law shot Mrs. Martin was because "she had lost her mind . . . and was insane at that time. She couldn't have been otherwise."

In the end, though, the prosecution destroyed the effect of Hallinan's work.

> Elkington: I will ask you, Mrs. Sonnenberg, if you did not state [in a deposition] that nothing was ever indicated to you that she was mentally unstable in any way?

Sonnenberg: Yes, I think I said that.

Elkington: That's all.

"It's hard to tell for sure," Hallinan later wrote, "what sticks with jurors and what doesn't, particularly in trials where the record is so voluminous. My strategy was to continue to work, privately, on John's sister and get in the last word. I told her that I came into this case through the Mansfeldts. We were kids together." Hallinan used on her the same logic he applied to some initially unsympathetic journalists. "I understood her loyalty to her dead brother, but I insisted that to stand by and allow Irene's conviction would do nothing but compound this tragedy by making orphans of her brother's children."

Just before the jury was locked up for deliberation, Hallinan struck where Elkington could not respond. The *Examiner* cooperatively ran a short and well-tailored clarification of Sonnenberg's testimony under her own by-line. In it she admitted her brother's "difficult side" and Irene's physical and mental health problems.

> I believe absolutely that she [Irene] was not in her normal mind that Thursday morning. . . . She was mentally distracted and hysterical for a considerable part of the preceding week. She was, I believe, temporarily unhinged and not aware of the awful thing she did.
>
> My brother was very dear to me. I took great pride in his success. But I was aware that my sister-in-law . . . was in a state of great anguish on his account. . . .
>
> Of course my brother didn't admit to me that he was having an affair with Mrs. Martin. He assured me they were but friends. Isn't that the usual attitude . . . ?
>
> We [Irene and I] do not see eye-to-eye on every issue. . . . But of one thing I have conclusive proof. She was a devoted and zealous mother. I profoundly hope she will be allowed to again function in this capacity with her three anxious children.

The remainder of her article was so well-composed and so neatly fitted to each of the pertinent needs of the defense that it suggested experienced, professional draftsmanship at

a time when Hallinan's personal relations with the staff
writers were at a career high.

Thus, through a supposedly independent press and a
supposedly hostile witness, Hallinan had the last word on
John's affair and Irene's insanity—whether they existed or
not.

Hallinan knew that statements more compelling than
Kispert's and Sonnenberg's were vital before somnolentia
could become an acceptable explanation, even to jurors who
otherwise were favorably disposed toward Irene. Hallinan
aimed his defense at the jurors' hearts and emotions but he
could not insult their intellects. The more convincing somnolentia became on rational grounds, the easier a juror could
vote according to personal sympathy. All Hallinan needed
was one among the twelve to prevent conviction. He had
introduced both drugs and mental instability into his opening
statement. To establish them more firmly, Hallinan brought
forward his star witnesses: the Mansfeldt children, Irene herself, and Dr. Joseph Catton who was a professional medical
witness from Stanford University.

Throughout the trial every San Francisco newspaper
illustrated its pages with the innocent pictures of the three
youngsters even though their aunt, Mrs. Sonnenberg,
shielded them from the inquiring reporters. To maintain the
favorable press interest and coverage without direct press
contact, Hallinan saw to it that pictures of the children at
home, with their Scottie dog, and then with her pups, reached
Irene in jail through the hands of the reporters. There were
enough extra prints, of course, for everyone. As the months
passed John and his two sisters remained unofficially seques-
tered in their Vallejo Street home. No one believed a jailhouse reunion would help anyone, and Hallinan preferred
to contain the intense anticipation of their public appearance
until it built to the point of rupture. When that moment
arrived, he called the children to the stand as his tenth,
eleventh, and twelfth witnesses.

That winter morning was unusually damp for San Francisco but not sufficiently unpleasant to thin the overflow
from the courtroom where a hushed and pensive crowd

stared in unrestrained sympathy. Numerous sets of opera glasses and even binoculars were set aside and the moisture wiped from the lenses, while young Irene, John, and Terry captured the hearts of everyone present. They were refined, sensitive, and attractive youngsters whom the public had learned to love in advance. They dressed in the styles of the 1945 adult world, all in suits. The eleven- and fifteen-year-old girls wore hats and medium heels and carried matronly purses. John wore a double-breasted suit, full-cut trousers, a white shirt and a wide necktie. From a distance he appeared to be wearing a Scout ring on his finger. All three tried to look and act grown up, but Hallinan took courage in knowing that their brave attempt would fail. They were kids who loved their mother and were intent on helping her.

No sooner did Bailiff John Kerrigan call the court to order than the sporadic sighs turned to audible sobs which spread from spectators to the recently seated jurors who began freely to wipe their eyes. Hallinan enhanced the sensitive mood by leading off with little Terry. Gently he asked what she remembered from the morning of October 4. The lovely, pixie-faced eleven year old looked past her father's friend, engaged her mother's gaze, blinked back her tears, swallowed hard and went down the defense line with its creator. At the end she filled with tears, sobbed quietly, and stepped down. Her emaciated mother blew her a kiss as the spectators wept unabashedly.

The older children came next, each in turn testifying in support of points Hallinan had outlined months earlier in his extensive opening statement. His questions highlighted each of their recollections: how their mother appeared drugged on the morning of the killing, that their father had thrown water on her to wake her up, that he had to help his wife walk but that she had fallen nonetheless. When the trio left the court, tears cascaded quietly down both girls' cheeks.

Their departure transformed the scene from unrestrained crying to heavy and complete silence. Hallinan's next witness was ready but Vincent hung back, letting the emotion of the moment take its full effect upon the jury, judge, press, and even the prosecutor—not to mention the mood-enhancing crowd. Whether jurors believed in somnolentia or not, now they might not even care. The children were irresistible, and through them Hallinan more than recaptured the sympathy Warrant Officer Martin had gathered for the prosecution. So well did the children perform that Elkington waived cross-examination because any attempt to demonstrate that the youngsters had been intensively rehearsed by Hallinan or were lying to save their mother would have been as futile as it would have been cruel. Any effort to do so, whether successful or not, would only have hardened the jurors' hearts against the prosecution and played into Hallinan's hands.

As the trial moved to its concluding phases, Irene's courtroom composure dissolved into a state of chronic weeping, punctuated by periodic outbursts and occasional collapses. Whenever she lost consciousness, MacInnis and Hallinan carried her from the close and stuffy chamber to the more breezy and photographer-filled corridor outside. Unexpectedly though, as her physical condition deteriorated her resolve to become more active in the management of her own case stiffened. Disagreements that Hallinan had formerly ignored reached the point where, in order to retain control of the case, he threatened to walk out of it entirely and he spared no detail in his graphic portrayal of what her fate would be without him. What had begun with Dr. Lennon's witness to her sanity hardened into her preference for conviction as a murderess rather than court-determined insanity. It became the measure of her sensitivity to madness that blighted the family trees.

At this point Hallinan knew they could not proceed at cross-purposes much longer. Hemmed in by Irene's psychological inflexibility, he decided to appropriate into his basic defense strategy her compulsion to proclaim her sanity. To do so, he stood deftly aside, allowing her emotional outbreaks to make her appear insane. The more frequently Irene jumped up in court to yell, "I don't want to be insane," the more likely her insanity would become believable in a juror's mind. Certainly the repetitive denial of that which offered the best hope of saving her life appeared as insanity. She lived her part every hour in court and in the end proclaimed it under oath for four days.

Besides transforming Irene's non-cooperation into a positive defense advantage, this device allowed Hallinan to evade even further the court's initial ruling that no insanity-related testimony would be admitted in the first phase of the trial.

When Hallinan did call Irene Mansfeldt to testify, he recalled later, "I still couldn't be sure she wouldn't say the things I wanted unsaid. At this point I could not rely upon her judgment. Still she had to go on." Not to place her on the stand would have weakened the defense immeasurably, not to mention what it would have done to his relations with his friends the reporters, who needed Irene to sustain their sensation.

The press gave Irene full-page coverage, complete with multiple photographs even though the content of her testimony was redundant. Hallinan had been thorough in getting before the court the extensive background, family and personal histories, stories of faltering mental health, the drugs, her suspicions, her love for the children, and her stated regret for her action; after all that, Irene seemed to be a corroborating witness to what others had established.

Several times she became excited, verging on hysteria. But that also supported the impression Hallinan cultivated. Frequently too, she tried to disengage from his verbal direction and go her own way in direct testimony. When his adroitness failed, he bullied her. Then he resorted to the novel procedure of objecting to the responses of his own client-witness. Judge Murphy sustained him and directed her to answer the questions as counsel asked them. In that way Hallinan kept her under reasonable control until he released her to Elkington.

Strangely enough, instead of being utterly drained by the added strain of having been manipulated by the counsel in whom she no longer had confidence, Irene sprang to life for the cross-examination. Her ghost-like manner, extensive weight loss, and deep, black shadows which encircled her eyes were all misleading, at least for the moment. When Mrs. Mansfeldt whimpered the jurors strained to hear. When she cried they dabbed their own eyes. And when she yelled they sat straight up in their chairs. The widowed mother of three dominated the scene. Before Elkington gave up and Hallinan guided her emaciated form back to the defense table, she twice more denounced her own insanity defense. But when Elkington confronted her with her self-incriminating statements she nonetheless explained herself in accord with Hallinan's psychological theory. "I was frightened even of Vincent Hallinan," she responded. "I figured that he might think I was insane. . . . I don't — want — to — be — insane." That was why she agreed with the police, so they would not think she was insane. Elkington could not shake her from that line through repeated and skillful attempts. Whenever he came close, "I don't remember that," became her refuge. That was her testimony and believable or not, she held to it steadfastly.

Only one requirement remained for the complete, symmetrical presentation of the defense in its most acceptable form; the appeal to authority. Hallinan had introduced somnolentia, had used Irene and the children to advance it, and intended to rest his case with the best available expert witness who could crown it with the dignity and respect the public reserved for medical science.

Months earlier he had engaged Dr. Joseph Catton, a Stanford University Hospital clinical professor with extensive experience on the witness stand as well as at the university lectern. Normally Hallinan devastated expert witnesses, who often sold themselves to the corporations and insurance companies to obviate or reduce the financial settlements for those maimed or killed in accidents which resulted from corporate negligence. Hallinan's contempt fed upon his own habitual destruction of such high-priced hirelings when he cross-examined them on their areas of expertise. These experts were, he agreed, "like a man in bed; they lie on one side and then turn over and lie on the other." He chose the Stanford expert not because of his paper credentials, the criterion of insurance companies, but because the doctor was the smoothest medical witness he had ever observed under cross-examination.

The doctor was tall, grey haired, and courtly. His baritone voice and friendly, learned bearing projected exactly what Hallinan desired: confidence and respect. Had Elkington not compelled Catton to admit having misled a jury in another celebrated criminal case, he would have symbolized all the innocence and sincerity of a country doctor. Still, he came out on top. Under direct examination he withheld damaging testimony so that in cross-examination, when the prosecutor seemed to have cornered him, Catton not only escaped, he did so with premeditation. To illustrate the tenuous nature of Catton's psychological theories Elkington applied them to the doctor himself. He demanded to know why what supposedly applied to Mrs. Mansfeldt did not apply to Catton. The doctor's answer was the reason why Hallinan engaged him and monitored his preparation.

> I have never tried suicide. . . . I have a happy married life, spiritually, mentally, and physically. Mrs. Mansfeldt has been frustrated at every turn. For instance during the first three years of her marriage that marriage was never consummated. There were subsequent periods when her husband, Dr. Mansfeldt, sought her embrace and proved impotent. She tried to divert her emotional energy into drama and music, still loving her husband enough to allow his futile approaches. She tried to relegate sex into the background of her life in order to forget her disgust and horror at his impotent advances. I never had the appearance of another man and my wife. . . . I never considered her taking narcotics or being engaged in a traffic in drugs. . . . And more important, I have never been conscious of a split in my personality.

In tandem with Hallinan's questions Catton traveled down their mental checklist of obsessions, phobias, hysteria, split personality, and drugs. Annie, he said, in direct testimony, had split off from the total personality of Annie Irene Mansfeldt. In this disassociated state, Annie did the killing and the explaining. The police questioned Annie before her personality reintegrated, after which she could neither remember the killing nor the explanation. Only her desire not to appear insane remained constant.

Dr. Catton, mature, dignified, and thoughtful, mobilized the mysteries of that respected world of presumed scientific certainty as effectively as the Mansfeldt children had concentrated the forgivingness of human compassion. He placed the seal of medical approval on Irene's interrupted consciousness.

Prudent legal procedure normally requires a prosecution to counter a defense expert with its own professional witness. In this case Catton's strength on the stand made it mandatory, so the district attorney's office engaged Dr. Mervyn H. Hirschfeld.

A professor of neurology at the University of California Medical School, Hirschfeld lacked the suave veneer of Catton but appeared every bit as sincere and forthright. He appeared younger than his Stanford counterpart, not so tall, and rather bald than grey. He lacked the glibness which Catton had perfected through long and concentrated encounters with attorneys and juries. But on direct testimony he was very damaging. After a one-hour-and-fifty-minute detailed and precise review of Catton's defense testimony by Elkington, Hirschfeld concluded, "There is nothing to lead me to believe that Mrs. Mansfeldt was in an unconscious or amnesic condition at the time of the shooting. . . . On the contrary, there are many things which make me believe she was conscious." Then Elkington's expert proceeded to list and explain the numerous reasons.

By 1945 Hallinan had mastered anatomy and substantial bodies of knowledge within allied sciences. What pertained to each case he mastered with scientific exactness. His memory was encyclopedic and frequently he even surprised himself with his ease of spontaneous recall, particularly when an expert made a mistake. As the years passed and the courts became more concerned with psychology and psychiatry he mastered major subdivisions of those fields too.

This time the expert specialized in diseases of the nervous system. He testified that Irene was conscious when she shot Mrs. Martin. "My strategy," Hallinan explained, "was to question him on a collateral phase of his testimony for which he was probably unprepared. So I started by getting him to admit, innocuously, that the brain was the organ which regulated the human conduct he had just explained."

Next, Hallinan asked the doctor to diagram the brain on the chalk board, using this as his first opportunity to remove Vada Martin's smiling photograph. Then Hallinan began pointing out the deficiencies of the doctor's work, promptly characterizing it as a "cartoon," and drew an improved representation with his own multi-colored chalk. Unknown to the court he had appropriately positioned tiny dots before the session began. Large and accurate, Hallinan's diagram covered the full board.

For two hours, Hallinan, without any notes and without a moment of confusion, grilled the expert on the structure and function of the parts of the brain which related to Irene's disputed mental state. To the doctor, confronted with failing memory, it seemed like two days.

Deep into his own improved diagram, Hallinan proceeded relentlessly.

Hallinan: This is the middle frontal gyrus, and this is the inferior frontal gyrus. Now, I want to get to some of these places we can locate accurately.

Dr. Hirschfeld: Well, Mr. Hallinan, I can save you a great deal of time and trouble.

H: I don't want you to save me time.

Dr.: I am willing to admit freely that I am not fully prepared to localize all the minute divisions of the brain surface . . . . I am not a neurosurgeon. I am a medical neurologist, and it is not necessary for me to keep these things in mind.

H: If you will just answer the questions, and not argue the reasons for them — the jury may find some reasons . . . .

H: What division is there of the anterior portion of the fissure of sylvius? Do you know what they are called?

Dr.: No, I have forgotten.

H: Where are they?

Dr.: Oh, I have forgotten these anatomical details for years.

H: That is not what I asked you.

Dr.: No, I can't answer that question, and it is of no importance.

II. Well, we have here in front the anterior ramus, the anterior ascending ramus. Now, do you know what the portion of the frontal lobe under the anterior horizontal ramus is called?

Dr.: Yes, I think it is the orbital gyrus.

H: They call it the porsorpitilis.

Dr.: That's right.

H: Do you know what the part adjacent to that and between the ascending ramus is called?

Dr.: No.

H: That is called the para-tri.

Dr.: I don't remember that.

H: Now, what is the part between it and the posterior horizontal ramus of the sylvian fissure called?

Dr: I don't remember that either at the moment. . . .

H: Fissure of rolando; there is a large sulcus that runs about in the fashion I have indicated; do you know the name of the sulcus?

Dr.: I don't remember.

H: That is the cingulate, do you recognize that?

Dr.: Vaguely.

H: What do you call the gyrus underneath?

Dr.: It is the —

H: It is called cingulate gyrus, do you recognize that?

Dr.: Well, I have forgotten that.

H: What would you say is the name of the portion above that?

> Dr.: I am trying to remember it. It slipped my mind. I thought I had it.
>
> H: Would you call that the sagittal, or something like that?
>
> Dr.: Maybe. I have forgotten. . . . Frankly, I am not following you very well. I am not interested in this thing at all. I told you, Mr. Hallinan, a long time ago that I wasn't qualifying as a neuro-anatomist, and you keep going on and on and I am frankly — oh, I am not a neuro-anatomist.
>
> H: Well, if a man gets up here and claims to be an automobile expert and he doesn't know a carburetor from a filling stem, some doubts might be cast on his qualifications.

Sprinkled through this devastating reduction of a previously composed physician and teacher to a helpless state of confusion, resentment, and humiliation, Hallinan delivered a concise lecture on neuro-physiology as befitted his client's defense. And in the end he forced the expert to discredit himself explicitly before the jury.

> H: Let me ask you this: you now tell us you specialize in neurology and psychiatry, is that right?
>
> Dr.: That's right.
>
> H: When you first gave your qualifications you said you were a specialist in diseases of the nervous system, didn't you?
>
> Dr.: Well, I am perfectly willing to qualify it —
>
> H: I asked you, did you say that?
>
> Dr.: I did. I didn't mean to say that I specialized in every condition of the nervous system. I specialize in certain conditions of the nervous system —
>
> H: The principal part of the nervous system is the brain isn't it?
>
> Dr.: That is true.

The evening *Call-Bulletin* considered this feat "pure Hallinan — an essence distilled from craft, wit, humor, intellectual brilliance and several parts of . . . just plain cussedness." Thirty-three years later Norman Elkington, then

Associate Justice of the California Court of Appeals, skipped the accolades but vividly recalled Hallinan's masterful tour de force: "It was brutal."

During his evening walks Hallinan began formulating his approaching summation. As usual, he dipped into his file of historical analogies and mythical allusions, which stored years of notes from readings among the classics and scripture. Each time he returned home with a segment fully developed he would try it out on Vivian, frequently working himself up to actual tears. For this case he prepared even harder than usual but received the very same criticism. "Vin, that stuff is crazy. History is fine. Classical names are great but forget the emotion. Be more logical, make a stronger appeal to science." Vivian's cool rationality just could not accept the emotionalism her husband always injected into his final arguments.

When he addressed human problems, particularly before large court audiences, the moisture which bathed his eyes so easily was genuine enough. But Vivian as a critic would never accept it and she could hardly believe that others could be induced to do so either. Vincent thought differently and persisted even though he recognized his wife's skepticism as a restraint on his latent garrulousness.

The next day all one hundred and thirty courtroom seats filled at six in the morning, as soon as the bailiffs opened the doors. When Hallinan arrived three hundred more potential spectators waited patiently outside, some seated upon camp stools and others carrying lunches. Inside he recognized rows of local attorneys, some accompanied by out-of-town associates who had rescheduled business trips to San Francisco to coincide with his summation. The large number of young people on hand, reporters told him, were Bay Area speech and drama students accompanied by their teachers. All had arrived very early yet only a fraction gained admittance.

Hallinan began in the manner Vivian liked, a logical development of each argument sustaining somnolentia. He loaded his words with the weight of testimony, particularly that of the children and Dr. Catton. Along the way he washed the entire courtroom in its own collective tears, Vivian excepted. Then he turned suddenly to the prosecutor and thundered, "You, Mr. Elkington, sit in your serene equanimity, asking why this tortured, half-insane woman did not display the wisdom of an Aristotle. What would you do if you saw your life ruined and the life of your wife ruined and the lives of your children ruined? What would you do in your infinite and exquisite restraint?" He pounded his clenched fist upon the counsel table directly before Elkington and, in a voice audible two floors below in the old concrete and marble Hall of Justice, he dramatically answered his own question. "You would go to him with your gun and you would say: 'You dirty son of a bitch,' and you would shoot him dead!

"This poor sick woman is no criminal you have to drag into the gas chamber the better to protect the people of the State." This was not murder at all, he told the jury, not in the first degree as Elkington demanded, not even second degree. He held out for acquittal and hoped for manslaughter, but privately admitted that a verdict of murder in the second degree would be a victory. He doubted that they would execute her, although nothing was impossible. Standing again beside John Mansfeldt's once beautiful bride, transformed now into little more than a human remnant, Hallinan looked to the jurors through his own blurred eyes and whispered, "Open your hearts."

Amid total courtroom silence he wiped his face and retook his seat.

He had no clue as to their findings when the jurors filed back five hours later. Certainly he would appeal if he had to, but on what grounds? Even the judge's final instructions to the jury had been a model of fairness. Happily there was no need to do so.

"Give us a smile, Mrs. Mansfeldt," one of the photographers yelled as the suddenly joyous Irene stepped swiftly through the swinging doors. She was beaming when Hallinan abruptly intervened, "She hasn't got anything to smile at."

Manslaughter was the verdict, and privately it delighted him too. "Never was I so relieved. It was like having a weight taken off my chest. That verdict was a gift," but it was professionally unwise to admit it and then to persist in the insanity phase with the same jury. So, instead, he told his client to wipe the smile from her face and he expressed their official disappointment. Just the same, he made it clear that he felt the jury acted in good faith.

At this point, with the possibility of execution eliminated, the accumulation of tense disagreements between attorney and client reached a climax. Manslaughter carried an indeterminate sentence of one to ten years in prison, the exact duration to be fixed by the prison board after six months. Irene had resisted the insanity plea all along even though it was her best hope for evading death or imprisonment. Now Dr. Catton sprang a surprise that upset the culmination Hallinan had planned. The Stanford doctor demanded that the plea of insanity be withdrawn and the conviction of manslaughter be allowed to stand. "When you get a victory like that," he insisted to Hallinan, "why should you have her thrown into an insane asylum where she'll stay longer than she will serve in prison if the insanity plea is withdrawn?" He argued that the insanity phase was a no-win situation, but he failed to convince Hallinan who listened and then let the doctor slide away. Characteristically, Hallinan pushed ahead.

To fix sentence, the prison board would review at least the outline of the trial. If the defense backed out now, dropped the not guilty by reason of insanity plea, and accepted the incredible manslaughter verdict, the initial defense could be reviewed as little more than a successful hoax. Why not go on? What difference would more rhetoric make? Particularly if it could mean freedom? An insanity verdict would place great discretion in the hands of the trial judge who had admitted broad psychiatric evidence over prosecution objections, who protected vulnerable defense witnesses and let Hallinan destroy those of the prosecution. The judge could hold a sanity hearing immediately upon a verdict of not guilty through temporary insanity, declare her to be then sane, and return her to her home and family. Within the bonds of courtroom propriety Judge Edward Murphy had given Hallinan all the unspoken indicators that he was well disposed toward the defense. Hallinan was convinced that "by the time the trial ended, Murphy was in our camp."

There was an even stronger reason for going on. Given his own basic metabolism, Hallinan hardly had a choice at all. He had to go on, with or without Catton, and did so in a most unorthodox manner. Hallinan turned over official direction of the case to co-counsel James MacInnis and withdrew; then he qualified himself as a psychiatric expert for the defense. Given his previous demolition of the prosecution expert not even Elkington objected to his lack of formal credentials as he took the stand and testified as to Irene's unsound mental condition. Vivian, who knew Mrs. Mansfeldt since 1932, followed him and did likewise.

Hallinan had to play to the end whether Irene wanted to or not. He had the hide of a rhinoceros himself and the stakes were high enough and the tangible costs, the non-psychological costs, were so slight that even Mrs. Mansfeldt could be made to endure just a little more, even against her will. Courtroom argument at this stage was a cheap enough commodity to expend for the chance of freedom. Conditioned by a lifetime of successful risk taking, Hallinan refused to accept Catton's characterization of this as a no-win situation. In this case manslaughter was a sweet prize, but Hallinan wanted even more. He wanted everything so he stretched for it. If he failed, the prison board would know that he tried.

Unfortunately, he never got the chance to test Judge Murphy's depth of sympathy. The three jurors who had compromised their initial acquittal votes in the first phase by acquiescing to the manslaughter verdict caved in during the insanity phase to the other nine jurors, who had voted guilty all along. At last Irene's wish became fulfilled. The jurors validated her sanity.

Annie Irene Mansfeldt delighted in the judicially adverse finding. She served twenty-five months in the California State

Prison for Women, Tehachapi, with dignity and grace. Her difficulty came in forgetting all those personal things her husband's friend had said about her and about John during his attempt to make her insane for a morning, but free for the aftermath of a shattered life.

8. Success Is Not Enough: In Defense of Harry Bridges, 1950

Harry Bridges occupies a unique place in United States history, though hardly a prideful one for Americans to remember. He was the most persistently and officially persecuted individual in American legal history even though, in retrospect, he seems a most inappropriate subject. He was a working man of limited formal education but immense organizational capacity who immigrated to the United States from his native Australia and found work along the San Francisco docks. What he encountered there in the 1920s resembled the story of *On the Waterfront*, the ugly and vicious exploitation of stevedores so vividly portrayed years later by Marlon Brando and Lee J. Cobb.

Bridges organized and led these wasted men. En route he clashed with and overcame the most powerful leaders of West Coast business. Before he finished he had closed down the Port of San Francisco and with it the city itself. To the popular mind, Harry Bridges was the cause of the general strike of 1934, not the legitimate grievances of rough and desperate men. When he declined a fifty-thousand-dollar bribe to sell out his union, the respectables, meeting in a formal boardroom, debated and narrowly decided against hiring a hit man to solve their labor problems.

160

Given the spirit of the times, the economic and social power of his antagonists, and their political and institutional connections, Bridges became the most visible, immediate target for defamation. His opponents first smeared Bridges as a tool of England, then switched when anti-communism became popular. From the 1930s onward the militant labor leader was assigned membership in the Communist party by popular assumption. Thereafter, business and patriotic groups pressed the government relentlessly for his deportation.

By 1945 Bridges had defended himself against multiple deportation actions: first, the investigations of Francis Perkins, the Secretary of Labor for Franklin Roosevelt; then a full-scale hearing brought by the U.S. Immigration Service and conducted by James M. Landis, Dean of the Harvard Law School; next, a rerun before Judge Charles B. Sears, again for the Immigration Service; followed by the U.S. Supreme Court acquittal.

For some American Legionnaires, deportation of this alien agitator became a virtual reason for being. Harper Knowles, a self-appointed defender of the true America and head of the Legion's Subversive Activities Commission, was one. He maintained the Legion's private dossier on Bridges and regularly offered it to law enforcers whose own incomes and expense accounts enjoyed periodic infusions of anti-Bridges money. Because of unrelenting zealotry such as his, the activities of the trade unionist became topics of discussion even at the U.S. cabinet level among successive attorneys general, secretaries of labor, and court justices. President Roosevelt knew what hours Bridges practiced on his mandolin and J. Edgar Hoover tried to find out what else he did in private. Roosevelt's naturally liberal instincts caused the president to look favorably upon Bridges and his militant efforts to unionize an exploited sector of the American workforce under provisions of New Deal legislation, not to the extent, however, of forthrightly terminating government cooperation in actions against the longshoreman. The FBI director, on the other hand, displayed no such instincts.

When Justice Frank Murphy offered his scathing rebuke of the public and private crusaders who endeavored to deport the waterfront labor leader at any cost, he innocently assumed that the decision of the Supreme Court was final and that conspiracy against Bridges would be silenced forever. Justice Murphy's mistake was not in denouncing the anti-Bridges conspiracy but rather in assuming that his denunciation would end it. In actuality, his 1945 opinion marked the mid-point in the unprecedented action of the United States government against an individual. After the Supreme Court ruled that Bridges was not a Communist and, therefore, should not be deported, federal agencies retooled. They spent the next decade trying repeatedly to prove the very same allegations despite the high court's ruling. Murphy, in fact, reviewed only the first eleven years. Another ten, even more oppressive, followed.

To every stage of investigation, formal hearing, trial, and unending appeals through the 1930s and 1940s, Bridges's regular legal counsel necessarily responded as if these actions were genuine and sincere inquiries into matters of national security rather than Red-baiting, anti-unionism identified by the Supreme Court. His first attorneys effectively challenged hostile witnesses, had Bridges deny the charges under oath, and bolstered his testimony with character witnesses. That defense strategy had been reasonable, conservative, and it worked, but only after years of appeal and then by a margin of a single vote on the United States Supreme Court. In 1949, it all unraveled and Bridges found himself once more back where he had started—as the accused. His safest option was to begin all over, prudently retracing his old defense steps along the well-marked trail, hopefully to the same safe destination. To do that, however, he chose the wrong attorney.

Before Vincent Hallinan entered the case he had only one brief association with Bridges. It was back in 1934 after a force of one thousand police, led by their mounted patrol, tried unsuccessfully to sweep the Embarcadero of the five thousand strikers Bridges used to close the port. After the dead were counted, Hallinan's assignment was to bail out the remainder of the union pickets. He also tried to restrain the city police as trespassers on the state port facility, but his stratagem miscarried. Some strikers objected to him anyway as being too bourgeois. Thereafter, Hallinan's knowledge of Bridges and his International Longshoremen's and Warehousemen's Union (I.L.W.U.) was limited to what he read in the unsympathetic San Francisco newspapers.

"When Harry Bridges looked me up," Hallinan recalled, "he was so scared of going to jail that I wondered if maybe he had foolishly joined the Communist party and therefore the government could actually prove it. But the problem wasn't Harry. It was me. I had never defended in a political trial and I was terribly naive. In the Bridges case I learned more about justice and its perversion than I did in thirty years of prior practice and thirty years since."

Bridges actually warned Hallinan that they would lose despite the evidence, despite his best defense effort, and that there would be grave personal and professional risks for any attorney who undertook the defense. Their mere association would link Hallinan permanently in the popular mind with the despised of the day — those assumed to be intent upon the destruction of the United States government and with it, the American way of life. A well-publicized court loss, in addition to their association, would shift any legal career into reverse.

Preliminary to accepting the case, Hallinan gathered a little family meeting that fifteen-year-old Patrick ended as soon as it began. "You'd take the case if they were going to hang you!" he told his father. So why all the fake concern? Already the older boys cared little for what people thought. And the little guys, everyone agreed, could not learn any sooner what integrity might cost. Hallinan accepted the Bridges retainer and by doing so took the first step toward the radicalization of what until then had been a quiet political life.

By Thanksgiving their gate posts were slashed in red paint, and for Christmas the hammer and sickle decorated their roadway. Instead of complaining to the Ross police the Hallinans struck back in a way their prim town disliked most. They left the paint in all its ugliness and thereafter hosted larger and larger picnics for left-wingers, strikers, blacks, the unemployed, and everybody's kids. The Hallinan guests, whom the neighbors considered revolting, habitually abandoned their jalopies along the meandering lanes, then addressed each other on civil rights, world peace, and colonialism over a powerful public address system. One year when the crowd was just having a loud, good time, the olympic-sized pool overflowed because so many children of all races had jumped in simultaneously. Even Dr. W. E. B. Du Bois and Paul Robeson attended and spoke.

More serious problems came later, though as side reactions to the Bridges trial. For the moment, case preparation called Hallinan back into the city where he and James Martin MacInnis, his associate from the Mansfeldt trial, plowed through the records of all Bridges's previous entanglements.

They discovered, for example, that since the general strike of 1934, the government had used 125 different witnesses trying to prove that Bridges was a Communist. On the face of it, the sources from which the authorities drew their accusers seemed limitless. "To get that many people to testify," Hallinan told Vivian, "Bridges had to pledge his allegiance to Russia on the fifty-yard line at half time of the Notre Dame–Southern California game." But of the actual 125, not one was above impeachment. Previous attorneys clearly revealed their self-interest and recorded their biases. Of course different witnesses might be procured this time, but given the vigor of unsuccessful previous actions, it was unlikely that the government reserved the best for last.

Characteristically, Hallinan abandoned the former defense strategy which tacitly acquiesced to the prosecution's assumed legitimacy. Instead he defined the renewed prosecution as a conspiracy and a fraud in itself, which was continued by known individuals within federal service and by the private interests to which they chose to be responsive. "This collusion had to be exposed and that exposure would be the only permanent defense Bridges could hope for." Besides his reasoning, Hallinan's combative nature and offended sense of justice foreclosed any less aggressive defense.

Once he and Bridges agreed on that basic strategy Hallinan put it more dramatically for public announcement. "In this case," he began, "a conspiracy will be proven, and the jury is going to see something like . . . those cryptogamic fungi that grow in the jungles . . . that have their roots in mycelium . . . hidden in the dark ground beneath the undergrowth of the thickets, that spring up in a single night . . . monstrous . . . fetid, nauseous, horrible . . . and as soon as the sunlight shines upon them, wither and fade away. Before this trial is over," he warned, "you may have to hold your noses."

Hallinan concluded from his preparation that the prosecution's case would be direct and uninspired. No genuine documentary evidence existed to prove Bridges was a Communist simply because he never joined the party. So the government would not present any authentic membership card, dues receipt, or signed application. Counterfeits were such a risk that their admission into evidence was most unlikely. The prosecution, as it developed, even refrained from presenting its much touted Communist party membership card made out to a Harry Dorgan (Dorgan was the maiden name of Bridges's mother) after Hallinan revealed that some entrepreneur had unloaded multiple copies on eager anti-communists at five hundred dollars each.

The rather complicated charge which brought Bridges before the Federal Court of Judge George B. Harris was conspiracy to defraud the United States government by means of a false oath denying membership in the Communist party of the United States. The commodity out of which the government allegedly had been defrauded by a perjured oath was the citizenship bestowed upon Bridges. His alleged co-conspirators were his two character witnesses, Henry Schmidt and J. R. Robertson. Both were old friends and long-time co-workers from the waterfront.

The convoluted nature of the indictment simply was lost on the American public whose mood was building to near-hysterical anti-communism. Bridges had already faced the charge of party membership and the Supreme Court acquitted him. Therefore, that simple, direct accusation could not be forthrightly resurrected. Neither could the straight charge of perjury be used since the statute of limitations intervened. Besides, the Supreme Court decision seemingly validated the truthfulness of Bridges's oath that he never was a Communist.

In order to bring the militant trade unionist before the courts again during America's anti-communist crusade, Justice Department lawyers broadened the old refuted accusations to include conspiracy and fraud. Doing so provided the advantage of artfully extending the statute of limitations sufficiently to include Bridges. To do this, the U.S. Attorney selected the Wartime Suspension Act which Congress passed during World War II in order to be able to prosecute the war profiteers after hostilities ended. This contrivance was exceedingly arbitrary because no relationship existed between Bridges's citizenship and any war-related frauds of money or property. His defense counsel argued this point in pre-trial motions and lost. Years later the United States Supreme Court ruled that the defense had been right. But in October 1949, the highly uncertain fate of Harry Bridges rested in the hands of his new, volatile chief counsel.

Hallinan, always a realist, still could not understand Bridges's pessimism. They had a strong case even though his client was highly unpopular, and Hallinan expected to win. That was why he was in it. Bridges persisted nonetheless that it would not be a trial at all but the same old witch hunt. The Russians had blockaded Berlin, and the American mood became transformed from suspicion into fear bred of hatred and ignorance. Communists had to be found.

On the eve of the trial the Cold War took a decided turn for the worse. President Harry Truman announced to a startled and apprehensive nation that the Russians had exploded their own atom bomb, thus ending America's short-lived post-war nuclear monopoly. A Gallup Poll revealed the nation's deep fear that Russia would use atomic bombs in order to destroy the United States and thereby rule the world. Anxiety drove the threat of war with Communist Russia up to the top of the list of issues in the poll leaving traditional economic and political concerns far behind. At the same time most Americans felt that the intricacies of foreign policy were beyond their understanding and ought best be left to Washington.

As additional anxiety, one which public opinion sampling techniques only hinted at, sprang from and exacerbated the fear of atomic war. Americans prided themselves on the folk history that the nation had won all its wars. This inaccurate though sustaining belief had for generations prompted a bravado which normally passed as confidence and patriotism. But renewed fear of communism twisted this prop of the national mood into a more distorted configuration. Of course America could still beat the world in a fair fight, so why should a nuclear-armed Russia be any different? Yet, the old confidence slackened, replaced instead by paranoia. Since America was in peril, the source of that danger could not simply be some foreign military power. For the mass mind to conceive of an invincible America in peril, the enemy had to be far more sinister. The natural corollary followed: only Americans had the mettle adequate to bring down America. Therefore, the ultimate enemy was not foreign, it was domestic. The enemy had to be within. Thus the internal security risk, the subversive, was born.

Not even Truman's national security program appeased the massive anti-communist mood of the day. When the FBI failed to uncover a single case of espionage from among the six million persons who were subject to the program, the popular anti-communist consensus remained unshaken. Secret Communists had to be more crafty and dangerous than even the flourishing new crop of anti-communist experts in and out of government led the populace to believe.

The critical and militant Bridges, who opposed the Cold War as being essentially American-inspired, became the symbol of the enemy within, just when the American mood approached its level of greatest intolerance. The federal courts, likewise caught up in this popular irrationality, allowed the reversal of the most noble feature of the nation's legal system — the traditional presumption of innocence. Bridges presumably was a Communist; therefore, the task was to get him convicted. The national mood thus threatened the law.

Bridges's pessimism indicated that he sensed then what scholars established a generation later. By failing to share his client's perception, Vincent Hallinan clearly demonstrated that in 1949, he simply did not understand his own America. He entered court under the assumption that if things were wrong, he could make them right.

Hallinan's success in the Mansfeldt case wedded him to the extended opener. It was unsurpassed as a technique for casting advance doubt upon a prosecution and for stealing the psychological initiative with the jury. Since 1945 he had used it regularly, even in petty little actions in which his clients' mothers hardly believed his defense line. And it always worked, even in trials over large matters and big money. What he liked best about his unorthodox procedure was the way it allowed him to work in, before the jury, material favorable to the defense which the trial judge otherwise would exclude.

Bridges definitely was not a sympathetic defendant like Irene Mansfeldt, and even if Bridges were wrong about the political nature of the case, Hallinan felt they still would need every possible advantage. In violation of accepted practice, Hallinan decided to open with a full two-day exposition. His decision was well considered, the technique certainly was well practiced, and, in this case, apparently it was safe.

The opening statements in Hallinan's past criminal cases had been rather satisfying experiences. But not this one. It turned into two days of unpleasant quarreling, during which Hallinan did succeed in placing before the jury a detailed statement of Bridges's labor and legal history. He developed the longshoreman's youthful exposure to progressive labor legislation in Australia, contrasting conditions on the early

San Francisco waterfront, union rivalries, strikes, vigilante interventions, hostile employer's accusations, and the help Bridges received from a few friendly groups including Communists.

Hallinan depicted his client as a militant trade unionist who had converted a transient labor pool of the exploited into productive, self-respecting men. In the process they listened to the advice of California Communists who had recent experience in labor organizing, the task which longshoremen were attempting for themselves. During the depression decade of the 1930s, when constituted authorities beat, gassed, and shot union pickets along the waterfront, San Francisco longshoremen could hardly reject anyone's voluntary interest and aid. The membership of the union considered policy suggestions regardless of origin, voted on what they considered best for themselves, and implemented as they could the democratic decisions. Bridges did associate with known Communists but he never became one. This was Hallinan's message and he got it before the jury.

The greatest difficulty Hallinan encountered during his opening statement was in his effort to bare the venality and perjury of ex-Communist witnesses who had testified against Bridges in the past and were anticipated once again. Judge Harris resisted his attempts at this. Hallinan persisted and what started as a tense situation quickly became explosive.

When Hallinan offered to show the conspiracy between the witnesses and those who were "coaching . . . each of these witnesses to take the stand and testify falsely," Harris seemed officially obtuse. The judge wanted to know how such a monstrous anti-Bridges conspiracy caused the labor leader to swear falsely during his naturalization proceedings.

"That isn't the point," Hallinan persisted. "The point is, why do they testify he swore falsely?"

Faced with Hallinan's willfulness, Judge Harris turned unabashedly to the prosecution table for help in containing Hallinan. "I noticed," Harris declared to the prosecution team, "that during the course of the remarks of Mr. Hallinan in his opening statement that you were prone to interrupt

. . . and then you desisted and remained seated. . . . Will you tell the Court precisely what you have in mind? I assume you desire a definition of the issues."

Sufficiently encouraged, the prosecutors objected to the broad scope of Hallinan's opener. In turn, Harris held that Bridges's history and the history of his previous prosecutions were irrelevant and that Hallinan should desist.

All this, of course, had an unsettling effect on the understanding between Hallinan and his client. Bridges, perceptive and experienced, understood the real dangers inherent in his attorney's new departure strategy of bringing the attack to the prosecution rather than passively enduring another siege. At noon this slackening of confidence took tangible form. The labor leader's family and friends dined together but they did not ask Hallinan to join them. Later that day, prompted by friendly reporters, Bridges and his co-defendants told Hallinan that he might be butchering their case. This was not because the new departure defense was wrong in itself but because Harris was not letting him get away with it in court. The judge apparently did not like being told that the government's case was corrupt. Hallinan's aggressive persistence aggravated him and maybe that was not too smart either.

Unaccustomed to taking direction from a client and unwilling in any event to accept a strategy imposed by a court which he considered unfriendly, Hallinan pushed ahead. He and Bridges argued heatedly in private that night and throughout the trial. Both were forceful men who came up the hard way to success in their respective callings and both were used to meeting disagreements head on. But when all the fury subsided, Bridges always returned to the fact that Hallinan was the expert who was laying "his reputation and everything else on the line to represent me. That took plenty of guts and Vince went in with everything he had."

All Harry Bridges and his union could do was to hold on for the ride, which became increasingly rough. Hallinan himself could easily have retreated, thereby abandoning the new departure, and reorganized behind the traditional defense lines, which acquiesced to the legitimacy of the prosecution, particularly since his client would not object. For any less seasoned campaigner, retreat would have been mandatory. Not for Hallinan. He explained it again to the doubtful Bridges and moved ahead as he could.

"If I didn't, Bridges would have a nice, neat, quiet, and short trial. They would say he was a Communist. We would say he wasn't. Harry would be found guilty and would have a far less meritorious appeal record. He deserved better than that from me and I gave it to him even though it took a little while for him to realize it. Besides," Hallinan thought, "to desist before an unjust prosecution united with an unworthy court would have been a collaboration. You know what I say to that."

Besides the logic of it all Hallinan was also temperamentally indisposed to follow the court's direction along the route of least resistance. He insisted, "That line was strictly a railroad."

By noon on the second day Hallinan's courtroom relationship with Judge Harris and the battery of U.S. attorneys reached bankruptcy, and the case had nearly five months yet to go. Between November and April suspicion turned to distrust and ripened into hatred. The defense watched unfriendly witnesses during off-hours for signs of collusion with the prosecutors. And the special assistant to the attorney general, attempting to explain his knowledge of private defense phone conversations, evaded the charge of wiretapping by admitting to having an informer planted at Hallinan's side. The infighting by then had become vicious.

To prosecute Bridges the Justice Department had selected F. Joseph "Jiggs" Donohue, a successful Washington lawyer, American Legionnaire, Bronze Star awardee, Air Force Reserve colonel, Army-Navy–Club member, and Irish-Catholic Democrat. The special appointment in itself bothered Hallinan even more than the man's credentials. Ever since 1925 when Special Prosecutor Preston Higgins all but lynched simple farming people down in Hanford, he suspected the motivation that supplanted regular, local officials with high-powered imports. This was particularly so for those with top level political connections. The un-explained assignment of a special prosecutor directly from Washington effectively removed trial direction from the San Francisco Office of the U.S. Attorney and told Hallinan the depth of official interest. After countless failures, the government needed a conviction so they brought in Donohue to get it.

Donohue looked his part and reflected the post-war image of the distinguished though hard-working barrister on temporary loan to government service. He sported a shorn, side-wall haircut, a well-pressed wardrobe, and polished army shoes. The eastern import was middle-aged, portly, and urbane. He cast himself in the role of an official government spokesman intent on safeguarding America's internal security as well as the dignity of the federal court. But in tight situations he knew where to place his hits. Besides their role as adversaries, Donohue and Hallinan shared a far deeper animosity, which compelled each to go for the other's throat.

Both sprang from America's most socially self-conscious, culturally defensive, and politically aggressive ethnic sub-culture — Irish Catholicism. To Donohue, Hallinan the atheist was a renegade. To Hallinan, Donohue was far worse. In Ireland he would not be an "informer" because Donohue was the manager of informers. In Hallinan's eyes he was the *gombeen* man in twentieth century dress, the village opportunist who prospered at the expense and misery of those who were oppressed by a tyrannical government.

The adversaries traded insults in and out of court, by-products of intense commitments under attack. Hallinan did what he could to upset the special prosecutor's prepared delivery by annoyingly standing at his elbow and objecting to his every sentence, sometimes every clause, much as Donohue had done during Hallinan's opening statement.

While Hallinan carefully responded to a personal denunciation from the bench, Donohue crowded him at the lectern and kept yelling into his left ear. In a less important trial over money or property, Hallinan would gladly have returned Donohue to his seat or the courtroom floor, whichever appeared first, after a smart left jab to the mouth. Even here he warned Donohue, who stuck tight to the G-men during recess.

In the end when Hallinan accused Donohue of having knowingly used perjured testimony, he publicly invited the prosecutor to sue him for libel. Never doing so, Donohue argued instead for Hallinan's immediate incarceration as a "mad dog" who roamed the courtroom "disregarding the rights of everyone," even Judge Harris.

Both attorneys tried, but neither could intimidate the other, and neither would back off. The basic difference was that Donohue had behind him the full power and prestige of the government and he knew how to use it. He knew that his actions would continue to be sustained by a friendly court. Harris's prompting of a more aggressive response to Hallinan's new departure defense told him that.

The first bomb fell on Hallinan after he challenged the prosecution over its initial self-proclaimed ex-communist witness. Hallinan had been truculent and unyielding from the start, so when Judge Harris unloaded on him it was hardly a surprise. What was unexpected though was the scathing quality of his rebuke and its duration, almost two hours.

In a prepared statement Harris characterized Hallinan's court behavior as "studied, persistent and inflammatory," and he accused him of trying "to impair the effectiveness of this court as an instrument of the judicial process." Harris announced his intention not to allow him to "run unbridled and roughshod" through the remainder of the trial and to that end he cited Hallinan for contempt of court. The real shocker, however, followed immediately. Harris directed the bailiffs to take him into custody and remove him from the courtroom. Furthermore, Hallinan's name was to be stricken from the roll of attorneys empowered to practice before the federal courts. He was to be imprisoned and disbarred.

Hallinan remained seated between his outraged co-counsel and his wilting client almost to the end of Harris's denunciation. Then he rose and asked Harris to disqualify himself from the case. Hallinan, always a willful and potentially explosive personality, offered to be sworn himself and to bring directly before the court a previous civil action in which Harris had been an unfriendly witness against Hallinan. Hallinan alleged now in open court that Harris harbored a "personal hatred" for him.

Harris hit the roof. "I say to you Vincent Hallinan . . . that you would have had no trouble in this case, but you saw fit to . . . impugn the integrity of the Court. . . . I think you know in your own heart, your own conscience, as you stand here, that everything you have said this morning is false, untrue, unfair, and scurrilous. Man to man, in an alley or in a courtroom, you couldn't look me in the eye and say that."

With the overflow courtroom silently gaping Hallinan coldly proposed to Harris, "Let me file an affidavit making the charge, and charge me with perjury, sir. . . . Then we will try it out."

Donohue insisted that his rival's incarceration should begin immediately. He claimed that even the interests of Harry Bridges would be better served but to this Bridges objected. By then he had seen enough. Reconciled to Hallinan's new departure defense, he bluntly informed Harris that "if things go wrong" without Hallinan, "I'll never, never, think that it was a square deal."

Confronted with the possibility of a mistrial, Harris countermanded his order and deferred execution of the six-month jail sentence until after the trial ended. The bailiffs released Hallinan and returned him to the defense table, where he was too outraged to wonder if he would be the one to serve time in federal prison, rather than Bridges.

On this unpromising note the trial resumed, still with over four months remaining. The flocking spectators and reporters, and for that matter Donohue and Hallinan too, had seen nothing compared to what was to follow.

The flow of prosecution witnesses followed Hallinan's prediction. In all, Donohue called seventeen men forward this time to testify against Bridges. Eleven were ex-Communists or at least claimed to be. Typically they elaborated on their background and any prior association with Bridges. Then they swore they saw Bridges at party meetings, had seen his membership card, or had watched the labor leader paste dues stamps into a little Communist party book. As in all the previous actions against Bridges, the San Francisco general strike of 1934 was portrayed as Communist-directed with Bridges being the agreeable agent of conspiratorial communism. Extraordinary witnesses maintained that Bridges met Earl Browder, head of the American Communist party, at his "American Kremlin" office in New York. Or was it in a fruit orchard in the Santa Clara Valley south of San Francisco? Accounts differed.

Since no documentary evidence existed that could put Bridges into the party, prosecution witnesses necessarily had to stand on their own credibility. Normally Donohue spent the better part of the day developing their direct testimony. Then Hallinan or MacInnis would trade off, usually for two or three days each, cross-examining the accusers, often with spectacular results. They brought early government witnesses around to admitting, under relentless questioning, to having committed the very offenses Bridges was denying. Some, as unindicted perjurers, appeared to be what the defense team labeled them—captives of the prosecution. The government, in the words of one nameless stevedore, "had these poor gutless bastards by the balls. What else could they do?"

George Wilson, formerly a close associate of Bridges who served as secretary of his Legal Defense Committee from 1941 to 1945, was an ex-Communist who had taken a government job which normally required a loyalty oath. As a most unwilling accuser he had to look directly across the courtroom at his old friends. Doing so, he hovered at the threshold of physical illness which prompted Harris to call an early recess. The reporters who flocked to the trial day after day felt that his distress over what he had to do permeated the courtroom and all but nullified his testimony. Hallinan realized little damage had been inflicted on Bridges so he resisted the passion most attorneys have for cross-examination and allowed Wilson to step down. Other prosecution witnesses, at least on the surface, appeared stronger. John H. Schomaker was one.

An ex-aide to Bridges, "Shoes" testified that his former chief was a card-carrying, dues-paying Communist who in the 1934 general strike took orders directly from Sam Darcy, the head of the party in California. He knew this because he was a Communist organizer himself while a member of the committee with Bridges. He swore he saw Bridges's membership application for the Communist party.

He was very clear and specific in direct testimony and he displayed good recall of events that had happened a dozen years before. When Donohue turned him over to the defense Hallinan pressed Schomaker relentlessly about all the details of his story to see if his memory was equally retentive when it did not advance the prosecution. It was.

Hallinan had nothing with which to impeach Schomaker from Bridges's legal files so he tried to draw him out and catch him in the loose ends of a manufactured story. On the second day he came close. Schomaker told of a party meeting in a private home where Bridges supposedly made a recruiting speech directed at the non-Communists in attendance. The year, Hallinan was pleased to extract, was 1938. That coincided with a deportation warrant then pending against Bridges. Even those who were convinced by the presumption of guilt which surrounded the trial that Bridges was a Red did not believe he was stupid. He knew his every move was watched and noted by the FBI. So the allegation that Bridges openly recruited for the party while denying membership strained Schomaker's credibility.

It was not much of a breakthrough but it was all Hallinan had when he switched to Schomaker's relationships with the Immigration Service. Here the witness could either admit to the close and cozy relationship, which Hallinan already knew about, or he could try to be evasive. Either way Hallinan planned on doing better. If he fled into the usual "I can't remember" defense about matters he discussed with government agents the week before, that would discredit his key testimony about events he recalled from the 1930s. If he were forthcoming, Hallinan could depict him as a captive, willing or otherwise, of the prosecution.

The strategy was simple enough but its execution was not. Each time Schomaker had half a chance he struck back at Hallinan. Yes, Schomaker revealed, over lunch he did discuss his testimony with Donohue. "I said, 'Hallinan is a smart guy,' and Mr. Donohue said, 'No, I think MacInnis is smarter.'" When the spectators laughed, Schomaker quoted another G-man, adding, "Not only do I think Mr. MacInnis is a smarter lawyer than Hallinan, but I think he is better looking." The crowd laughed again.

For the time and effort invested in a three-day cross-examination Hallinan's reward was meager and he was painfully aware of it. He developed the details of how the government cushioned his life with transportation, meals, drinks, and housing; how agents took his wife shopping and babysat their daughter. After detailing the extreme closeness of the relationship, he asked, "Are you in custody, Mr. Schomaker?"

It was progress. But not much.

Since 1919 when Hallinan began cross-examining liars in the old San Francisco Police Court, he had come to recognize that "it takes an extraordinary mind to abandon the guidelines of truthfulness and still be able to keep a manu-factured story intact under vigorous, experienced cross-examination. I encountered only one such mind in my life and it wasn't Schomaker's."

Armed with nerve and an absolutely unrelated old transcript Hallinan leaned into Donohue's best witness for one last try. Pretending that the document in his hand was some prior Schomaker testimony before another body, Halli-nan slid artfully around Judge Harris's direct request for its identification. Skillfully he continued the evasion and pressed Schomaker, who for the first time looked acutely uncom-fortable. His composure ebbed.

As if he were reading from some earlier sworn statement by Schomaker, Hallinan persisted, "Do you remember being asked this question: 'Are you a member of the Communist party?' Answer. 'Who? Me? No.' ''

Squirming in his chair the witness responded, "That is very possible, but I don't recall. . . . I don't recall saying it in that *[sic]* words, no."

Hallinan backed away and claimed victory. This was an admission, "direct or implied, that he was willing to testify falsely." Otherwise Schomaker would have responded in the negative without hesitation and without qualification.

Even this success was costly. It took three days and in the end Harris cited the transcript trick as further cause for holding Hallinan in contempt.

Fortunately for the defense Donohue lacked Hallinan's selective restraint in cross-examination. In his attempt to take back the ground Hallinan had gained he asked one of those foolish questions which allowed a hostile witness to express an opinion. Donohue knew that Schomaker had held up rather well considering all Hallinan put him through but he could not leave well enough alone. When he asked Bridges what reason Schomaker would have to testify falsely against him under oath, the articulate and engaging Bridges let Donohue have it.

Schomaker, he said, was elected to a union post of trust and responsibility back in the difficult early days. There was little money in it and his wife frequently complained to Bridges. Besides that, Bridges did not think Schomaker could handle the job. So it was easy for Schomaker to sell out union interests when he had financial troubles. From the money he was offered himself, Bridges knew how union officers always had that option. "It isn't a new story. It happens all the time. . . . Even members of the bench, you know, sometimes sell out. And the best way to cover up," he concluded, "is to be an expert anti-communist."

Next, the prosecution brought forth three extraordinary witnesses. Manning Johnson and Paul Crouch were professionals, kept men who derived incomes from testifying before internal security committees and at anti-communist trials. Bridges never saw these two before they took the stand against him. The third, introduced as Lawrence Ross, was an amateur whose career in government service MacInnis would severely truncate.

Johnson, a black man, joined the Communist party as a youngster and quit years later when religious enthusiasm supposedly overcame him. After his asserted rebirth he earned a livelihood as a government witness, appearing in twenty-four trials around the country before traveling out to California for his appearance against Bridges. Besides these, he was a regular witness before the House Un-American Activities Committee. When the congressmen were on tour Johnson traveled in their entourage, naming a labor leader in one state or a liberal teacher in another.

As he took the stand in San Francisco he displayed all the aplomb and ease of the veteran he was. His testimony elevated Bridges from a disciplined card-carrier who followed party orders to an officer, an elected member of the Communist Central Committee. This ex-Red knew this, he swore, because Bridges attended the 1936 party convention in New York and he saw him there as party election returns were announced from the stage. Johnson swore he recognized Bridges standing off in the wings.

Adroitly MacInnis had the witness commit himself to the day and time, then spent the rest of the afternoon tearing at his story. Throughout Johnson's testimony Bridges sat at Hallinan's side reconstructing in his own mind his activities of the summer of 1936. His memory, occupational routine, and his accurate records brought everything together.

His regular practice for years had been to report the results of the union's annual convention to the San Francisco Bay Area locals. In 1936 he did just that and on June 28, at the time Johnson swore that he saw him in New York as an elected official of the Communist party, Bridges actually spoke at a union meeting in the port town of Stockton, California. His files contained the meeting's minutes as well as the press coverage of the event. His driver of thirteen years before was available to testify too. Then unexpected luck boosted the defense even higher.

After the Stockton meeting Bridges had accompanied several union men to a nightclub where one passed uncalled-for remarks about some patrons in formal attire. Bridges intervened, introduced himself, and apologized. He did not wish to dampen the spirited good time of what appeared to be the aftermath of a wedding reception. Now, over a dozen years later, the bride's brother called Hallinan's office after reading Johnson's testimony in the paper. He brought the press photos of the wedding to corroborate the date and offered his own testimony and that of the others as well.

Bridges's unalterable decision to stick with Hallinan no matter how rough the ride started to look better. This was the first break in the case and Hallinan handled it adroitly.

Since his police court apprenticeship Hallinan regularly defended criminals who actually had committed the offenses alleged. That brute fact always reduced his legal options and moderated his courtroom brashness. Now and then his clients, assuming he cared, lied to him about their innocence and if he based his case on that mendacity, the roof usually caved in on them both. But Bridges was different. "Harry was honest, uncorruptible, and he had a social conscience. He told me the truth and my review of fifteen years of perjury against him convinced me that he was innocent and a victim too."

The Bridges case was the most vexing of Hallinan's career but still not sufficiently distracting to distort his assessment of the prosecution. The content of all the hostile testimony really did not make Bridges a Communist or not a Communist. Actually it was disorganized information about Bridges meeting with different groups, some of which had Communist members. It proved nothing about Bridges's alleged membership. The witnesses who testified along that line usually were little men, former associates of Bridges, who were themselves at the mercy of the government prosecutors. Hallinan seldom pressed them on cross-examination for fear of forcing them to be more damaging in order to save themselves. There were exceptions, like Schomaker. And there were the professionals who constituted another species altogether.

Since Hallinan was unshakably convinced that Bridges was honest in protesting his innocence, that meant that the heavy artillery Donohue was wheeling into line were liars. But far more important, Hallinan reasoned, as strangers to the case they lacked a sensitive feel for what they could get away with, an advantage which the locals who testified under duress to less incriminating matters possessed. By trying to inflict critical damage on Bridges with its least perceptive accusers the prosecution was making itself vulnerable.

To try to compensate for the absence of documentary evidence against Bridges, Donohue regularly brought his witnesses over identical matters. They corroborated one another's claims, vouched for each other, and thereby tried to build credibility.

In any case, Johnson's testimony made him a sitting duck who could be blasted out of the water at any time, so Hallinan decided to hold his fire and use him as a decoy for whomever else might corroborate his story.

The very next witness, Paul Crouch, represented patience rewarded. He too swore that he had seen Bridges at the same New York convention as Johnson had. Crouch went down the line in support of the preceding testimony under the well-cultivated illusion that Hallinan was trying to use him to refute Johnson.

In Hallinan's non-political cases this would have finished the prosecution. He could enter the evidence of perjury through the direct testimony of Bridges, offering as he went the abundant documentation as lettered exhibits. Or he could confront the perjurers in person. Normally he preferred creating on the witness stand a one-hour hell for those he caught lying for pay or consideration. By this stage of the trial he had become fully aware of the political nature of the case so he let Johnson and Crouch escape the personal confrontation. Instead, Hallinan redirected his brimstone toward the court and the prosecution.

At the morning's opening session, with the jury seated and the perjurer ready to retake the stand, Hallinan piled up his documentation upon the clerk's desk. Ceremoniously he explained his perjury evidence in mock apology, telling the court that held him already in official contempt how he felt bound to raise this unfortunate matter in order to preserve the integrity of that same court. The situation was embarrassing but the court had to be protected. That these words came from Vincent Hallinan, rather than the officious attorney for the government, conveyed the derision resting in the speaker's intent, even while his speech itself remained a model of courtroom propriety. To conclude the scene he offered a prepared document to Judge Harris for his signature, ordering Donohue's first two professional witnesses to be taken into custody as a preliminary to perjury prosecution.

Everyone—including Harris, Donohue, and the reporters—was stunned.

> Of course we didn't expect those characters to be arrested. This nonsense political scientists spread about the separation of powers in the three branches of the federal government is just that. Nonsense. The federal courts and executive agencies are all tied together. How could those who managed and coached these professional liars turn on them and not expect reprisals when the witnesses got caught for doing as they were directed? Can you imagine what the likes of Johnson and Crouch could have spilled about our government's prosecution if they were subjected to the prosecution themselves? The judicial branch would not allow agencies of the executive branch to be so exposed.

By declining to take the witnesses into custody and perfunctorily asking the United States Attorney's Office to look into the suspected perjury of its own witnesses, Harris fulfilled defense expectations. "Suborners of perjury were asked to see if they were suborners of perjury."

At that point Hallinan reclaimed the documents he had spread before the court and returned them to the defense table. Certainly he would enter them into evidence, but later, when he called Bridges himself. Until then he held the axe in abeyance so Donohue would have to carry on under that impediment if no other.

While the Bridges defense committee publicly agitated

for indictments, Hallinan refused to let it die in court. In subsequent cross-examination he asked Crouch if he had been indicted for perjury yet. "I couldn't resist the question. In a trial like that you have to get your little satisfactions where you can." But much more was coming.

The next witness gave his name as Lawrence Seton Ross. He was the prosecution's surprise witness, billed by the newspapers as one whose education and detachment from the case would carry more weight with jurors than seasoned professionals. His performance, following on the heels of Crouch and Johnson, should have turned acute embarrassment into abject shame. But it did not.

Ross was smooth and self-assured. His story followed that of the other two. Yes, he had been a Communist and yes, Bridges had been elected to party office in New York during the 1936 convention. Ross protected himself though. No, he had not personally seen Bridges there and he tried to offer possible avenues of escape for Johnson and Crouch. But in the end MacInnis destroyed Ross too.

In digging into Ross and his educational background MacInnis detected his mild reservation as to precisely what years he attended the University of Kentucky. No one seemed to notice this except MacInnis. Could Ross, he wondered, name a few of his fellow classmates from good old student days? No, Ross responded, "I'm afraid not."

Ross persisted that he was the son of a southern planter, born in Bell County, Kentucky (before births were registered there), where he attended school and later drifted into communism. But now he was restored to the democratic faith and served as the editor of a southern trade magazine. MacInnis simply did not believe him but, not having anything in Bridges's file, he spent Friday afternoon nailing down the specifics with Ross and killing time for a weekend of deeper research.

The special prosecutor's restiveness rose with MacInnis's growing confidence and before the weekend adjournment Donohue intervened with a violent objection to continuing the cross-examination over to Monday. He protested that already Ross had endured considerable sacrifice in testifying and had to return to Memphis, Tennessee, to bring out the special edition of his *Cotton Trade Journal.* By then Hallinan had a return telegram to the effect that Ross neither attended the University of Kentucky nor the local secondary school. That school's principal also informed Hallinan that he had provided this same information by telephone to the Immigration Service chief right there in Harris's courtroom.

"In other words," Hallinan recorded, "we now knew that the prosecution attorneys had definite information that their witness was lying. It took no great acumen to understand that they were trying to ferret out how much we knew and that they intended to slip their witness out of the court's jurisdiction."

Over the weekend the defense forces discovered there was no Lawrence Ross! His entire identity was a fraud. The witness was actually Lipman Rosenstein, not from Bell County but from Poland. His father was no southern aristocrat but rather a New York garment worker from the Bronx, where young Rosenstein grew up. The whole cavalier identity was a fiction. Further, the defense unearthed four previous examples of his perjury, one identical to that for which Sam Darcy, head of the California Communists, had been convicted.

Hell broke loose in Harris's court on Monday and at the end of it all, Vincent Hallinan was the one cited for misconduct.

Harris allowed Donohue to take the lectern first that morning rather than to have MacInnis continue with the impending exposure of perjurer number three. Donohue put as good a face on the corruption as he could, then he asked the judge to allow Ross, not MacInnis or Hallinan, to be heard. Harris did not refuse.

Ross excused his repetitive perjury, cited scripture, and blamed Communism. By telling the truth now he claimed even to be jeopardizing his second marriage. His wife, if he could be believed at all, not only was solidly anti-communist, she was an anti-Semite as well. He discreetly omitted that at the moment she was being comfortably chauffeured home to

Tennessee by an Immigration Service employee. Apparently Ross had brought his family along for a winter holiday to California in what began as a government-subsidized trip.

At the culmination of this sham Donohue pledged his own cleanliness to Harris "as an officer of this court and as an attorney." After the exposure of his third successive perjurer the special assistant to the attorney general of the United States vouched for his own purity. "I knew nothing of this situation," he intoned, "until I talked with Mr. Ross *[sic]* on Saturday."

MacInnis did a superb job in handling the Ross cross-examination and Hallinan recognized it. But Donohue's assurance of personal sanctity drained what limited self-restraint Hallinan had left. He did not bother claiming the lectern and when he spoke he directed his words at the Washington special prosecutor as well as at Harris. "Donohue," he began,

> doesn't seem to realize the implication that everybody who sits in this courtroom entertains as regards him. He thinks that he still has prestige. He gets up here and he vouches for these witnesses, as though it were some sort of moral Morris Plan that he is co-signing; but he is more bankrupt than the witnesses are. . . . He tells how he had been sent here as special attorney for the United States government and I submit, Your Honor, that I have not seen inferior merits or inferior qualities better rewarded since Caligula made a consul of his horse and Charles II knighted a beefsteak. I haven't seen the gentleman's equal in legal perspicacity since poor Jimmy Carroll died down in the San Francisco police court.

Undoubtedly Donohue understood the Caligula and Charles II references but as an outsider the clarity of Jimmy Carroll probably escaped him. If Donohue did not know that the shadowy, nearly sightless Carroll had become a local legend by bribing the police to change their testimony, Judge Harris knew. From the sensation Hallinan's remarks made, everyone understood his reference except his target—the special prosecutor from Washington.

So raw was the trial Harry Bridges received in San Francisco's federal court that in the end new spokesmen of the original conspirators against him came forward and testified in his behalf. Belatedly the waterfront employers tried to kill the fungus of anti-Bridges suspicion they had cultivated since 1934, but it was too late. What they had helped begin in self-interest was beyond their control and the presumption of guilt prevailed.

Despite the evidence, the jury decided that Bridges was a Red. During this period of pervasive anti-communist paranoia the free citizens on the jury chose to believe the Schomakers, Johnsons, Crouches, and the Ross-Rosensteins who spoke for the government and their decision was congratulated by the court. "You have found the golden truth," Harris commended his jurors, "shining in the fiery crucible of this trial."

Hallinan's fury exceeded all bounds. By then he fully understood how powerful the anti-communist mood of America was and how it touched the Bridges jurors. But he dealt not in entities so amorphous. "Harris was the one. If I have to live forever, I'll piss on that man's grave."

In the aftermath of nationally significant trials, chief participants normally disperse to the original orbits from which they had been attracted. Ross-Rosenstein was one. Joyfully reunited with his now ethnically more tolerant wife, he patriotically proclaimed that America's future now was secure. The country, he announced to the Memphis press, had "at last rid itself of the most influential and . . . dangerous supporter of Communist ideology in the American labor movement."

Donohue retired satisfied too, firm in the knowledge that he had prevailed over a major "subversive attack with constitutional means." His only residual fear was that Harry Bridges would jump bail and flee the country. In a singular misjudgment of the man he pridefully saw convicted, Donohue warned that "as president of an international and communistically-dominated union" Bridges had "everything to gain by escaping beyond the reach of American justice."

Of the professional imports, only Manning Johnson gained a modicum of national recognition. The John Birch Society established a memorial fund to provide annual scholarships for deserving Negroes in honor of this "great American patriot who tried to expose the Communist hands behind most of the 'civil rights' agitation."

Except for the select professionals, most of the participants resided in the San Francisco area, in rather close physical and occupational proximity at that. Little men who had been unwilling cooperators with the prosecution at least escaped the fire of federal prosecution but had to climb back into the frying pan. They had to continue to work as longshoremen within the structure of the I.L.W.U. and alongside union men who gave first loyalty to Harry Bridges, the leader who had salvaged their wasted lives on the waterfront. With the passage of the years, hard feelings subsided and they retired with the bonuses Bridges had negotiated for all union men, including collaborators.

Some disappointed government men joined the popular Christian Anti-Communist Crusade. One went insane, driven perhaps by the anti-communist obsession. Only after this Red scare mellowed and post-Watergate Americans shook off their blind faith in the government did retired agents readily admit to Bridges that the case was a frame-up. They added, of course, that if he quoted them they would have to call him a liar.

Bridges himself never fled American justice. By sticking with Hallinan's new departure defense, Harry Bridges rejected docility and resisted a system gone wrong. In time the U.S. Supreme Court reversed his conviction on the ground that the statute of limitations did apply. In fact, the arbitrary use of the Wartime Suspension Act against him was a perversion of legislative intent.

Naturally Hallinan appealed his own contempt sentence but just like his first contempt citation in the Windmill Murder back in 1925, it stuck. He served his time and began an entirely new life, that of an active political dissident.

The judicial afterlife of Judge Harris continued but not

without stigma, at least in the minds of those liberal San Franciscans who remembered the Bridges case. When the Immigration Service, not satisfied with two rejections by the Supreme Court, brought Bridges to trial yet again on the same type of testimony in a civil suit, Federal Judge Irving Goodman's conclusion on the evidence before him could hardly have gladdened Harris's heart. "Only a weak yielding to extra-judicial clamor," Goodman wrote, "would excuse acceptance of the testimony of the witnesses . . . as proof of the allegations of the conspiracy."

Supposedly Bridges had won. But from 1934, when he organized a militant union and struck the San Francisco waterfront, until 1955, when Goodman dismissed the final Immigration action against him, Bridges had been locked in exhausting legal combat. During those years his wife left him and he lost his home. He subsisted on $135 per week, the rate set by his own policy which prevented International Long-shoremen's and Warehousemen's Union officials from earning more as officers than the best-paid stevedore; thus his income was considerably lower than those derived by executives of other major American labor unions. His greatest financial difficulty, however, stemmed from the government's vindictive parting shot. The Internal Revenue Service taxed as personal income the hundreds of thousands of dollars that Bridges's legal defense committee had raised and spent defending him from the intolerance of the U.S. government.

In time, the public recognized and accepted the aging militant. In 1970 a flamboyant San Francisco mayor, Joseph Alioto, appointed Bridges to membership in the Port Authority. By then the waterfront had experienced twenty-two years of industrial peace under Bridges's democratic labor leadership and no one even wondered about the propriety of an old red fox in charge of the chicken coop.

Time also brought to Bridges the opportunity for reflection during which his admiration and respect for his counselor sublimated memories of their near nightly arguments. He realized that he was despised throughout the anti-communist decade but also that he was a visible member of a substantial union, which provided him with a mass base of support. "But Vince was on his own" and nobody besides Vivian and the boys backed him when the Red smear stuck to him. "When Vince went to jail and lost his livelihood he never threw it up at me." His wife and kids never did either. "One thing about that Hallinan family," Bridges concluded, "they sure hang together."

Harry Bridges never served a federal prison term but both of his attorneys did; Hallinan for making life so acutely miserable for devoted servants of the state while unmasking official fraud and calling it by its name; MacInnis for a spirited reaction to Harris's courtroom treatment of a Catholic priest who testified as a character witness for Bridges. Besides, MacInnis objected sixty-seven times to Harris's final two hours of instructions to the jury.

Throughout his years of civil, criminal, and political practice Hallinan never had a permanent or even long-lasting partnership. In his early days he associated himself with older men who taught him what the textbooks left out. As those turn-of-the-century figures passed on, he and MacInnis came together and remained associated long enough to try two of San Francisco's most celebrated cases. The Bridges case was one of national historical significance and it permanently altered Hallinan's life.

Hallinan admired the legal talents which allowed the younger MacInnis to dismantle Lawrence Ross and reconstruct Lipman Rosenstein for the benefit of Donohue, Harris, and the jury. But federal prison terminated that association too, not because they were incarcerated but because after one month MacInnis did his obeisance to Harris who commuted his sentence to the time served. Hallinan missed Vivian, Patrick, Terence, Michael, Matthew, Conn, Daniel, and poolside life in Ross. But he was incapable of following suit. He would not write to Harris for his forgiveness. Hallinan preferred serving out his time.

Irene Mansfeldt with James Martin MacInnis, Hallinan, and matron (1945).

Left: *Hallinan with second cousin Eamon de Valera, President of Ireland (1948).*

Below: *Yosemite rescue of Kayo (1949).*

Right: *Harry Bridges, Mrs. Bridges, Hallinan (1950).*

Below: *End of first prison term and start of presidential campaign (1952).*

Hallinan and Charlotta A. Bass (1952).

"Hallinan, CP [Communist Party] attorney of S.F., would be a good candidate for the Independent Progressive Party (CP group) indeed!"

— General Staff–Intelligence
Sixth United States Army

"Progressive Party is Moscow's top U.S. political agency. . . . It may offer him the role of a top commissar in a Soviet America."

— Confidential Security Information
Consolidated Index Sheet

9. Hallinan for President, 1952

The surveillance of both Vincent and Vivian Hallinan by federal agents was an unexpected side effect of the Bridges defense. For FBI purposes, Hallinan ceased being a random name on the pages of the monitored left-wing press when he started speaking out publicly against prosecution tactics. After the trial he went on a national speaking tour and thereby became a target of pointed attention. J. Edgar Hoover added Hallinan's name to his secret and unauthorized custodial detention list. Hallinan's mail was monitored, his wife was watched, and he was followed. Their conversations were recorded and ideologically unorthodox remarks found their way into the classified files. Agents and secret informers followed them through art sales, hotel lobbies, and even into Harry Bridges's living room and their own gymnasium. Most prominent among the items of presumed incrimination was their growing contact with blacks. Interracial sympathy was a prime FBI indicator of a questionable loyalty and in the event of sudden difficulties with Russia, Hoover planned to put Hallinan behind bars for the duration. None of this, of course, became known until the Freedom of Information Act and Hoover's death.

But for the Bridges case, Hallinan might easily have resisted Vivian's urge to political radicalism. He was a regular Democrat and "I usually threw my vote in local politics to whatever Irishmen were on the ballot." His first vote in 1920 did go to the jailed Socialist Eugene V. Debs. That was a temporary flirtation prompted by his college valedictory on "Radicalism." As long as President Franklin D. Roosevelt lived, the Hallinans had remained undisturbed by the general domestic policies and programs of the national government. Even as World War II raged in Europe and Asia, and Roosevelt started hedging against the increased possibility of American participation, they did not object to his realistic preparations. When the war ended both Vincent and Vivian were convinced that the future of world peace required the continuation of Roosevelt's policy of cooperation with the Soviet Union. They had five sons by 1945, and Vivian planned more, none of which she intended for atomic destruction in any Third World War.

Mankind, they became convinced, needed a functioning alternative to capitalism almost as much as it needed permanent peace. Unfortunately, Roosevelt was gone and President Harry Truman's policies seemed directed more toward his own re-election than the creation of a tension-free, post-war world. In essence, Truman's 1948 campaign strategy operated on the elementary political principle that the greater the international tensions short of war with Russia, the more American voters would rally behind their incumbent President. Truman successfully played this anti-communist card, which, along with a variety of other moves, provided the combination for his spectacular upset over Governor Thomas E. Dewey. To the politically sensitive Hallinans,

Hallinans, the survival of a Missouri politician hardly merited the awesome risk to mankind. By getting tough with Russia, Truman made Russia get tough with America. By nurturing the anti-communist paranoia already alive in the American mind, Truman aggravated a national fixation. The result, they feared, would be the absolute suffocation of creative thought addressed to the nation's real problems at home and abroad. Such an end to genuine debate over foreign policy alternatives, which already characterized congressional approval of the Truman Doctrine, would make the Cold War and an armament-based economy permanent; war itself would be the logical result. Agreement among the leaders of both national parties on this "bipartisan" anti-Soviet policy abroad and the new red scare at home made the advocacy of serious alternatives virtual treason. Speaking out against anti-communism simply became a dangerous act.

To do what little a private citizen could to interrupt this scenario, Vivian Hallinan joined Henry Wallace's third-party movement in 1948. She considered his new Progressive party to be the legitimate heir to Roosevelt's New Deal and with her she dragged a willing but, at first, somewhat distracted spouse.

Henry Wallace had been Roosevelt's long-term Secretary of Agriculture until the president elevated him to vice-president for one term in 1941. After Roosevelt's death in 1945, Truman removed Wallace from the cabinet following Wallace's public opposition to the new president's cold war politics. When Wallace responded by entering the 1948 presidential race against his former chief and against the administration's aggressive anti-Soviet stance, knowledge-able political observers felt that the well-known Wallace would win enough liberal votes to reduce Truman's support and thereby guarantee the election to Dewey, the Republican Governor of New York.

During Wallace's highly successful, early swing through California, the Hallinans listened appreciatively as he questioned basic administration foreign and domestic policies. Even before Wallace asked why the United States Government should continue to support Chiang Kai-shek with arms to use against the vast majority of his own people, the Hallinans had heard enough. At a San Francisco Cow Palace rally the politically inactive couple gave the usherette a check for the Wallace campaign which was so large and out of keeping with the welter of small cash contributions that the managers wondered if it would bounce. No sooner did it clear the bank than a smiling field worker appeared and invited them into politics.

Vivian's "maiden" appearance was hardly what the term traditionally implied. A group representing Women for Wallace surprised her one morning, arriving at Ross while she was having tea on the sun-splashed veranda. They wanted Vivian to chair an organizational meeting in San Francisco. She readily agreed. Not until the group left did she realize that when the maid brought more refreshments she had remained seated behind a rather large table. Throughout the short meeting her unexpected guests probably never did notice that she was eight months pregnant with her sixth son. Later, when Vince came home, they realized the awkwardness of the situation so Vivian offered to stand aside. Upon consultation with the national campaign headquarters, the Women for Wallace decided instead that no better symbol could speak out for world peace.

Five days after the birth of Daniel Barry, Vivian and Vincent met with Henry Wallace at the Palace Hotel; then Vivian held a party at Ross for Mrs. Wallace. Their driver fetched the guests of honor from San Francisco and chauffeured them across the Golden Gate into the seclusion of their Marin County villa.

Mrs. Wallace was entirely uninterested in Progressive politics, but shifted her gaze from the man-made lake to wonder why "Henry did not have more people like the Hallinans of Ross in the party?" Wallace agreed, but for his own reason. "Yes," Vincent recalled, "He made me his party's chairman in a reactionary county where even my humanitarian sister wouldn't join the Progressives. But he made Vivian West Coast head of Women for Wallace. He flipped over Vivian. If I faded out of the picture altogether, it would have been all right with Wallace."

As county chairman Hallinan did hold meetings in his gymnasium even though the turnout always was an embarrassment. Aside from the remnants of an artist's colony in Sausalito, there were insufficient radicals — even liberals — to clog the lanes meandering past the residences of his Republican neighbors. Were it not for the FBI and the boldly curious, even fewer gym seats would have been occupied. Nonetheless, his chairmanship did give him a place on the party's State Central Committee and a further introduction to third-party politics.

Besides Wallace, Vivian introduced her husband to Calvin Benham "Beanie" Baldwin, the politically knowledgeable, sustaining force behind the Progressive party. The mild-mannered and slightly pudgy New Dealer had been drawn into government as a young man of ideals during the Roosevelt administration. Baldwin was a special assistant to Wallace in the Department of Agriculture where he discovered the underside of farm life: tenant farming, migratory labor, share cropping, and the hidden but very stark reality of debt peonage which stalked parts of back-country America. By 1944, as Roosevelt approached his fourth national campaign, he asked Baldwin to leave Agriculture and manage the CIO's Political Action Committee. Baldwin's charge was to bring the labor vote into line for what was to be his chief's last campaign. Months later with Roosevelt dead and Truman and the New Dealers heading in different directions, Baldwin became for the Progressive party what James Farley had been for the Democrats and what a latter-day Lawrence O'Brien became for John F. Kennedy and Lyndon Johnson. Although he looked more like a confectioner's assistant, the displaced New Dealer was a talented political manager, but one with a basic distinction. For Baldwin the long-range solutions to the systemic problems of America were not in the creation of more agencies or a permanent war economy. For him the further socialization of American society was paramount. He was a low key socialist but not anti-communist, like members of the American Socialist party.

Harry Truman's historic victory over the supremely confident Dewey, plus the disappointing failure of the Wallace peace vote, hardly dampened the newly acquired Hallinan enthusiasm for Progressive politics. Characteristically, the effect was quite the reverse. They watched Truman transfer the irresponsible "soft on Communism" smear to the Progressives by red-baiting Wallace and applying his cold war rhetoric to the domestic scene. Repelled, the Hallinans stepped up their political involvement, particularly with the outbreak of the Korean War and Truman's executive decision to commit American troops. Once Americans started dying in Korea, Wallace not only appeared to have been an insightful political leader, to the Hallinans his prior utterances seemed prophetic. He had warned against American involvement in colonial areas and the risk of war inherent in the assumption that military force would stabilize restive peoples and protect American interests.

The Hallinans pictured Syngman Rhee as a Korean Chiang, a tyrannical dictator behaving in the classical mode of selling out his own people to American interests in order to preserve and enrich himself. They predicted his ultimate, postwar fate but did not imagine Korea's subsequent corrupting influences within the United States Congress itself. But when they met with the Progressive Party National Committee, the Henry Wallace they encountered, instead of being bullish, seemed utterly chastened.

Henry Wallace and Vincent Hallinan had but one lengthy, private discussion on that occasion. Wallace's disagreement with the party's growing anti-war militancy was apparent even to the political neophyte from the West who tried to impress the former vice-president with the need to stick together, to struggle even harder for what Wallace stood for in 1948. "He listened but said little. It was evident," Hallinan realized, "that I could have no influence over him."

Shortly thereafter, Wallace took his leave from the

Progressive party, announcing through the *New York Times*, ". . . when my country is at war and the United Nations sanctions that war, I am on the side of my country and the United Nations."

Hallinan explained why Wallace's peace posture collapsed at the very time when war in Korea represented the unfolding of his worst predictions in much the same way he excused so much of the human frailty he witnessed in life:

> Henry Wallace was a limited person. Yes, he was an intellectual, a writer, administrator, and an experienced national politician but his mind remained bound by the traditional values of the agricultural, mid-America that shaped him. He was a gentleman, a Christian believer, and a liberal capitalist. Each of these characteristics was mentally, emotionally and, I think, dynamically limiting for him. He had the right perspective on what American policy ought to be, only his limitations prevented him from ultimate action on his own convictions. He was a patriot in the most limited of ways. He could not oppose the Korean War, largely because too many reds opposed the Korean War.

Vivian's analysis was even more revealing—of herself and her concept of the family unit:

> How could you expect him to challenge the mindless traditionalism of his own America when the chips were down? So far as I could determine none of his family was with him. His wife appeared uninterested in his work. I never saw a child or relative campaign with him. What man can stick up for ultimate convictions in the face of near universal rejection without the support of his family? In 1948 he did the right thing, and that took courage. Four years later it required more and he didn't have anyone close enough to sustain him. I felt bad.

Baldwin, because of his openness to far left political personalities and policies, remained in the party as national secretary and campaign manager. It was his wing that determined the anti-Korea posture and declined to go along with

Wallace's support of the war. After Wallace departed, Baldwin remained surrounded by a line up of national party officers most of whom had made themselves odious to mainline America.

W. E. B. Du Bois, the peace activist-intellectual, and Paul Robeson, the world-renowned vocal artist, highlighted the strong black leadership element of the Progressive party. Their anti-war, pro-black militancy attracted national attention, federal indictments, and ultimate prosecutions. Hugh DeLacy, a one-time university teacher and former congressman, reflected the disaffection of both politicized intellectuals and progressive office-holders whose professional careers were truncated by their irrepressible, liberal views. Hugh Bryson of the Marine Cooks and Steward's Union became the West Coast's radical labor contribution to the party's decision-making body. He organized the 1948 Independent Progressive party in California and later was convicted under the Taft-Hartley Act for affiliation with the Communist party. Harry Bridges, with his own legal and union troubles, began restricting his own political action but his strong affiliation with the Progressives was fixed in the public mind. In addition to Shirley Graham (Du Bois) and Eslanda Robeson, the national leadership element was fortified by Alice Liveright and Florence Luscomb. Liveright came to progressivism from an established Philadelphia family. Luscomb, who at age eighty would walk from Boston to United Nations Headquarters, New York, to protest the Vietnam War, traced her lineage to the Mayflower. Polishing off the veneer of political respectability was Elmer A. Benson, the third-partyish former senator and governor of Minnesota. Summing it up for the American mainstream, *Time* magazine concluded that Wallace's "dusty rose Progressive party" had become "shocking pink." Some flaunted memberships in organizations proscribed by the attorney general and those who did not were considered guilty by association.

The Hallinans were attractive to the Progressive leaders for obvious reasons. Vincent was slated to go to jail for defending a prominent member of the Progressive party, a labor leader whom the government refused to let alone. Vivian, like her husband, was an articulate speaker and additionally, she was a good organizer. Both shared the Progressive opposition to the Cold War and favored socialistic solutions to America's problems. Both willingly contributed to the party's treasury and could well afford to continue doing so. And neither was put off by Communists or those the government alleged to be Communists. As far as Vincent was concerned, "to be branded a Communist by some ignorant committee chairman was to me a strong, favorable recommendation. Communists? I was all for them."

An analysis of the correspondence between Baldwin and his state party leaders shows that what Progressives wanted most was for some well-known Democrat, disaffected by Korea, the Cold War and McCarthyism, to denounce Truman and declare an independent candidacy, much the way Wallace did in 1948. Baldwin and those who surrounded him would gladly have supported any Democratic party nominee who genuinely shared their "radical" opposition views. The forlorn fantasy that a peace candidate would be nominated by a major party, however, never impeded their own realistic plans.

As 1951 ran out and no nationally recognized Democrat converted to Progressivism, Baldwin and the party leaders decided that they had to generate their own national ticket, or else Americans would have no alternative in November to the bipartisan Cold War and Korea. To emulate Wallace and abandon the field was, to them, unthinkable.

The first inkling Vincent Hallinan had that he was being considered for the top nomination came in New York during the deliberations of the National Committee in January 1952. Vito Marcantonio, the former congressman from New York, had declined to allow his own name to be considered because of personal and local political reasons. His long established radicalism which usually paralleled shifts in Communist party policy made him appear to be at least a fellow traveler. On the floor of Congress his immediate and solitary denun-

ciation of Truman's commitment of American forces in
Korea endeared him further to the Progressives, particularly
since that act cost him his congressional seat. Marcantonio
would support the Progressive ticket, but he would not head
it. Actually he was considering running for mayor of New
York.

Du Bois, Robeson, and National Lawyer's Guild President, Earl Dickerson, likewise were considered. All three
were blacks; all were prominent in the party. As head of the
Peace Information Center, Du Bois had successfully defended
himself in the Federal Court for having gathered signatures
for the Stockholm Peace Petition. The Justice Department
maintained that his action constituted an offense of an "un-
registered foreign agent." With a turn-of-the-century German
education and a Harvard Ph.D., he was a forceful writer and
an eloquent speaker. Though he was still vigorous, his Progressive friends were unwilling to subject him to the imposition of a presidential campaign at age eighty-four.

Robeson absolutely refused to be considered. As a militant advocate of black rights in a day when that in itself was
considered evidence of disloyalty, Robeson was a lightning
rod for the gathering storm of civil rights protest. Like
Marcantonio, when the Communist party's position on issues
shifted, Robeson adjusted accordingly. The long established
and well-publicized militancy of the baritone, most famous
for his portrayal of Othello, hardly endeared him to his
fellow Americans. Adolphe Menjou, in characteristic serious-
ness and dignity befitting of his Hollywood roles, tipped off
a congressional investigating committee of the one sure way
to identify communists. They were the ones who applauded
when Paul Robeson sang.

Dickerson, rumored then to be the richest American
black, had heavy commitments to his business, The Supreme
Life Insurance Company of America. Despite the private
efforts of Du Bois, he would not accept the nomination
either.

Throughout the protracted deliberations, Hallinan's
name remained prominent. Among those mentioned, he

possessed the best balance of qualities for a straightforward national campaign. Some committee persons even considered his impending imprisonment to be an added advantage. If he would have to surrender himself, as appeared increasingly likely at the time, the party could portray him as another Eugene Debs whose 1920 Socialist campaign for president enjoyed that identical point of honor.

Years before, Hallinan had turned aside friendly suggestions of California Democrats who urged him to enter state politics as preparation for a run at the U.S. Senate. To an habitual outsider, the vision of a lifetime immersed in compromises was not an attractive one. As a lone wolf he liked striking his own deals, making his own decisions, and carrying them out personally. It was the prospect of electoral success rather than defeat that kept him from embracing the California Democratic party. Since the presidential nomination of the Progressive party hardly entailed the liability of success, he did not say no.

He accepted the nomination because he believed in what the party advocated: peace in Korea, civil rights for blacks and all Americans, an end to repressive anti-communism, restoration of civil liberties, improvement in the rights of organized labor, and redirection of the national economy. He wanted the war-oriented economy transformed into programs of public works designed to serve broad economic and social needs and not the interests of finance capitalism. That these goals were the goals of the Communist party prompted no reservations. Hallinan felt perfectly comfortable in the company of blacks, socialists, fellow travelers, and Communists too. He was convinced that from the Progressives came the most rational and most promising responses to America's foreign and domestic problems. All these things allowed Hallinan to accept. One added factor all but compelled him. The run for the presidency promised to be a splendid adventure for a family of insatiable experience-seekers.

Because of the Progressive party's unique commitment to racial equality and because of the presence in leadership positions of prominent black activists, the assumption that a black ought to be on the top ticket was natural. Even party leaders at the state levels who disliked that prospect could not argue against it in principle. Hallinan's previous personal contacts with blacks had been few. He had belonged to the lily-white Olympic Club in the days when San Francisco's slight black population was insufficient to generate applications even if they had been welcome. His early and enduring friendship had been formed in an Irish and mixed European ethnic neighborhood which, before World War I, housed no blacks. After World War II, his irreligious proclamations hardly recommended him to the greater body of church-going blacks. He felt that, as witnesses and clients, they shared the same characteristics as their Caucasian counterparts and he always welcomed blacks as jurors. "They are understanding of life's problems and compassionate of human frailty."

As a rough equalitarian Hallinan understood the position of disadvantage and discrimination which blacks occupied in American society. Once, when he encountered an aged black man on a narrow sidewalk, he glimpsed what permanent subordination could do. Before Hallinan could move close enough to the building to slip past, "the old gentleman stepped into the gutter, took off his hat and bowed. It turned my stomach."

Normally, Hallinan sublimated such momentary flashes to the standard liberal assumption of America, a land of opportunity, equality, and inevitable progress. The passage of time and government action, he had felt, would moderate and ultimately end discrimination. In the meantime he continued to treat those few blacks he encountered just the same as whites. Upon closer personal association in 1952 he concluded, "That was a mistake. They are not the same."

Vincent Hallinan acquiesced in the Progressive leadership's selection of Charlotta A. Bass, a black woman, as the party's vice-presidential nominee. The former editor of the *California Eagle*, the West's oldest black newspaper, was not his first choice. Hugh DeLacy was. DeLacy was an Irish

American but showed it less than Hallinan. His name went back to the twelfth century Norman invasion of Ireland. He lost his Seattle congressional seat in 1946 to a demobilized navy officer who promised to do more for the naval yard in their district. Besides the bond of political radicalism he and Hallinan shared a fondness for books and an easy gregariousness. DeLacy regretted never having been brought up a Catholic as Hallinan was because, "It's a church I would have enjoyed revolting against." Vince's own revolt was anything but joyous, but he never begrudged "the Norman" his dig.

When Marcantonio proposed Mrs. Bass, Hallinan reminded the National Committee of their own intentions not to make the election a symbolic protest but to make it a competitive, forthright campaign for the largest possible vote just as the party tried to do four years earlier with Wallace. Prejudice against blacks was strong throughout America, particularly in the South. So, Hallinan argued, why fly in its face? Without a black on the ticket maybe they could resurrect old southern populist votes by stressing the actual issues.

The immediate black Progressive reaction was direct and not what Hallinan anticipated, that is, a recognition of the unjust reality and a resolve to fight for the principle of equality. "Earl Dickerson angrily asked me who the hell I thought I was. He told me, 'You have no right to say that.' I discovered then and there," Hallinan recalled, "that I had been mistaken in assuming absolute freedom of expression among blacks. It was not to be done. I learned that being black is more than just being a human being with a different skin color who was discriminated against. It entails bitterness, suspicion, and over-sensitivity. If you say one little thing that may be taken as patronizing or trenching upon black dignity, it is interpreted as the truth behind a false front of friendship and toleration. When you understand the psychological history of American blacks, you realize why this limitation is there." Even prominent blacks with otherwise strong self-esteem, Hallinan felt, shared that same problem. Among them he included Charlotta Bass, a distinguished, successful, and mature professional woman. Despite her general good sense, the retired newspaper publisher demanded the perquisites normally associated with the vice-presidential nomination of a major party, trappings which the financially bankrupt Progressives could not provide.

Months later, one campaign incident was to convert his principled stand for full racial equality into a personal and emotional commitment. It committed his heart as well as his conscience to Mrs. Bass. In Washington the two of them spent a morning conferring about a joint television appearance. At noon Hallinan suggested lunch but Mrs. Bass said it was a long way to the railroad station. "I honestly thought she meant that they had good food there. But no. She meant that it was the one place in the then segregated Capital that she knew of where a black woman might eat with a white man in public. I couldn't believe it. It was an outrage. She thought I did know it and was pretending otherwise."

Before this emotional bonding took place Bass and Baldwin made one final effort to keep Hallinan from jail by petitioning President Truman for commutation of his Bridges contempt sentence. It failed. So, on April 1, Hallinan surrendered himself into federal custody. He left to Vivian, Patrick Sarsfield, Terence Tyrone, and Michael de Valera the responsibility for maintaining the family's public commitment to the Progressive cause. Meanwhile, the presidential candidate tended the prison chicken coop on McNeil Island, Washington.

Over the Fourth of July the Progressive party gathered in Chicago for its third national convention. They wrote their platform, planned their campaign strategy, and sought media attention for the candidates and the issues they identified as the critical matters confronting America. The Hallinan-Bass ticket already had been selected by a broadly based, ad hoc committee and had been approved by the state organizations whose wishes had been communicated through the committee representatives. This nominating procedure was necessitated, in part, by restrictive legislation against third parties. Some states required third parties to submit the name of their candidate far in advance of the summer conventions which chose the major party candidates. In each state, Progressives had, first, to figure out unique requirements to get on the ballot; then they had to scramble to comply. Otherwise Hallinan and Bass would not be on that state's ballot for the November election.

The public relations experts engaged by the Republican party were packaging Dwight Eisenhower for political marketing as a combination of staunch military hero, national father figure, and Mr. Clean. Totally lacking any political record of his own, the spotless "Ike" Eisenhower accepted "corruption in Washington" as a campaign issue. From the start, Richard Nixon, California's anti-communist senator and Ike's running mate, was a burden. Disclosure of his private slush fund proved such an embarrassment to the general that he contemplated dropping Nixon for a more fragrant running mate. In order to stay on the ticket as much as to appeal to the American people for their election day approbation, Nixon used the television medium masterfully. During prime time he explained why accepting money from California oilmen was not for him a venal act. Melodramatically and demeaningly he confessed that besides money, he also accepted a cocker spaniel, Checkers, which his young daughters had come to love. As a good and kind father, he intended not to return the pup either. For Progressives, the "Checkers" speech embodied Nixon's intellectual poverty and ethical legerdemain. But Ike liked it and decided to retain "my boy" Nixon on the Republican ticket.

For Progressives Dr. Du Bois set the intellectual tone of the campaign. As the possessor of the most cultivated, trained, and acute mind of all twentieth-century political activists, the aged Du Bois had all but despaired for racial equality in the United States. Since the 1880's he had weaved his cerebral way through Harvard, the University of Berlin, various American professorships, and untold publications.

En route he could not forget Georgia blacks burnt at the stake and their organs, "crispy cooked, for 10 cents," displayed in an Atlanta grocery store. Between this horror and his Progressive keynote fifty-three years later, Du Bois's life led him from mainline American politics to an acceptance of Marxism. His most powerful and cogent historical works rested upon its precepts. Few Americans were intellectually equipped to understand the depth of his mind and in a decade of intolerance, he and his ideas were dismissed with hostility. Undoubtedly, when at age ninety-three in 1961, he publicly applied for Communist party membership and two years later became a citizen of Ghana, such terminal behavior was accepted as retroactive corroboration for anyone who had considered him an over-educated and disloyal black.

For the Progressive convention delegates, Du Bois summarized the history of Western imperialism and its heritage of war, subjugation and exploitation around the darker parts of the globe. In Chicago, Los Angeles, and New York he warned that America ought not to follow England and France into wars to maintain the interests of industrialized nations and to suppress revolutionary nationalism among third world peoples. At the time when the spokesmen of both major parties were defending America's Korean involvement Du Bois thundered, war "is a vicious human habit, a throw-back to primeval barbarism, an anachronism which shames religion and retards civilization. . . ." Concluding in a more poetic mode reminiscent of autobiographical portions of his *Souls of Black Folk*, written fifty years earlier, he appealed to science, history, psychology, and sociology for earthly redemption. Otherwise, the new atomic age would bring war, "the supreme disaster."

On the campaign trail Vivian normally followed Du Bois to the lectern with a less dramatic but more direct expression of concern for the mothers and children in future America. Cognizant of how the protective quality of motherhood became paralyzed when the flag waved and the bugle called, she denounced the destruction of the nation's youth in Korea and called upon all mothers to register their opposition. "I am not accepting the statements of . . . corporation lawyers whose interests have elected them senators. Or the words of professional murderers who operate under the title of generals." Emphatic and to the point, her remarks earned for her a separate classified security file which bulged in its own right.

The presence on a national ticket of Charlotta Bass was in itself striking enough as an historical first. In spite of how *Time* misrepresented her as a Russian-influenced, disaffected radical, she had left the Republican party, only after thirty years of loyal service, because she despaired at the intraparty segregation, even of volunteer workers such as herself. She aimed her hardest oratorical punch at the two major parties. "Can you imagine," she asked, "the party of . . . Eisenhower . . . calling upon a Negro woman to lead a struggle against high taxes . . . ? Can you conceive of the party of Truman, of Russell of Georgia, of Rankin of Mississippi, placing in nomination a Negro woman, like myself, to carry on a battle . . . against segregation . . . ? Would the Democratic or Republican parties nominate a Negro woman whose platform can be stated in these words: Peace, end the war in Korea now?"

Between feeding the chickens and playing jailhouse lawyer, Hallinan had plenty of thinking time. Unlike the well-financed Republicans and Democrats, he could count on having no speech writers. Baldwin's skeletal staff could type, mimeograph, and send out mailers, but beyond that Hallinan would be pretty much on his own. Baldwin, as campaign manager, constructed the itinerary for Hallinan's national campaign and identified the single issue most appropriate to each speaking engagement. Exactly what the candidate would say and how he would say it was Hallinan's responsibility. Baldwin offered to help but, in fact, he was overwhelmed by the details not only of the Hallinan-Bass speaking tours, but by state and local party matters as well. So Vincent fell back upon his recall from reading among the leftist papers and magazines on Vivian's ever-expanding subscription list. Beyond these, he was well-informed by habitual attention to the eastern press and national magazines for news of world affairs. From this mental data bank and the experience of traveling in Europe, the incarcerated candidate outlined a series of speeches, each one focusing upon a major issue. For his contribution to the Progressive party platform he relied upon Vivian who, with Patrick, spoke for him at the Chicago convention. Actually, constructing a platform which supported party principles and also was compatible with the positions of Hallinan and Bass presented no problem. The leading personalities of the party already were galvanized by the unpopular views they shared. By the time Hallinan did see the platform, his prison reading had prepared him even for the farm policy. On the issues of Korea, permanence of a war economy, the need for future American-Soviet cooperation, institutionalized racism, civil liberties, and the welfare of labor, Hallinan was in full and knowledgeable accord with the platform. Progressive views were his views.

When he stepped aboard the prison launch, which was to take him ashore at Steilacoom, Washington, his head was filled and his briefcase stuffed. At mid-passage a two-masted yacht chartered by Progressives hailed him with "Hallinan for President" and a serenade of Irish melodies. As the last chorus of the "Soldier's Song" blended into the "Siege of Ennis," he felt that same old adrenaline surge. He stifled the incipient thought that similar music probably fortified the legion of fallen Irish heroes whose names Vivian regularly appropriated for their sons. Whatever, he was impatient for his own coming fight and ready to tell America just what he thought. The Progressive party gave him an opportunity afforded few individual citizens of a mass society so he intended to make the most of it.

Already General Dwight D. Eisenhower and Governor Adlai E. Stevenson had been on the campaign trails since the Republican and Democratic conventions one month earlier. The Republicans were hungry for office after their twenty-year exclusion. Herbert Hoover had taken credit for the prosperity of the roaring twenties so Americans continued to blame his party for the soup kitchens and tar-papered Hooverville shacks of the depressed thirties. To overcome this built-in disadvantage the Republicans marketed Eisenhower as an attractive commodity, a good tactic but one which could not be relied upon as sufficient in itself to overcome fixed public opinion. Behind the famous Ike smile and open-handed show of good will the Republican planners also advanced a southern strategy designed to crack the once solid Democratic South, which had shown signs of crumbling four years earlier. Strom Thurmond, governor of South Carolina, had bolted from the Democratic party in 1948 and, as a candidate for the Dixiecrats, actually polled more votes for racial segregation than Henry Wallace polled for world peace. To hasten the desertion of southern Democrats and attract the region's enfranchised white voters, the Republican party wrote blacks off altogether. Following his party's political strategy, Eisenhower headed south where he campaigned against a Fair Employment Practices Commission by telling receptive southern whites that such compulsory legislation would aggravate race relations. Returning to Harlem, the general falsely claimed that he had tried to eliminate segregation in the military.

The Democratic party hardly offered Negroes anything better. They responded to the Republican southern thrust by retreating from their own advanced 1948 platform plank on civil rights. Democratic leaders planned to retain the historically loyal South where whites controlled the election apparatus and blacks voted only at white sufferance. Prominent among those Democrats who withdrew the party's previous commitment to blacks was Senator John Sparkman of Alabama. After the avowed segregationist completed his task, the Democratic Convention chose the Alabamian as Stevenson's vice-presidential running mate. On this ticket Sparkman symbolized Democratic abandonment of blacks to the interests of the white South in order to maintain party harmony and retard Republican electoral advances.

Hallinan's personal position and Progressive platform plank on civil rights were identical. Alongside Bass, he spoke out for the advancement of blacks in every sector of American life. Once out of a segregated federal prison, he devoted a major portion of his opening address to "the emancipation of the Negro people from political, economic, and social degradation." In San Francisco's Civic Auditorium he called for a compulsory Fair Employment Practices Act, for an end to the poll tax and other devices used to disfranchise blacks, for new laws to combat lynching, and for federal action to end segregation in education, housing, and the military. Predicting the black revolution of the next decade, Hallinan foretold the rise of a "new militancy" supported by the bulk of fifteen million black citizens left with no other recourse. The major parties which traditionally converted legitimate political needs into reform and administrative action were selfishly ignoring a major sector of the populace because it did not have control of its own vote.

Hallinan analyzed and explained the broader meaning of black political impotence, a facet seldom recognized by disinterested whites. Southern states, by restricting the vote of those unable to pay the poll tax, screened out the blacks at whom the tax was aimed, and with them, poor whites as well. The effective result was government by a reactionary minority. Briefly lapsing into the mode of a political science lecturer, Hallinan contrasted the congressional representation of South Carolina with that of Washington State. Both states had had the same number of congressmen, only those from the poll-taxed South were elected by about one-eighth of those casting votes in the Pacific state. Besides that, the long tenure of congressmen from one-party southern states gave them important committee chairmanships under the seniority system which then allowed them to kill liberal and pro-labor legislation.

This "vicious caste system," he maintained, "is making its victims a class of American untouchables." It had to end, if not in justice to its victims, then for the health of the body politic. "A prime condition for progress in this country for all the people—white and black—is full political, economic and social equality for the Negro people."

Among the four thousand who attended his opening campaign rally were the ever-present federal agents. They listened and summarized Hallinan's "strongest language" for pages 281–87 of his expanding confidential security file. Undoubtedly, they concluded, Vincent William Hallinan was pro-black.

By the time Vince entered the campaign, Vivian already had logged eight thousand miles through eleven Midwestern, New England, and Middle Atlantic states. She had appeared at the party's Madison Square Garden rally with Du Bois in May where he rendered a powerful and well-reasoned defense for the existence of third parties in the American political system. Again in October she returned to the East, that time with her released husband who delivered the major address at the American Labor party's New York rally. Radical New York was Marcantonio's preserve and he shared it uneasily with the Progressives. Once he adroitly scheduled Hallinan to speak across town while he was to meet with the moneyed crowd and solicit contributions. Vince sent Vivian to make the scheduled appearance and he attended the quiet fund raiser himself. Marcantonio's reprisal was unanticipated though. He omitted young Patrick Hallinan's name from the next rally program. At Madison Square Garden Hallinan corrected the slight by introducing his son to the audience anyway. "I couldn't let a guy shorter than me get away with a mean trick like that."

With family loyalty satisfied, Hallinan ripped into the post-war foreign policy consensus shared by both major parties and by Stevenson and Eisenhower personally. He rejected the bipartisan foreign policy through which the presumed protagonists within the national two-party system had agreed not to disagree and thereby choked off effective discussion of diplomatic alternatives.

The prevailing American view of the world fixed on the Soviet Union as its point of orientation. Hallinan, of course, accepted Soviet importance but refused to go along with what he considered the mindless cant that characterized the USSR as the epitome of evil in the world. The other two parties accepted as genuine the assertion that the Soviets intended to spread atheistic communism by internal subversion and direct military aggression to the rest of the world, including America. According to the prevailing bipartisan prospectus, the post-war world ought instead to reflect American, not Russian, institutions and be amenable to American strategic interests as well. To advance these interests and to thwart unacceptable counterdesigns inspired by Soviet concerns, the Truman Doctrine first propped up the unsteady rightist regimes in Turkey and Greece. Next, Marshall Plan funds rehabilitated Western Europe along capitalistic lines and then the North Atlantic Treaty Organization provided for coordinated military planning as a counterforce to the Soviet presence in Eastern Europe.

None of this made sense to Hallinan, whose own reading of world events prompted a more cynical interpretation. To him the Truman Doctrine followed the misguided American tradition of assisting unpopular regimes in suppressing their own citizens, whose legitimate goal was the overthrow of their tyrannical rulers. The Marshall Plan, which most liberals accepted, appeared to him to promote American corporate interests by preventing, at a most critical point in European history, nationalization of key industries and thereby reserved the opportunity for dominance by American-multinational corporations. Most of all, Hallinan objected to everything the North Atlantic Treaty Organization fostered. American proponents of an expanded military justified large budget increases by the threat they asserted Russian Communists posed to a Europe which they claimed was vital to American security. Hallinan and his wife had returned from Europe with the distinct impression that Europeans were unconcerned about any Soviet menace. Furthermore, their representative governments refused to expand their own forces and reacted strongly against America's containment action in Korea.

Since the American demobilization in 1945, the superior status of Russian forces was regularly alleged by those intent upon expanding the military budget. By 1952, Hallinan was sick of that procedure and turned the argument on its head. For the United States to embark upon a new militarization program, he reasoned, was as provocative as it was unnecessary. On this single point he agreed with Senator Robert A. Taft of Ohio, the conservative Republican who lost his party's nomination to General Eisenhower. Russia's interests were not in attacking the United States or Europe. Europeans seemed to understand this but American leaders could not or would not grasp what, to Hallinan, appeared elementary.

The entire Cold War, according to the bipartisan formulation, resulted from the tension caused by Russia's global military designs being contained by American resolve. Because his first-hand European observations and his review of international affairs caused him to reject this analysis, Hallinan wondered why Washington policy-makers did not form similar doubts. For his answer he chose a mixture of economic expediency and intellectual sloth mixed with a modicum of venality. By 1952 he recognized the permanent and growng presence of a military, war-primed economy. Defense had become a big business. Its needs did indeed stimulate the economy and, in the short run, it did prevent recession. The military and its growing coterie of defense contractors, Hallinan felt, were dependent upon permanent threat, whether real or bogus. The role of the president within this matrix had degenerated into that of prime inducer of public fear of communism which then allowed him and his party to exploit the irrationality for political advantage. Meanwhile, senior congressmen, particularly those from the near-rotten boroughs of the poll-taxed South, drew to their own economically limited districts the arsenals, proving grounds, depots, repair yards, training camps, and service schools which would, according to the bipartisan Cold War analysis, defend the free world. Eight years before President Eisenhower became sufficiently aware of this threat from within to bring it to national attention, Hallinan warned America about the dangers inherent in the military-industrial complex. It was a main campaign theme.

For all their professionally generated private wealth, the Hallinans were not at all opposed to massive government spending. The tragedy of the bipartisan foreign policy and Cold War, they both concluded, was that the American response prompted aggression abroad while at home it siphoned the nation's productive and creative energies away from obvious human needs. "The corporation that feeds on billion-dollar arms contracts and drapes itself in the glitter of false patriotism," Hallinan told a campaign dinner at New York's Hotel Astor, "is as bipartisan as the war program from which it springs." Before it was too late, before the political and military leaders of the nation, in consort with an expanding, permanent lobby of defense contractors, shackled America forever to a war economy, the productive capacities of the people ought to be redirected toward efficacious work. With spending for war becoming fixed, how easy it would always be to misinterpret wars of revolutionary nationalism through the distorted ruby prism of anti-communism. He pointed at Korea and predicted the same for Asia, Africa, and Latin America. That was what Hallinan saw in the future.

Two full years of fighting and dying had elapsed since President Truman ordered United States troops into Korea. Surprisingly, even though the polls clearly showed the near-universal disapproval of the war by the American people, both major political parties wished to avoid Korea as a campaign issue. When Truman engaged American ground forces in 1950, only Congressman Marcantonio stood to voice his opposition. In a crisis atmosphere both Republican and Democratic congressmen rallied around the president, thus demonstrating the reflex action bipartisanship commanded. As the 1952 campaign progressed, ignoring the number one concern of the voters became difficult, then impossible. In Stevenson's case, even if he wished to do otherwise, he was tied to the party whose leader had committed American forces to Korea and kept them there fighting through the election campaign. Unable to ignore this, the Governor backed Truman's "police action" as an aspect of the Cold War that turned hot. America simply had to pay the price in blood and treasure, whatever the amount, to defend the free world. Besides the political necessity of this posture, Stevenson's behavior indicated that he accepted the Cold War assumptions as sufficient justification for American deaths in Korea.

Eisenhower, the respected military commander who had won victory in Europe, began his first political campaign by telling the American Legion convention that Eastern Europeans lived unwillingly under communism and there would be no peace with Russia until they were liberated. When legionnaire applause subsided, Eisenhower offered no plan for implementing such a provocative proposal. On Korea itself he apologized first for having no proposal at all. Thereafter, he oscillated between support for General Douglas MacArthur's plan to carry the stalemated war into mainland China and, on the other hand, to turn the conflict over to Republic of Korea forces ("let it be Asians against Asians"). Throughout the campaign and quite inconsistently with his support of MacArthur, General Eisenhower stressed that all-out war in Korea was to be avoided. In the end he acceded to the American hunger for peace, announcing, "I shall go to Korea." Just what his personal presence was expected to achieve remained as unknown to the voters as it was to Eisenhower himself.

Hallinan observed that Eisenhower would be the only American sure of making the Korean trip on a return ticket. Eisenhower's total lack of reflective thought on how even to begin addressing America's most critical problem sustained Du Bois's public assessment of the war hero. "Eisenhower showed in every word his lamentable ignorance of the meaning of the modern world."

To Hallinan the war in Korea was the tragic result of reactionary American policy in Asia. The cold war mindset had prevented Americans from assessing the Communist revolution in China as a successful national liberation. The corrupt Chiang, the recipient of abundant American support since the 1930's, had used the arms, money, and experts to suppress and exploit his people for the benefit of American interests. He did this to the extent that American wishes did not interfere with his own. Hallinan saw Korea as a transplanted China. Only the names, the landscape, and the timing had changed. Like Du Bois, he maintained that French imperialism in Indo-China was as brutal and as doomed as that of England elsewhere around the globe. The children of America, he warned, should not be made into "foreign mercenaries engaged in the most useless and stupid of all undertakings — to repress freedom." Korea should be united, it should be industrialized, and its industry should be free of American economic influence in order that it serve its own people and not the world export market. For Americans to take up the heritage of colonial exploitation of less developed peoples was to do what England began in Ireland and continued in Africa and the Middle East. Asian "colonialism is finished forever, and it will hereafter be impossible for any American or European country to successfully exploit" Asian nations. America must "not sink back into the predatory and parasitical model of Victorian imperialism."

Progressives applauded, special agents took more notes, and the rest of America looked elsewhere for the traditional anti-communist analysis.

Hallinan's solution to the Korean War was as direct as it was unacceptable to Eisenhower, Stevenson and the two major parties. The peace talks had been in session for fifteen months at Panmunjom, north of Seoul. Based upon current Pentagon casualty figures, 963 Americans were being killed or wounded weekly which brought the war total to over 122,000. Death continued to claim Americans even though negotiations had settled all major issues but one. The American side refused to repatriate all communist prisoners, maintaining that America's higher commitment to freedom required that those Koreans and Chinese who chose not to return to their communistic homelands should not be forced to do so.

Over the CBS network Hallinan sarcastically concluded, "No other war in history has been fought to give enemy prisoners the right to decide whether they want to go back home when the peace is signed." Further, he interpreted the Korean prisoner of war riots, the forceful suppressions, and the actual fear American military police felt at being assigned to the compounds on Kojedo Island as belying this claim to higher virtue. He doubted the assertion that North Korean and Chinese prisoners were, in significant numbers, exempted from the natural desires for home and family. He wanted to "end the fighting at once at the demarcation line . . . agreed to a year ago. Settle the prisoner of war question by peaceful negotiations after the killing has been stopped." Twenty-seven years later, reflecting not only upon Korea but on Vietnam as well, he added, "I would have ended our military interest and fighting presence in all of Asia as unilaterally and personally as Truman had instituted it. And the world would have been infinitely better off."

Basic Progressive strategy was, first, to attack the Republican party for not addressing America's actual needs: peace, civil rights, civil liberties, and the economic-labor problems of the post–World War II era. Next, they underscored how lamentably deficient the Democrats were on the same check list. The Progressive explanation, which the Hallinans advanced through their twenty-seven-state campaign, was that neither major party advanced the will of the American people. Both political parties were the captives of the major corporations which, through financial power, molded national policy to serve corporate interests. Party leaders, office holders, the military, the media, and on down to the little people — all went along either in patriotic exuberance, ignorant bliss, or calculated design. Hallinan and Bass spoke directly to what they and their party identified as the needs of the people. Only they and the Progressive party

offered Americans an alternative to the old parties, which
continued to place the interests of finance capitalism above
those of the people. Among themselves and in their most
optimistic moments, Progressives looked for a massive alternative vote that would form the basis for a new national
political realignment resting on a multiracial labor base.
England's Labor party was, to Hallinan, a worthy example.

Branded as Red, this message was not a popular one, so
the Progressives had to struggle to make it heard. The
Daughters of the American Revolution tried to deny Hallinan the use of San Francisco's Civic Auditorium for his post-
prison speaking debut and they would have succeeded except
for the chance presence of a circumspect Irishman in the
city's civil service. The property director, Eugene Riordan,
lined up the city attorney and then held off the DAR, which
wanted the facilities reserved for the "decent, patriotic,
loyal citizens of our fair city." Besides the passing ire of the
Sequoia Chapter of the Daughters, Riordan earned a niche
in Hallinan's surveillance file.

The City of Angels harbored no such guardian for Paul
Robeson. When he agreed to speak and sing, the Shrine
Auditorium of Los Angeles, which had been reserved for the
event, closed its doors to the Progressives. Generally the
managers of such facilities were eager for additional incomes
as long as well-known radicals did not attract public attention. This penchant for avoiding guilt by association reached
its apogee in Chicago when the manager of the Ashland
Auditorium, which the Progressives rented as their national
convention center, requested that the party not put its name
on the marquee. Those few radio and television stations
which complied with the Federal Communications Commission decision to give Progressives equal time had the
political beliefs of their executives investigated. These
findings also found their way into the surveillance files.

The meanest and most senseless move toward curtailing
free expression concerned Vivian Hallinan's family history,
My Wild Irish Rogues, which Doubleday had published
earlier in the year. In essence the book was a light-hearted

family romp with Vince and their six hearty sons. The message it contained—liberalism, humanism, and rationalism in child rearing—was all but smothered in the constant action. At the conclusion Vince's problems with the government were briefly noted by a sympathetic wife. In the thickening security files this book became a "flagrant employment of the COMMUNIST PARTY line, including references to racial discrimination . . . and vicious attacks upon the U.S. Government." When Vivian married Vincent in 1932, the report gratuitously concluded, "It was a case of one warped personality marrying another."

Since Doubleday was a major publisher whose respectable and combative president, Douglas M. Black, was also president of the American Book Publishers Council, the only recommendation was that *My Wild Irish Rogues* be removed from military libraries surreptitiously, so no freedom of the press advocates could create an incident.

To try to overcome the media black-out, Hallinan insisted on addressing the troops in Korea as "the only candidate interested in saving their lives." The Armed Forces Radio accommodated General Eisenhower and Governor Stevenson but the Pentagon turned aside Hallinan's request for FCC-approved equal time, "because of problems of cost and availability of time." Truman ignored his further request for the same national security briefing provided to Stevenson and offered to Eisenhower. The Washington *Evening Star* editorialized its regret that security interests prevented equal treatment to all legal candidates for the same office and added that Hallinan would make the most of this "embarrassment to our tradition of freedom and fair play." In Southern California the press was less delicate. Maybe the AFL and CIO leaders could, an editorial suggested, ask Truman "to give Hallinan a military briefing—if Hallinan would ask Josef Stalin to give [a] similar briefing to Stevenson and Eisenhower!"

Hallinan's attempts to engage the Democratic and Republican candidates in direct exchanges likewise failed. The Progressive party simply did not enter into major party campaign strategy. Fighting each other for the prize, they would not be distracted or annoyed. Still the Hallinans kept it up. Concentrating their efforts in the industrial centers of the Northeast, they spoke in private homes, rented halls, university campuses, and from the backs of sound trucks. Always asking, why continue the killing? Why prosecute those who speak out for a better America in a safer world? Abolish the Taft-Hartley Act and restore freedom to union labor under the old Wagner Act. End segregation and all forms of racial discrimination. But most of all, end the war. Only rarely did they succeed in obtaining national media attention for the Progressive message.

Nevertheless, Hallinan campaigned just the way he did everything else. He could hardly have exerted any greater efforts if he had an actual chance of being elected. Rarely, except in Wisconsin, did he expend his energy where he was not on the ballot. In that state his urge for self-gratification, he rationalized, was compatible with the best in Progressivism.

America had two prominent Irish-Catholic politicians who, Hallinan was convinced, despoiled the United States Senate by their presence and destroyed the rationality and tolerance of the nation by their utterances. The behavior of Republican Senator Joseph McCarthy of Wisconsin and the legislation of Democratic Senator Patrick McCarran of Nevada betrayed everything that was noble and heroic in a heritage they shared with him. To think that McCarthy, who gave his Irish name to the despicable American "ism," sprang from the same genetic base as generations of Irish rebels. The thought appalled Hallinan.

Since J. Edgar Hoover's Security Index was such a closely guarded secret, Hallinan never knew that he himself was targeted for "custodial detention" under McCarran's Emergency Detention Act. Had he known, he would have been enraged.

McCarran, in America, sponsored laws which duplicated the detention which Terence MacSwiney, Lord Mayor of

Cork, starved himself to death in a British jail protesting. Does the Senator from Nevada represent the flowering of the Irish political heritage in America? In mercy the best another Irishman can say is that maybe the barren desert Pat McCarran called home is just too far from the green mossy banks of Cork's River Lee. Still, he and Joe McCarthy betrayed what Daniel O'Connell lived for and what Robert Emmet and MacSwiney died for.

When Eisenhower welcomed McCarthy aboard his Wisconsin campaign train, Hallinan headed for Madison. Over station WIBA he denounced McCarthyism as "the open face of fascism in American political life" and warned of Eisenhower's acceptance of the Senator's support. Even a vote for Stevenson, he added, threatened civil liberties since the Democratic candidate "abjectly solicited . . . the support of McCarran, McCarthy's Democratic twin." Hallinan's summary view, as election day approached, became fixed.

This year there is only one way to make your vote count against McCarthyism and McCarranism, against the war in Korea, against Taft-Hartley . . . against Jim Crow and every form of race discrimination. That way is to vote for the Progressive Party. . . . Any other vote is worse than wasted. It is a vote against yourself. The bigger the vote for the Progressive Party, the greater will be the pressure on both old parties to adopt the program that you want.

Vote Progressive. It will be the most precious vote you ever cast.

McCarthy's final election ploy was the single most exasperating indignity of the campaign for Hallinan. "That bum called Stevenson a Communist but not me!" Eight days before the election, the Wisconsin red-baiter devoted a national address to demonstrating falsely that the Communist party supported Stevenson when, in fact, the official endorsement of its National Committee had previously gone to Hallinan.

On election eve back in Ross with the whole family, Vince perceived faintly that the far left actually had abandoned him and the Progressive party. By October the Communist party realized that Hallinan's campaign had not attracted mass labor support and quietly concluded that third party politics was futile. In disappointment Communists faded out from behind his candidacy even though the official Russian Communist party publication, *Pravda*, had praised him, as had *The Daily Worker* and the *Daily People's World*. The Communist party of the United States actually was on the run. Its leaders were in jail or in hiding. Its members paid no dues and dared not to meet. To the most dedicated Communists, the candidate who failed to attract and deliver the laboring masses became "an ignorant chauvinist." He rode in out of the West and snatched away their most cherished possession—their cause. Without being one of them, neither Communist nor black, he dramatically voiced the grievances which for them had become an identity and a reason for being. To watch a non-ideologist, who had not shared in their long sufferings for communism and for black rights, gallop off with their surviving treasure was insufferable despite his open-handed good will. To the most persevering Communist, Hallinan's third party candidacy was a mistake and Hallinan himself was a thief.

One by one the radicals bailed out on Hallinan. I. F. Stone in the *Daily Compass* abandoned him for Stevenson. Leo Huberman and Paul Sweezey split in their *Monthly Review*, leaving the impression that a vote for Hallinan was not being used to prevent Eisenhower, the militarist and potential fascist, from gaining office. Norman Thomas, the perennial Socialist who this time watched from the sidelines, was strongly anti-communist. He opposed the Progressives. Organized big labor supported Stevenson and radical locals, for the most part, supported local Progressive candidates on a selective basis to the exclusion of Hallinan and Bass. Stevenson even succeeded in reconciling mainline black politicians to the Democratic ticket despite the presence of the

Alabama segregationist and a virtually anti-black platform. Black New York Congressman Adam Clayton Powell, who had walked out of the Democratic convention in July, rejoined the fold by November. Even Earl Dickerson, the Chicago insurance magnate who had challenged Hallinan's right to express a reservation about the Bass candidacy, accepted Stevenson and Sparkman and what went with them, the southern strategy and war.

That blacks at large, to the extent that they could vote at all, cast their ballots for Stevenson, Sparkman, and Korea was bitter enough—particularly for Bass. The nadir, however, was the hostility that emanated from the *California Eagle*. The newspaper, which a Southern California white Progressive of limited means kept afloat, turned viciously upon its former editor and her unorthodox political associates. The Progressive party, according to the *Eagle*, was a "stooge" for communism and used Bass as black "bait" for Negro votes.

As far as the election of 1952 was concerned, blacks, laborers, Communists, and soldiers all seemed to be just a bunch of Americans and, in effect, voted and abstained from voting much like all the others. Until the bitter end the Hallinans, Bass, Marcantonio, Du Bois, Robeson, DeLacy and their co-workers struggled on under the unflagging direction of Beanie Baldwin to get the message across in the twenty-four states in which they were on the ballot.

The result was a humiliating 140,000 votes, which prompted Baldwin to observe that, "The vast majority of the American people never knew we had candidates in the field or what their program was." The media blackout succeeded largely because America was unwilling to receive the Progressive message no matter how Hallinan delivered it.

The only pique Hallinan ever evidenced was against the doctrinaire features of American Communists. Four years after the campaign he defended the Communist party officer, Marion Bachrach, relying once more upon his extended opener. Listening to Hallinan's explanation of what communism meant to his client and her immigrant family, the New York judge, who had a not too dissimilar background, concluded that for her no intent to overthrow the government by force or violence existed. So Hallinan took Bachrach by the hand and together they walked out of the prosecution. Unfortunately for her six male co-defendants, their establishment-oriented attorneys, headed by the respectable Newman Levy, had refused to allow the unorthodox Californian to extend his opening remarks to cover them. Their independent defense failed and each was convicted under the Smith Act, which Hallinan had denounced during his campaign. In closing out his part of the case Hallinan returned to the Communist party the check which was to cover the monies he had expended on the defense.

When he supported Baldwin's still-born efforts for a revived socialistic party embracing what remained of the left, Communist leaders had become angry at him. Before heading home to California his assessment was that, "the Communist Party, unhappily and without any fault on the part of its members who had been persecuted unjustly, was miniscule and without any force in society. Communists could achieve nothing and ought to get out of the way for any humanitarians who may be able to achieve anything at all." Aside from being rigidly doctrinaire, Hallinan felt that the basic trouble with the Communists was, "there wasn't enough of them to do any good."

To Hallinan, Russia had always been the best hope and example of an alternative and just economic system. But "American Communists were crazy to be as concerned as they were about Russia. If Russia sank under the waves, they should still try to bring socialism to this country." Rather than being persons dangerously devoted to a foreign power, Hallinan saw too many Communists as isolated intellectuals, a blend of pathos and comedy. "When they fretted about how they should explain Khrushchev's latest revelation I always recommended, 'Why don't you just say you don't know anything about it?' " He found that an admission of ignorance by American Communists was unacceptable.

"Invariably they told me, 'People expect us to have an answer.'" They did not have any answer because Moscow no more confided in them than in Hallinan. Never a rigid ideologist, he could stand on any ground which encouraged greater social control of the creation and distribution of wealth.

Long life allowed Hallinan what few participants in history enjoy, the opportunity to read the judgment of the scholars. In June 1979, he returned early from Hawaii because the unseasonably high winds off Maui spoiled his swimming. The San Francisco courts were on their own vacation recess after the traumatic Dan White murder trial and the verdict riots. His own case preparation, as always, was ready so he filled the unplanned leisure reading "The Election of 1952," by Stanford historian Barton J. Bernstein. In balance, he thought the account was fair enough and certainly represented thorough primary research and careful reading in the secondary literature. Though most of the extensive essay concerned Eisenhower and Stevenson, Hallinan liked Bernstein's conclusion that it was Hallinan who focused upon America's actual problems. Posturing in the main ring, the others largely ignored the real problems of the country. Hallinan's eyebrows raised, however, when he read that as a candidate his incisive analysis was "overwrought."

> In writing history as opposed to living it, even sensitive and well disposed scholars from the new left too often lose the vital ingredient. If they had just been released from federal prison, or just escaped a southern lynch mob, or — closer to home — if they had just been denied tenure and with it a career and a way of life, then their perceptions might be a bit different. I was anything but "overwrought." I was too damn nice. I attributed a dignity to the campaign for the presidency that was a mistake. Richard Nixon's Checkers speech was deplorable, yet, it allowed him to survive and claw his way to the top over the mangled bodies of people better than himself.
>
> Instead of talking like the stereotype candidate, I should have put on an act that would have embarrassed Elmer Gantry. "Listen you slobs," I should have roared. "You think

you are safe in your patriotism. And you think, so what if the Government nailed Harry Bridges and a bunch of Commies out on the Coast? Well, hates and fears change and the next American dark age may hate and fear you. Not because you are a Communist, but because you are a Catholic, or a Baptist, or a Jew, or maybe because you are just a God damn working man with nothing more in this world but a boy you don't want killed in senseless and unjust wars." I did not do a very good job. Given the condition of our country, I should have been overwrought.*

Hallinan remained convinced that the best way to protect your children, yourself and the nation was to protect the least, even the worst, among you. In November 1952 the best he and Vivian could say was that they had tried. In doing so, they reached out and found a new and exciting personal experience together. It was called failure.

* From an interview author had with Hallinan on subject of the Bernstein essay.

> "Dear Dick: I thought you would be interested in . . . Vincent William Hallinan . . . who attended the trial in Moscow of Francis G. Powers, the U-2 pilot."
>
> — J. Edgar Hoover to Richard M. Nixon
> August 22, 1960

10. The Protest Movement of the 1960s

The federal government was able to strike back at Hallinan because he gave it the opportunity. Born into poverty and a pre-income tax America, Hallinan became a man far more concerned with earning money than accounting for it to tax collectors. The thought of being prosecuted, or even audited, never entered his mind. If it had, he would have smiled with a bemused self-confidence.

As the years passed and Vivian's apartment holdings increased, the Hallinans formed the Clay Jones Corporation which held their properties. Vince also established a trust fund for the sons. As inflation gained momentum at the end of the war, the Hallinans continued to file their customary tax returns but instead of forwarding what was due, they deferred payment and accepted the added interest charges. Among their considerations was Vince's conviction that it was financially wiser to use the money for property acquisition which was inflating faster than the Internal Revenue Service penalties.

In 1953, the year after Hallinan's radical candidacy for president, he and Vivian were indicted on fourteen counts of

226

tax evasion. Basically, the IRS maintained that between 1946 and 1950 the Hallinans' expenditures exceeded their stated earnings, and yet they became wealthier. Through the net worth method, the Justice Department and IRS intended to prove that the Hallinans evaded sixty-five thousand dollars in taxes by under reporting legal fees and by deducting improper business expenses.

This prosecution followed a combined total of seven working years of preparation by three federal agents. Before resting the government's case, Prosecutor Mecklin Fleming would present 50 witnesses, 296 documents, and amass a total of 2,699 pages of testimony during an eight-week trial. He also requested and received a confidential report from the FBI on the venire of potential jurors from which he selected those who would judge the Hallinans.

Given Hallinan's lifetime of legal and political notoriety and then his atheism and radicalism besides, the press gave the case full and detailed coverage. He had supported his parents since 1922 when he moved them to their first home, and he maintained other family members as long as needed; then he helped with their children. After the formation of the Clay Jones Corporation, Vince made Pat Hallinan its secretary and began deducting as a business expense of the corporation the eight hundred dollars a month he gave to his father. After Pat died Vince paid the salary to his mother whom he maintained for years in an elaborate rest home.

When Prosecutor Fleming asserted that the payments were excessive for Pat's qualifications and were gifts, not business expenses, Hallinan reported: "What I pay my father for his services is nobody's business but ours. To earn it he did everything that the ordinary corporate executive does except that he didn't play golf." Hallinan also cited the legal precedent for the continued payments to an executive's widow.

Pat's salary was only the start. Other payments, deducted as salaries, included monies he gave to numerous relatives as well as large bonuses to those who were helpful in critical cases. When he made big money, he spread it around.

He was generous with those who were close to him, but hardly prudent with the IRS.

On the grill and alone, the long-providing brother and uncle received the sort of extended family support he expected. Atheism and radicalism on his part and religion and anti-communism on theirs all but neutralized his beneficence. Annie voted for Eisenhower in 1952 rather than for her brother because, she told him, "The Church knew you were a Communist." The houses, the trips, the medical care, the cash, the parental support, help with children—all these generosities together could not compel or excuse false testimony. Not one relative would say on the stand that she did indeed work for what Vincent gave her.

The trial and the resulting publicity dragged into the public domain minor though interesting matters: the number and quality of fur coats Mrs. Hallinan purchased, her jewelry, where she shopped for shoes, how many pairs she owned. The most significant revelation concerned Ross. Their estate, like the other properties, was owned by the corporation, which in turn was owned by Vivian and Vince. Its renovation, the gym, the pool and the up-keep, all of these were deducted as business expenses.

Explaining that consumed a good part of Hallinan's six days on the witness stand. "The corporation," he said, "purchased Ross as an investment. All those improvements were further investments. It is quite obvious that everything there is far too large for any single family—even ours. We intended selling it at a profit to an institution, a school. If we included free rent as income, our services there could have been deducted."

Hallinan had an answer to every question, and his attorney, James C. Purcell, extracted what mileage he could from the IRS's previous approval of deductions for which they now prosecuted his client. Purcell also stressed tax errors which favored the government. The basic trouble was that most jurors found Hallinan's answers unsatisfactory and Purcell's counterpoints insufficient.

Throughout the trial the prosecution and the news media missed few opportunities to detail Hallinan expenditures and donations to organizations which the attorney general listed as Communist or pro-Communist. The government's appeal to political prejudice was not blatant, but it was real.

Vivian's defense rested on the correctness of her business records and denial that she ever participated in preparing the disputed joint tax returns. The jurors accepted this position and acquitted Vivian, but they convicted Vince on five counts, a total evasion of $37,000. His punishment was eighteen months in jail and $622,000 in accumulated fines, costs, and penalties. That amount, plus their two defenses and Hallinan's subsequent fight against disbarment, elevated their total losses to about three-quarters of a million dollars.

Perhaps if Hallinan had not been such an imposingly unpopular figure, he might not have attracted such relentless attention. Perhaps he would have. Tax disputes were not clear-cut and experts regularly advised clients to act excessively and then let the IRS react. Inquiries, audits, fines, negotiated settlements, civil suits, and criminal indictments were options available to the government. Hallinan maintained that the authorities "gathered together as much tax avoidance as they could and made it appear as tax evasion. If it hadn't been for the Bridges case and the Progressive Party, the most they would have done would have been to file a civil suit." Instead, the government chose its strongest option first and obtained a criminal conviction.

The years of meticulous preparation and the special FBI investigation of the jury both suggest that the government was particularly intent in its efforts to convict its long-term antagonist. The Justice Department did not convict Hallinan through perjured testimony or contrived evidence. There was, in fact, an abundance of damaging evidence. Whether he deserved a criminal indictment and confinement in prison is less clear. The holdout jurors argued that the whole trial was "a political persecution." The last one to yield to the admonitions of the majority insisted through fourteen hours of deliberation that his fellow jurors were prejudiced "because Hallinan was an Independent Progressive Party candidate and because he defended Harry Bridges."

The Federal Penitentiary on McNeil Island was far less congenial the second time around. The authorities did not assign Hallinan to the prison farm or to any work which could earn him "good time" and thus shorten his confinement. He entered and lived in the mainline cell block with broken, violent, and irrational men. Denied parole, Hallinan threw himself into physical fitness and self-improvement activities — wrestling, handball, and more language study. He also became a father confessor to forgotten wretches who had lost all hope.

As elected head of the inmates' organization he forced the desegregation of the federal facility in compliance with President Eisenhower's executive orders, which had gone unheeded until he pressured the prison administration. Later, he wrote a sweeping critique of prison conditions, which he submitted to the U.S. Senate Committee on the Judiciary and the Senate Standing Subcommittee on National Penitentiaries. Hallinan concluded that "there should be an end to the conscious program designed to degrade and humiliate the convicted man to the last extent. A prison . . . as operated in these United States . . . is a symptom of a diseased social system."

Personally he had no problems in jail; again he demonstrated that he could get along anywhere. When some black prisoners tried to provide bodyguards for him in the big yard during his desegregation efforts Hallinan declined. "It would have been provocative." He sat with them at meals and pretended anger and disappointment when they continued to eat together after desegregation freed them to mingle. He would not let them alone until they moved around. To counter the threat of inter-racial violence, Hallinan spread the rumor that the warden had a long list of names. Each convict on it would be moved immediately to Alcatraz, the hated maximum security prison in San Francisco Bay, at the first sign of trouble.

Hallinan did receive time off for good behavior and he departed with the same general impression as before. "Jail is an interesting experience." It had no apparent effect on his life other than to interrupt it.

During his confinement Vivian sold the Clay Jones building to cover the fines and losses and to be ready for the expenses of her husband's inevitable battle with the California Bar Association. Following his tax conviction, the Board of Governors recommended his suspension from legal practice for three years. The State Supreme Court had declined to disbar him, despite provisions of the Business and Professional Code that mandated disbarment upon a felony conviction. The Court did, however, reject Hallinan's novel appeal against even a suspension. He claimed that the tax conviction did not demonstrate moral turpitude as the Bar Association maintained. "It penalized me for keeping my own money, not for taking someone else's."

So from 1957 to 1960 Vincent Hallinan was unemployed for the first extended period of his life since 1909, when he delivered groceries in Petaluma. To fill time, he and Vivian wanted to travel. Unfortunately, the State Department revoked their passports.

Federal agents prevented Hallinan and Paul Robeson from crossing into Canada to address the Mine, Mill, and Smelter Worker's Union in Vancouver, British Columbia. When Vivian applied for a new travel document, she was turned down for having done all the things she was proud of. "It has been alleged," the Passport Office Director wrote her, "that you were associated with the Civil Rights Congress; that you were an active member of the Independent Progressive Party . . . ; that you posted $10,000 cash bond in behalf of Loretta Stack, Smith Act Defendant . . . participated in affairs sponsored by the Californians for the Bill of Rights, the National Lawyers Guild . . . and the Veterans of the Abraham Lincoln Brigade." When Vivian read her rejection over the public address system at their next Ross picnic, her pause at each punctuation mark brought sustained applause from the lunching radicals and strikers. In this period, too, the oldest Hallinan son was barred from military service because of his alleged close association with his father and mother.

Once the courts restrained the State Department from curtailing the free travel of U.S. citizens, the FBI notified American embassies abroad that the Hallinans were coming. The FBI's formal alert notices read as if Hallinan controlled a subversive organization of international scope, which somehow would sabotage national security.

Vivian and Vince traveled through Asia first and brought home from that troubled part of the world a report that was hardly surprising. The U.S. military presence ought to be eliminated and replaced with a humanitarian assault on hunger, disease, and ignorance. What communism had done for nearly a billion Chinese represented a modern world miracle. Instead of supporting and arming corrupt, reactionary Asian regimes, the United States ought to encourage revolutionary change throughout Southeast Asia.

Likewise the Hallinans publicized their equally critical and unpopular report of their trip to Cuba. They had vacationed in Cuba during the 1930s when poverty, disease, and particularly the juvenile prostitution appalled them. The intervening years of Fulgencio Batista's pro-American dictatorship changed none of these basic features of Havana life. Fidel Castro, they said, did. What the Hallinans saw in Cuba after Castro's takeover resembled Theodore White's before-and-after observations of the People's Republic of China. The glitter and luxury of the old foreign enclaves were gone but so, too, were the beggars and the whores. The well-being of the masses improved dramatically.

From the lecture platform and at the press conferences Hallinan warned repeatedly that the American government was not above invading Cuba to reestablish a regime responsive to American business interests rather than the well-being of the Cuban people. He was particularly apprehensive about the unofficial, yet significant, attention that agencies of the federal government were giving to anti-Castro Cubans in the United States.

Groups of these Cuban exiles did what they could to intimidate Hallinan on the lecture circuit as he persisted in praising Castro, warning of reactionary U.S. policies, and the prospect of a Cuban invasion. Unable to shout him down, a Cuban mob in Los Angeles charged the stage with tire irons and knives. The police drove them off and exchanged gun fire with them outside.

Elsewhere conventional patriotic groups debated Hallinan over Cuba, internal security, and communism. By then the 1950s generation of university students was rousing itself and Hallinan began attracting a small but hearty following of unorganized young radicals. The most enterprising among them attended the University of California and San Francisco State.

The Soviet Union, not Cuba, was the nation that attracted the Hallinans' greatest interest and respect. Vince remembered the 1917 Russian revolution against what he concluded later had been an exploiting aristocracy and a superstitious and parasitical church. Despite its uncalculable losses in World War II, Russia elevated itself to first-rank status among world powers. Hallinan considered "Russia . . . an example to the world and the hope of the future of mankind." He admitted the purges and the Stalinist abuses but he always stuck to his basic position of approval under hostile criticism.

Because of their well-known, critical views on American foreign policy, Vince and Vivian had no difficulty obtaining visas from the Soviet government. As a welcome guest, Vivian toured medical and educational institutions and saw the sights. Vince spent much of his time spectating at Russian trials, touring jails, and conversing with Moscow lawyers and legal scholars. What he saw and heard fortified his favorable predisposition. Even in the largest Russian cities, violent crime did not constitute a significant problem. There were, of course, numerous sociological explanations such as limited mobility, no transiency, and insignificant unemployment. Pay was low and work was hard, but everyone had some. High culture such as opera and ballet attracted these working-people who were not out of place in their common attire. The absence of a drug problem in European Russia also pleased him but Hallinan, the non-drinker, made no comments about alcoholism.

Hallinan approved of what he saw in Russian court, a restrained advocacy between prosecutors and defense attorneys. The state employed both, and from what he observed, there were no phony defenses or framed prosecutions. The lawyers were not flamboyant buccaneers out to make a name or a fortune or to capture higher political office. The material facts normally were agreed upon, and mitigating circumstances or degree of remorse constituted the normal areas of contention.

Punishments appeared mild by American standards and he thought Soviet prisons were more humane. The prisoner's psychological life, for example, was a matter of official concern. Well-behaved prisoners were allowed to receive their wives or family for private overnight visits. Ex-convicts were placed in receptive, stable environments and regular employment.

His personal critique of American prison life identified sex perversion as a primary problem which caused most of the others. In U.S. prisons the brutalizations and killings were related to homosexuality. Since prison authorities pretended that it did not exist, nothing was done to protect the weak or to restrain the strong. "In America perverted sex was good enough for the cons."

The only matter over which the Hallinans and their Russian hosts disagreed was intolerance of homosexuals. Communist views were identical to those which prevailed in the capitalistic West; they were hostile and rejecting. Homosexuals could not be trusted, the Russians insisted, because they could be blackmailed. Vivian told their hosts that the U.S. Central Intelligence Agency (CIA) agreed fully, but the Russians preferred to drop the subject at that point.

Following the Russian tour the Hallinans published observations in *Clash of Culture: Some Contrasts in American and Soviet Morals and Manners*, a booklet which led to unexpected results.

Since the end of World War II, the United States regularly violated Soviet airspace with illegal reconnaissance flights, first with stripped down B-36 bombers, then with increasingly sophisticated, specialized aircraft. The Russians knew of these encroachments but maintained diplomatic silence, because no nation ever admitted to espionage without being caught. A Soviet protest that lacked irrefutable evidence would provoke an automatic American denial and would focus world attention on the inferiority of Russian military technology which could not guarantee the nation's borders.

By the late 1950s the Lockheed Corporation's specially designed photo reconnaissance plane, the U-2, operated comfortably at sixty-eight thousand feet. Its pilots, confined in space suits, glided through the outer reaches of the earth's atmosphere as automated cameras and radars worked away. The U-2 displaced its primitive predecessors in the top-secret reconnaissance program targeted against the Soviet Union. The graceful craft became "the black lady of espionage" to the Russians who tracked her by radar but failed to bring her down.

Hallinan, of course, knew nothing about the U-2 program that the CIA sponsored. The agency kept its secret even from the U.S. Congress and all but a handful of men in the Defense and State departments. The CIA obtained its pilots clandestinely through access to Air Force personnel files. The officers they identified were screened and then offered agency contracts at thirty thousand dollars, then three and one-half times their Air Force pay. They were also promised full military retirement credits and promotions for the years contracted out to the CIA. Since the Russians could not fly, or shoot, high enough to interfere with a U-2, the pilots were assured of their personal safety. There was only one imperative. The ultra-modern espionage technology fitted into the unique jet gliders could not fall into unfriendly hands. In an emergency, destruction of the aircraft and its contents was preferable to compromise. The pilots were instructed to push the "destruct" button, which would allow them ample time to abandon the plane before it detonated.

Improved Soviet rocketry caught up with the U-2 program on May 1, 1959. The unfortunate pilot, rather than taking his employers at their word and pressing the destruction button, chose simply to open the canopy and push himself away from the disabled spy plane. He also circumvented the automatic ejection system built into his seat. One result was that instead of searching for scattered debris, the Russians captured the CIA's highly sensitive equipment intact along with the potentially most compromising evidence of all — the pilot.

He was Francis Gary Powers and he embodied the most dramatic cold war encounter between the Berlin blockade and the Cuban missile crisis. The Soviet government promptly charged Powers with espionage and tried him and, indirectly, the United States too. The Russians held all the cards and they invited the world to watch.

First the Russian authorities placed Powers incommunicado. They ignored official U.S. efforts to see him and to provide him with American legal counsel. A year later the CIA subsidized two Virginia hill country lawyers to accompany Barbara Powers to Moscow for her husband's trial. The Russians never allowed them to speak with Powers and the best they could do was to watch him through binoculars at the trial itself. Likewise, the Russians ignored the defense that the CIA offered for their employee.

Hallinan's invitation to return to Moscow as an observer at the U-2 trial came from the Legal Section of the Soviet Friendship Societies. He had become acquainted with Russian lawyers during his previous visit and they undoubtedly were familiar with his glowing review of their legal system which the American Russian Institute published. Hallinan's views on American cold war policies were known in official Russian circles since *Pravda's* favorable comment on his 1952 presidential candidacy. His arrival in Moscow triggered J. Edgar Hoover's unfounded reminder to Richard Nixon that Hallinan was a Communist.

As late as August 1960, fifteen months after the U-2 went down, the U.S. government's intelligence community was still in the dark. The CIA, for example, wanted to know from Powers if the plane really was shot down by a Russian rocket at sixty-eight thousand feet or if engine trouble caused him to lose altitude and fall into the known range of Soviet missile batteries. Even after the trial a CIA debriefing officer wanted to know if Barbara Powers was sure the man with whom she spent her conjugal visit was really her husband.

Besides Powers's immediate family, Vincent Hallinan was the only American to speak with the captured pilot. Yet, as desperate for information as the U.S. was, no official contacted Hallinan before or after he interviewed Powers. To find out what Hallinan learned and what transpired between him and Gary Powers, special agents of the FBI waited in line outside Harry Bridges's union hall and bought tickets to Hallinan's public lectures.

Except for special technical training and an infatuation with flying airplanes, Gary Powers lacked distinction. He was thirty-one years old and had never voted in an American election. He knew little of the culture of his own country, and nothing about Russia. He liked card-playing, he introduced his young wife to PX shopping and military drinking parties, and he felt at home whenever he returned to Pound, Virginia. In Moscow his mind was a jumble of loyalty, patriotism, self-interest, and regret.

Placed at the focal point of international tension, Powers was in an unenviable position. The Russians had the goods on him and on America too. Espionage was a capital offense and a Russian lawyer was to defend him. It was over the quality of the Russian defense that Hallinan and Powers basically disagreed.

Roman A. Rudenko, the prosecutor general of the Soviet Union, presented the government's case. A veteran of the Nazi war crimes trials at Nuremberg, Rudenko addressed the personal responsibility of Powers but he stressed that the programmed espionage was America's crime. Particularly, it was the crime of the CIA. Rudenko introduced piece after piece of U-2 espionage equipment, intended bribe money and jewelry, personal weapons, maps of Russia, and an avalanche

of paraphernalia that disproved the CIA cover story that
President Eisenhower had maladroitly asserted: the U-2
was a weather reconnaissance plane that had strayed off
course.

Soviet law required the accused to testify, so if Powers
refused to do so, it would be held against him. Hallinan
thought Powers was a careful witness.

> He gave the prosecution nothing it didn't have on him al-
> ready. There was a lot, but not everything. When Rudenko
> asked him if he was sorry, Powers behaved intelligently and
> said that he was. Rudenko was humane though. He did not
> follow that answer with what I assumed would be his auto-
> matic rejoinder. He did not ask Powers if his sorrow and
> regret were over the failure of his mission and his capture or
> over his violation of international law and sovereign rights of
> the Soviet Union. The Russians did not make Powers publicly
> crawl to save his own skin.

A second feature of the prosecution demonstrated to
Hallinan that they were less interested in convicting Powers
for flying across Russia than in convicting the U.S. government in absentia for sending him. As might be expected, the
U-2's destruction device advanced this objective. Rudenko
called a Soviet expert who testified that the mechanism had
no time lag whatsoever. If Powers activated the device,
it would have destroyed him with his equipment. Accordingly, the CIA misled its own pilots and would have made
Powers a victim had he been innocent enough to follow his
instructions. Next, Rudenko surfaced the real shocker.

Not only was the destruct mechanism a booby trap, the
pilot's escape system was also rigged. Had Powers chosen to
save himself through use of the standard ejection seat, he
would have died at the hands of his employers. In either
case, Hallinan noted in his journal, "He and the plane would
have been blown to smithereens together."

Powers directed his strongest retrospective criticisms at
his defense counsel, Mikhail I. Griniev. In *Operation Over-
flight*, Powers contemptuously dismissed Griniev as a mem-

ber of the trial team that specialized in losing important state cases. Not once, Powers complained, did Griniev object to any statement by the prosecution and, in his final argument, his defense attorney joined with the prosecution in condemning the CIA and the U.S. Government.

Hallinan did not agree with these criticisms either. For Powers to interpret Griniev's defense as collaboration with the prosecution was, Hallinan thought, "junk thinking" by the pilot.

> Would Powers prefer his defense attorney to absolve the CIA and say the whole idea was his, that he overflew the Soviet Union on his own initiative? Or did he expect his attorney to claim that he was framed; maybe they got the wrong guy? No. Griniev dumped on the U.S. for the proper reasons. The U.S. was guilty and his client needed that defense.
>
> I did not detect any omission of defense evidence which any competent American counterpart of the Soviet attorney would have included or any incriminating concession which would have been better left unsaid.
>
> Cold War realities notwithstanding, the Russian legal system defended Gary Powers far better than he would have done himself and as well or better than any first class American lawyer. If those two hillbillies the CIA covertly commissioned to defend Powers were allowed to do so by the Russians, Powers would still be in a Russian jail.

Griniev's actual defense stressed Powers's working-class background, his difficulty finding civilian employment in the competitive capitalistic economy, and the fantastic wage offered by the CIA. Hallinan thought this was the only realistic defense: "Admit the act they caught you in, express regret and sorrow, and build up as many mitigating circumstances as possible."

In private Hallinan told Prosecutor Rudenko that the Russians should dedicate a statue of Powers in Red Square for all the favorable Cold War publicity that accrued to Russia. Rudenko smiled and seemed silently to agree with the thought if not its physical manifestation. In any case, he did not ask the three-man military court for the death penalty which was authorized; he asked for fifteen years in prison. The three generals who constituted the military court decided on ten.

It was Hallinan's old gall and talent for manipulation that enabled him to interview Powers at all. His initial request had been turned aside by the Soviet prosecutor general. Next, he explained to Rudenko that when he returned to the United States he would be asked by reporters if he had spoken with Powers. "If I have to say, 'no,' they will ask me if it was because I failed to take that much interest in my countryman or was I denied that privilege by your government. I asked Rudenko, 'What will I say to them?' Then he arranged our meeting."

Hallinan always had a kindly and sympathetic manner with people in trouble unless he had professional reasons to act otherwise. Powers was a limited young man who was in no way prepared for his place at the contact point of international tension. Considering this, Hallinan thought he had conducted himself quite well throughout his ordeal and he tried to cheer him up by offering some practical reassurance and advice. Hallinan doubted that Powers would have to serve very much of his sentence, since the Soviets already achieved all they wanted by the trial. He suggested to the pilot that his detention could be made easier by a show of cooperation.

I told him that if they expressed a desire that he study their history or government, he should go along. He might even learn new and interesting things which could broaden his understandings. To make his jail time pass more quickly I advised him to study the Russian language. It was a good investment in himself and would demonstrate a cooperative spirit as well.

Hallinan left him with two thoughts. "Powers would not be personally abused in a Russian prison as Americans are at home. And he would be returned home far sooner than he expected."

Instead of accepting or ignoring Hallinan's remarks as personal advice, Powers chose to interpret them as Communist propaganda. In his account of the interview, however, Powers destroyed his own credibility by also characterizing his single American contact as a chain-smoker who was extraordinarily nervous. That Hallinan, a lifelong foe of all tobacco products, somehow lost his consummate self-confidence in the presence of Gary Powers is difficult to accept.

Hallinan's final statement to the press before he departed Moscow was hardly designed to change J. Edgar Hoover's conviction that he was a Communist. "The safety of the world," he announced, "depends now upon the good sense, patience and forbearance of the Soviet government, and the maintaining of their own military strength at a stage which will not invite a reckless attack by the American top brass."

In 1952 he campaigned against the growing military establishment at home, against what President Eisenhower would shortly term the "military-industrial complex." By 1960 Hallinan felt it was too late for America. "This case," he told the world press, "demonstrates that the American people have allowed not only their own safety but that of the rest of the world to be threatened by a stupid, arrogant military."

The next morning he checked out of the New Moscow Hotel and left for home and for renewed FBI surveillance

This was the proper moment for Hallinan to retire from active legal practice. Since the Bridges trial he had spent most of his time pursuing left-wing politics and then defending himself and serving time in and out of jail. He had previously announced his retirement, twice in fact, but when he returned from Moscow at age sixty-three, he admitted to himself that he was incapable of inactivity. The time might be right, but he would never be. For twenty more years he would walk to his office in the morning to continue doing what he did best; even in the 1980s he would have no real intention of quitting.

His three-year suspension was over in 1960, and he

publicized his comeback in the normal Hallinan style. He announced his candidacy for the Ross Council on an anti-dog platform. He attacked the doggie set that ran the town as relics left over from the hunting and gathering stage of civilization. At the same time he sued a prominent attorney for malpractice and assumed the defense of a blind musician whom the police arrested for public begging. He won the malpractice case, lost the begging case, had fun, and kept his candidacy in the papers for a week. Even though he lost that too, he let people know Hallinan was back in town and opened for business as usual. What he expected and what he got, however, were entirely different.

The 1960s marked the emergence of a new generation, the protest generation, which rocked American institutions and permanently altered the national culture. First came student activism, then came militancy. The silent, personal success-oriented generation of the 1950s gave way to articulate idealists who began the student movement to reform America by direct action. The lunch counter sit-ins protesting segregated dining facilities in Greensboro, North Carolina, were the first spark. The second was the protest against the House Un-American Activities Committee (HUAAC) in San Francisco. The young black students in the South protested the comprehensive abridgment of the civil rights of their race. The young white students in San Francisco protested the unconstitutional abridgment of every American's civil liberties by HUAAC.

Hallinan had campaigned vigorously against racial segregation and political repression in 1952. He approved of student direct action in both areas of national concern in 1960 and was present when the northern wing of what was to coalesce into the massive national movement erupted. When it happened, he was more than ready: "I was glad a young America finally caught up with me."

The House Un-American Activities Committee had made itself odious to a sizeable segment of thoughtful Americans by its chronic abuse of liberals, radicals, and intellectuals. For years the fear of internal subversion, which the committee both sowed and reaped, invested in its members patriotic distinction. During the height of America's anti-communist crusade, any criticism of the committee was in itself taken to be evidence of disloyalty. Hallinan's personal distaste for HUAAC sprang from the Bridges trial ten years earlier. The professional witnesses that he and MacInnis contended with had been groomed by their regular appearances before HUAAC during the anti-communist hearings the committee staged across America.

When the ultraconservative, southern-dominated committee scheduled its public investigation of Northern California subversives, it had no expectation of losing control of its own proceedings. By 1960 the times had changed, particularly in unpredictable San Francisco, and HUAAC was about to be updated. In San Francisco HUAAC itself became the issue and the target. Old leftists, including Harry Bridges, some California Communists, and an assortment of labor radicals were subpoenaed in order to be subjected yet again to the decade-old questions, smears, and insults.

Bridges was as unintimidated as ever. The U.S. Supreme Court had overturned his 1950 conviction, his union was still behind him, and he was secure from further prosecution. In fact, for the first time since 1934, he was getting some enjoyment out of his notoriety. He thought that several of the most persistent anti-communists were deranged and in public debates he never missed a chance to aggravate their acute paranoia. It was the students, however, from Berkeley and San Francisco State, still dressed in dark business suits and sporting crew cuts of the 1950s, who stole HUAAC's show. They were subpoenaed as witnesses because they criticized the committee in their student newspapers and because they picketed the hearing site, San Francisco City Hall.

The focal point of the anti-HUAAC sentiment was a denunciatory petition, signed by over five hundred California writers and intellectuals, which asked HUAAC to abolish itself, as a service to America. Bay Area Central Labor Councils agreed and added their weight to the movement. Hallinan participated as counsel to labor radicals who had incurred the wrath of committeemen by trying to spread the California brand of militant unionism to the unorganized South.

To the shock and amazement of the congressmen, witness after witness refused to cooperate and refused to be silenced. The more arbitrary HUAAC members became, the more aggressive and offensive the witnesses became toward them. For the first time in the twenty-three year history of the congressional committee, which had called Franklin Roosevelt a Communist, HUAAC got a strong dose of its own patented medicine. To their faces and in front of a growing battery of television cameramen, the anti-communist crusaders were lambasted as dangerous frauds. By their habitual disregard for the constitutional rights of witnesses and harassment of non-conformists in the name of internal security, HUAAC subverted the highest American ideals. "This Committee is un-American!" shouted witness after witness.

The students took the lead; the old leftists followed. One Hallinan client, a warehouseman, was characteristically direct. He called his inquisitor "some kind of nut" and turned to the chairman and yelled that his congressional colleague was "a madman." Of the forty-one subpoenaed witnesses, thirty-six defied the committee. The others worked for the FBI or were too slow to understand what was happening.

To aggravate the increasingly volatile situation, HUAAC tried to pack the house but did not quite succeed. Police restricted students, who had arrived early, from the chamber and admitted American Legionnaires and Daughters of the American Revolution through side doors. Outside the students continued to picket peacefully.

Inside, members of the old left locked arms and serenaded the committee with "The Star Spangled Banner" and "America the Beautiful." They demanded that the newsmen turn on their floodlights and expose to the American people the mentality and general quality of the men who governed the nation. Startled, and on the defense, the committee shut off the microphones, which by then were useless anyway over the roar of songs and demands. The assembled witnesses then started chanting "Open the Doors, Open the Doors," a demand which the students outside picked up and repeated until it echoed around the massive City Hall rotunda. The beleaguered HUAAC chairman then yelled, "This isn't a court. We make our own rules here." But in the noise and excitement nobody heard him or cared.

At this point the police forcibly removed another Hallinan client. It was the union organizer's third ejection from the same hearing. Clearly the situation was beyond committee control even with the substantial and growing help of the San Francisco Police Department. At the noon recess the old leftists, except for Vincent Hallinan, literally went out to lunch. It was during that hour that the first northern blow was struck in the revolution of the sixties that established a new relationship between the individual citizen and agencies of the federal government. Before the decade ended civil rights advanced, a president declined to seek renomination, and war was rejected by the very generation which was expected to provide its combat leadership.

To clear the corridors of the nation's most beautiful neoclassical City Hall, the uniformed police broke out high pressure fire hoses and turned them on the students. When the youngsters embraced each other and clung to the ornate fixtures and protruding masonry the officers used physical force. As in similar incidents, precisely how the clubbing began constituted a hotly disputed point.

Hallinan anticipated some decisive action and skipped lunch with his old radical friends. "I just felt like hanging around." According to the police version a student seized an officer's club and began beating him with it. Hallinan, an eyewitness, branded this explanation "a lie" and pointed his finger at the officer who, he said, beat the student with the help of six other policemen. "I tried to intervene and they roughed me up too."

When the soaked and bruised students still refused to vacate the second floor, the police dragged them by the ankles and bounced them down the slick rotunda steps amid the cascading water. On the sidewalk outside the police arrested them and carted them off to jail.

The student movement which began in San Francisco possessed a definite Socialist-Marxist intellectual base. As it gathered adherents and spread through the North it became less concerned with ideology and more concerned with action. These young people identified persisting abuses in American life and assumed responsibility for correcting them through direct confrontation with authorities who, they felt, had tolerated racism and repression long enough. Hallinan liked this relationship which subordinated ideology to action.

He had been the closest thing to a campus radical St. Ignatius College had in 1916. He voted Socialist in 1920. He welcomed support he thought the Communist party was giving him for president, and he told the party to stand aside when he thought its presence prevented other elements of the American left from advancing progressive goals. The imperatives of ideology never tied him down.

There were immediate, personal reasons for Hallinan to go along with the new left as well. Before the civil rights, anti-war movement came to an end each of the Hallinan sons had enrolled at Berkeley. They were all politically active and to varying degrees opposed radical discrimination, the war, and administrative suppression of dissent on campus.

For twenty years, those middle decades during which most fathers of Hallinan's age try to fend off and redirect the youthful energies of growing sons, Vince remained true to his philosophy of child rearing. He drew every son into shared family activities. By 1960 his six boys had grown up but he had not grown tired. He intended not to intrude in the youth movement, but, "I wasn't ready to expire politically either. Age was not going to consign me to the 'Old Left' and let them have the 'New Left' for themselves."

In their second foray into San Francisco, the students swung the election for mayor of the city to the liberal Democrat by picketing the drive-in restaurants owned by his conservative opponent. Student intent was to embarrass

Supervisor Harold Dobbs and to open up employment opportunities for blacks. Long-term Congressman John F. Shelley,
an aging labor stalwart, appeared on local television and
steered a successful course into office between frontlash and
backlash. He made the most of the embarrassment the
students caused his opponent. Besides determining an otherwise even race, the active intervention showed the students
what their power could do.

The third generation of Hallinans made their political
debut in a world their grandfather never anticipated, but one
he could, perhaps, have understood. Old Pat was a radical
activist in his own day who protested in the only way he
knew. The differences between him and his grandsons were
that Pat was not much of a student and nonviolence as a
controlling principle never appealed to him. Between his
Union Labor nomination for state senator and the birth of
the American student movement, the Hallinans had moved
up professionally, economically, and educationally. Their
social isolation was their own choice. What remained the
same through the generations was their propensity towards
radicalism and their physical combativeness.

The national student movement originated at the University of California and announced itself in San Francisco.
The election of Mayor Shelley had been merely a demonstration run. The movement's first local objective was the
elimination of discriminatory hiring practices. Its first tactic
was nonviolent sit-ins at San Francisco's Sheraton Palace
Hotel and the Auto Row car dealerships. The young Hallinans helped with the organization and staging of both events.
They participated in both protests and were arrested.

The prominence of Terence Hallinan allowed the media
to splash the emerging movement with the old Red paint. He
had gathered with a handful of like-minded classmates and
formed the original Du Bois Club. The yong Hallinan took
credit for creating the roundly lambasted organization,
served as its original chairman, and issued the call for the
formation of the national Du Bois organization. According to
him the Du Bois Club was "an activist-Socialist group started

on the initiative of independent young people." He denied fronting for communists and admitted young people who claimed to be communists. Both were entirely compatible, he said. The Du Bois Club broke the University of California ban on communist speakers and claimed two thousand members in colleges across the country. Besides their California initiative the national movement of Du Bois Clubs spread as a student reaction against the war in Vietnam.

Before each sortie into San Francisco, the students used the Berkeley campus, particularly the Sproul Hall Plaza, as a recruiting ground and a staging area. The California Regents responded by trying to curtail this use of University property. This reaction and student counter-reaction created the premier campus disorder of a violent decade and from it sprang the Free Speech Movement. When University administrators tried to regulate student political advocacy, the students staged a sit-in at Sproul Hall. The police cleared the building, arrested students, and left a tottering University administration with seriously reduced options. By the time the students closed down the University of California, Matthew Hallinan was among the principal strategists.

Nightly television covered the battles which began between determined activists, and the campus and Berkeley police. When the students prevailed, the authorities mobilized the California Highway Patrol and the National Guard. Protest demonstrations and violence spread to the communities, and the Free Speech Movement, Sproul Plaza and Sather Gate all became household words across America. The television offered eager university students throughout the nation an exciting glimpse of what was within their power. Each day nonnegotiable demands escalated with the surge of student power.

The Hallinan sons' roles in the movement were highly significant. At first Vince was chief rooter for Vivian, Patrick, Terence, Con, and Matthew. Police Chief Thomas J. Cahill recalled one arrest quite vividly. "Vincent Hallinan was right behind me yelling encouragement all the time we were hauling his family away. 'At a girl, Vivian!' If all the

Irish stuck together like they did, we could still run San Francisco."

Hallinan always was incapable of spectating for long, so when the jailed demonstrators needed legal representation, his resolve to remain in the background melted. Overwhelmed by the flood of arrested demonstrators, the superior court judges proposed trying them in groups of one hundred and fifty. Hallinan objected, arguing that he was the chosen counsel for each demonstrator and that to try different groups simultaneously before different judges would deprive students of the attorney of their choice. He claimed to represent everybody and demanded individual trials. For days Hallinan was half-attorney and half-choreographer as he dallied before one judge, then darted to the next. Whenever he lost a motion, he would wave grandly to the assembled students and off they would go, following him to the next courtroom.

Once the small-group trials began, he tried to argue the illegality of the institutionalized racism in employment and the propriety of non-violent protest. "San Francisco considers itself a liberal and progressive city. I think it is. Yet, racial discrimination prevents a black man from being a bartender or waiter in San Francisco's most historic hotel and prevents him from selling the very automobiles black people buy and drive." His objective was to publicize further the economic plight of blacks and to stall for time so that public hostility toward the young activists would dissipate.

Two years later Vivian and four sons each received a modest fine and thirty days in jail. By then Patrick was an attorney himself and had taken over the case by agreeing to accept whatever punishment the court decreed for the other Hallinans. Vivian declined a suspended sentence because it would not extend to all other demonstrators. When sentenced to jail she appeared excited, possibly because she read her husband's report on prison life. She served her time as spokesperson for the younger girls, some of whom may have been taking drugs and started coming apart in jail. "That sentence was a small enough price to pay. I'm glad we were there to step forward and influence events." Her sons served their time too, one surrendering a bit tardily after having become a Phi Beta Kappa graduate from California in the interim.

The larger result was the establishment of a Human Rights Commission for San Francisco and more open hiring practices for blacks. Sparked by direct action in California, the northern wing of the civil rights movement rolled ahead nationally.

Caught up in the movement as a national director of the Du Bois Clubs, Terence headed south to help register black Mississippians to vote. Vince had been south the year before with a group of lawyers for a tour of court and police facilities. "What they showed us looked all right but civil rights workers were disappearing out of these jails. Not even their bodies were being found. When Kayo was arrested down there I phoned the jail and was told, 'No, surr. No one by dat name heer.' Vivian and I spent that night at the airport waiting for a plane to Mississippi. The fear that overcame me was something I never knew before. It was horrible."

Actually, with all the national publicity generated by the burning of freedom-ride buses and the deaths and brutalization of civil rights workers, the FBI had intervened. Young Hallinan, with other white students, was removed from the local jail on the instructions of Attorney General Robert Kennedy. "That intervention made up for all the other reasons I had to despise Hoover's private army — almost!"

As the decade of student unrest advanced, opposition to the expanded war in Vietnam outstepped all other campus concerns. Again California led and again Hallinan participated.

The San Francisco–Berkeley region all but erupted in major demonstrations against President Lyndon Johnson's escalation of the conflict. California was the jumping-off point for men and munitions for the Asian war. The militant students aimed individual protests against the Northern California military installations and the civilian suppliers who profited from the killing. Vince appeared regularly as an anti-war speaker and protest marcher, but, as in 1952, few who were not already convinced believed his punch line. "Americans are the most hated people to ever inhabit the globe. . . . By supporting the repressive regime in Saigon we are part of a criminal conspiracy against the Vietnamese people." He protested to President Johnson in a scathingly satirical letter which, when unanswered, he redirected to the syndicated political satirist, Arthur Hoppe, who made the most of it.

Complete with historical references, Hallinan claimed that to kill one enemy soldier Julius Caesar spent seventy-five cents, Napoleon spent twenty-one thousand dollars, and by World War II we spent fifty thousand dollars. This inflation, he argued, made Vietnam an outrage. It cost twenty billion dollars in 1966 for a body count of fifty-eight thousand. Hallinan's solution was to take the war away from a "wasteful, bureaucratic Department of Defense and turn it over to private enterprise." After all, professional hit men worked for twenty-five thousand dollars and volume deals certainly would command discounted prices. For the government to spend $311,827.58 for a bemedaled field marshal might be acceptable but not for "a skinny, malnourished, undersized, pajama-clad guerrilla." Americans simply were not getting enough death for their tax money. By returning to the private sector and allowing "free competition in an open market we can once again put killing people back on a sound financial basis."

Vivian, as usual, was less playful and more direct. She threw herself into the work of the Rankin Brigade to oppose the war and served as chair for the Women's International League for Peace and Freedom. In January 1968, they gathered three thousand women who marched on Washington and demanded the withdrawal of American troops from Vietnam. Together with Jeanette Rankin, who as a young congresswoman from Montana had voted against war with Germany in 1917 and war with Japan in 1941, Vivian addressed the protestors and presented petitions to the Democratic leadership in Congress. The war then was massive and growing. It was two months before President Johnson

announced his intention not to seek renomination and immediately before he abandoned the effort to blast a way out of
Vietnam.

In March Vivian disrupted the popular Merv Griffin
television show with a spontaneous verbal brawl with writer-
diplomat Carl Rowan for his cutting remarks on extremists.
She was in the audience as Griffin's guest.

Vincent Hallinan's most pointed effort in support of the
student movement against racial injustice and war was
personal, gratuitous, and obscure. Only a single student
among the thousands of activists benefited and he hardly
said thanks. Wayne Green, a nineteen-year-old black, had
been arrested and tried for attempted murder by throwing a
Molotov cocktail. The incident happened at night on the edge
of the U.C. campus after an anti-war demonstration. Two
men, both California Highway Patrolmen, had been seriously
burned. Green's first trial ended in a hung jury because one
man refused to vote guilty and held out against the other
eleven. He was George French, a Berkeley inventor who had
no contact with the University beyond the occasional use of
its libraries.

The anti-war militant had been defended by a young and
recently admitted white attorney and an older black lawyer
with considerable experience in criminal cases but none with
political overtones. As the first trial unfolded, the defense
team was lucky to have had the independent-thinking inventor in the jury box. The prosecutor, Frank Vukota, was the
most formidable of California veterans with an extraordinary string of convictions and death verdicts.

Two police officer-witnesses testified that they saw
Wayne Green throw the deadly projectile. They were located
at a distance of about sixty-five feet, were on the opposite side
of a row of sycamore trees, wore gas masks, and were dodg-
ing rocks at the time. They placed Green on the grassy knoll
directly east of Sproul Hall and overlooking the plaza where
the students and the police regularly skirmished. The officers
were sure of Green's identification because they knew him by
sight as a troublemaking anti-war demonstrator. One officer

stated that earlier on the very evening of the fire bombing Green had insulted him.

Green's first defense team produced six witnesses who were standing on that same knoll. They were apolitical types who mostly held administrative positions in education and government. None had ever participated in a demonstration and none had connections with student political action groups. Only two were previously acquainted and two others contacted the authorities on their own when they read in the papers that the police arrested a black man. Each of the six swore that the man who threw the fire bomb was not Wayne Green. They did not know who he was but they knew that he was white. He was dressed like a typical hippie, not a black militant.

During cross-examination the prosecutor bullied each defense witness into confusion and retreat. Vukota concluded that their testimony could not be believed because the details of one were at variance from the details of the others. He referred to the defendant as the "colored boy" and in his final call to the all-white jury denounced protestors and anarchy. He warned the jurors that the failure to convict would mean an endorsement by them of the violence that threatened the security of the nation. He rang in his own military service in World War II and finished with a glorification of the flag, his own right arm lifted toward the massive banner on the wall and his voice lowered to a reverent pitch.

In the jury room George French disregarded the rhetoric and appraised the credibility of the rival sets of witnesses. To focus the unstructured discussion he outlined the police testimony, listed reasons why the officers should be believed and why they should be doubted. Then he did the same for the six defense witnesses. He concluded that credibility rested heavily with the defense. He was shocked to discover that not one juror agreed with him. What followed insulted his scientific mode of deduction and shattered his innocent interest in the judicial process.

Racism, superpatriotism, and paranoia erupted against perceived anarchists, weirdos, and drug-crazed radicals. It all gushed forth and for three days French endured the personal abuse of jurors who had claimed lack of bias as a condition for their selection. Then the foreman gave up and announced a hung jury.

The obstinate juror drove to San Francisco and un-burdened himself on Hallinan. Then he put the matter directly to Vince in a way that was less than flattering. "He wanted an old fighter who knew how to roll with Vukota in the legal gutter and come out on top with his knee deep in the bully's groin. . . . Of course I took the case. If I were fifty years younger, I would have taken Vukota too, in the Court House corridor when no one was around. You couldn't turn a guy like French away."

This case would be easy, he thought. He could at least balance Vukota and the evidence was with the defendant. Hallinan was starting to find that preparation was not as much fun as it used to be but, "It's still the only key to consis-tent winning." He was seventy-two now.

Hallinan moved across the Bay to an Oakland hotel within walking distance from the Alameda County Court House and refined his defense. He phoned Vivian twice a day, ran the forthcoming trial through his head a few more times, "and I waited for Vukota to come on. I have a vin-dictiveness I should not be proud of, but I am. Getting him for what he was doing to this kid was going to be easy but I didn't want to miss. I had to be prepared."

Buried somewhere in the files left by the first attorney, Hallinan found a cryptic record of a phone conversation with a Joyce Levec. The female caller stated that the boyfriend of a girl she knew threw the Molotov cocktail, not Green. The first defense team did not follow the matter up because it looked like compounded and inadmissible hearsay—gossip upon gossip. In the meantime Levec dropped out of sight and even if the web could be untangled, the attorneys doubted that the boyfriend would confess to attempted murder to save Green.

By the time Hallinan sat down behind the defense table he had located Art Gottlieb, the alleged firebomber boy-

friend, and he even converted Gottlieb into an effective witness for Green. Hallinan's strategy was several steps beyond
the legal ingenuity of Green's first hard-working defense
team.

Hallinan had also concluded from new witnesses that the
police and the district attorney's office knew about Gottlieb
but were suppressing the evidence linking him to the crime.
Green was the man they wanted. He was black, anti-war,
anti-racism, anti-university militant fond of calling the
campus police "fucking cops." Instead of releasing Green
and going after a low-profile but guilty white student, they
kept after the offensive but innocent black.

The prosecutor opened the second trial with his standard
accusations against the lawless elements engulfing the
university community and he listed the specifics he would
prove against Green. Hallinan already knew Vukota's case
from the previous trial and, in accordance with the U.S.
Supreme Court discovery rules, he had the list of prosecution
witnesses and the content of their testimony. It was obvious
to him that Vukota had nothing new.

Hallinan had used his extended opener successfully in
pre-discovery days when no other prominent attorney would
risk premature disclosure of his defense. After discovery
rulings by the courts, the conservative nature of American
attorneys continued to keep them tradition bound. They still
held their opening remarks until after the prosecution completed its case. This major evolution in the legal system, for
Hallinan, merely reinforced what he had been doing for a
generation. He knew the prosecution from the first trial transcript, and the only new development was that he knew who
actually committed the crime. The case was ideal, again, for
his specialty, the extended opener.

Hallinan roared that Vukota would prove none of his
charges because Green was not the firebomber. He named
Gottlieb and promised to produce him in court. He named
the disinterested witnesses, all with impeccable credentials.
He stressed that those who had offered their testimony to the
authorities that "a white man did it" had been turned aside.

For the moment Hallinan reserved his own Molotov cocktail —the official suppression of evidence—that he intended to smash over Vukota's head. When he retook his seat next to Green, he had done more than hold open the jurors' minds. He lifted his client's spirits and let Vukota know that if they grappled, it would hurt.

Hallinan had unraveled the Joyce "Levec" (really spelled Levesque) mystery on his way to locating Art Gottlieb. After the Berkeley police arrested Green, she reported that Gottlieb had done it. The police listened to her story and ignored it. Hallinan knew there would have been a written report on her statement and he knew Vukota would have read it.

The Alameda prosecutor "was not dishonest himself," Hallinan recorded in his journal. "He was a super patriot. . . . He had been aggrandized by a commission in the army and now by his position in the District Attorney's office. The system which had recognized and elevated him was sacrosanct. That system's central image was the cop. The 'thin blue line' between its edifice and anarchy, communism, hippies, long haired, dope crazed freaks—the terrifying concepts of the ultra-right imagination. . . . The almost paranoid effort to produce a conviction by unreliable and unsubstantial evidence was the activity of a sick man."

In a workmanlike manner Hallinan defused, dismantled, and destroyed a prosecution's attempt to railroad a youngster who was "guilty" of opposing the Vietnam War, of opposing racism, and of opposing a university administration which had tried to retard student activism. Perhaps most insufferable of all, Green was guilty of being unpleasant about all these problems. He was, however, not guilty of any crime, particularly the attempted murder of two highway patrolmen.

Hallinan instructed Green to talk back to Vukota this time during cross-examination and to stand up for his anti-war principles. "If the jury doesn't like what you say, they will at least give you credit for being honest." He gave Green one other instruction. "If I hear you call Vukota 'Sir' like you did in the first trial or if you slump back in your chair, I'm going to go right up to you and smash your face. This guy is trying to take your life away for what somebody else did. We have to make his infamy clear to the jury not just by what we say, but by what we do. For them to know it is not enough. They have to feel in their guts what Vukota is doing until it sort of makes them sick. Every time he yells at you, yell back. Say, 'No, Vukota, I didn't do it and you know I didn't!' "

Skirting the hearsay rule, which had handicapped the first defense team, was easy. Hallinan called Gottlieb to the stand and directly asked him if he threw the firebomb. In their pre-trial conferences, Hallinan had instructed him to decline to answer that question on constitutional grounds in order to protect himself. Hallinan also made sure that Gottlieb never admitted anything directly to him. Therefore, Hallinan's knowledge remained no more than hearsay.

Before his witness could answer the question, the judge intervened and reprimanded the silently pleased Hallinan for putting Gottlieb in legal jeopardy. It was the judge who, in the presence of the jury, instructed the witness on his rights not to incriminate himself. That unanticipated assistance allowed the jury to interpret Gottlieb's refusal as prompted by the court, rather than by Hallinan.

With that much accomplished, Hallinan brought the judge's attention to the infrequently exercised exception to the hearsay rule that allowed him to place an admission of guilt before a jury without any legally binding confession by Gottlieb. When the primary party is "not available as a witness himself," others who heard the admission can testify to that fact. By taking the Fifth Amendment, Gottlieb had made himself unavailable to the court.

Once the judge accepted that, Hallinan called Gottlieb's schoolmates, who testified that he told them that he did it. Gottlieb threw the firebomb to get even with the police for a beating they allegedly gave him at a previous demonstration.

Next, Hallinan called Joyce Levesque, who testified that she had reported all this to the campus police. Hallinan then served a subpoena on the officer she spoke to, then on Vukota's investigator, who received that officer's written

report. In the end Hallinan succeeded in obtaining the report
itself, which had been retained by the prosecution.

As Hallinan followed the paper trail from Levesque to
the prosecutor's office, Vukota objected that none of this concerned *The People* v. *Wayne Green.* But it did. The report
named and described Gottlieb, just as Levesque testified, and
it destroyed the State's credibility. At this point Hallinan
succeeded in making the prosecution the suspect.

It was a lifetime of cases just like this — little people — that
gave me such respect for the way the Soviets treated their
nobodies, even the way they treated Powers. By trying to
frame the wrong guy our public servants let the right guy go.
I wondered how the cops who got burned liked that move.
The two cops who perjured themselves could hardly change
their testimony from black to white and accuse Gottlieb.
Vukota couldn't do an about face and start a new prosecution
based on a suppressed document I had to get the court to
order into evidence.

Sure I got the kid acquitted in the end, but look at the costs
to everybody. Not financial, moral. Now, with a perspective
of ten years, cerebral Americans agree Vietnam was wrong.
Instead of prosecuting students every patriotic American
should have joined them. No one worthy of consideration has
justified racism, the covert, contributing reason for Green's
prosecution and near-conviction.

For the life of me I can't understand why we suppress
dissent and corrupt our institutions in the process. The
students of the New Left were the best thing that happened
to America in the 1960s. I am profoundly grateful that they
let me lend a hand even though most of them thought I was
somewhat beyond that embryonic age of thirty and no longer
worthy of their trust.

Hallinan took the bus into the city and walked to his
Civic Center office. En route he passed the imposing public
buildings that he had watched rise from the ashes of 1906.
All were dark except for the night lights in the Emergency
Hospital, but the architecture did not interest him anyway.
The shadows let him think of the people who were gone:

Mulvey and Supple, Judge Golden and Egan, the Auditorium crowd that applauded when he pleaded for sanity instead of a permanent war economy, John Mansfeldt. He wondered what had become of Mansfeldt's children. At least Harry Bridges was safe and thriving, still tormenting professional anti-communists.

In his deserted office behind the Opera House, he dumped his notes into a folder, scrawled "Green" across the lip, and shoved it into the "history" file. He phoned Vivian to come and get him, not because he was tired, but because his reflections took him back to the way he felt when they rode together after the Egan trial in 1932. He loved that mood and wanted to recapture it even in his imagination.

"I realized the reverie was dangerous though." A new world had grown up out there and he still wanted to be part of it. "I wanted just one more big one, to go out in style."

He did a few push-ups, turned on the outside light, and looked out the side window to see if Vivian's Mercedes was in the lot.

The fourth Hallinan to win U.C. boxing title, surrounded by his five brothers (1959).

Mikhail I. Griniev, Soviet defense counsel for Francis Gary Powers, and Hallinan in Moscow (1960).

Vivian Hallinan being arrested at San Francisco civil rights protest (1962).

Right: *The Hallinans and the Robesons (1965).*

Below: *Eightieth birthday with Vivian, their six sons and families (1977).*

Above: *In training for the distance, age 82 (1979).*

Left: *Hallinan at work (1980).*

> "'Hold fast to what you have but never regret
> what gets away.' I read that somewhere. Oh, it
> seems like a hundred years ago. One other
> thing too. 'Never believe a captive.'"
>
> — Vincent Hallinan
> July 22, 1980

11. The Distance

Vincent Hallinan never developed much of a fantasy life for the simple reason that he did the exciting and gratifying things ordinary persons dream about during their most solitary moments. Even at eighty-five, he subordinated his wishful thoughts to a fixed and active daily regime.

He had everything he wanted, more than he once knew existed. His $1,080,000 fee in the contested will case of Lillian Ryan Stulsaft faded in comparison with his sustained earnings through a still active sixty-three year legal practice. Vivian's success in the San Francisco real estate market dwarfed even his lifetime gross. Hallinan liked money because of the influence and access it allowed, not particularly for himself, but for the advancement and interests of his sons and his grandchildren.

About the only physical comforts he allowed to creep into his later years were the fringe benefits he derived from living with Vivian. She kept him moving into newer homes with better views of San Francisco. She kept getting the new furniture, trading in automobiles, throwing out old mattresses and hiring more domestic staff members. "I told Vin that we did not work like hell to live like hermits. He acquiesced but his heart isn't in it. He is indulging me." Where he drew the line, however, was at traveling.

Hallinan liked walking to work, liked defending wacko psychiatrists who probably deserved to have their licenses revoked for what they did with their female patients. He liked tilting with police witnesses and taking on technical experts of all kinds in court. Even though there were few spectators the courtroom remained the place where he derived his satisfaction from doing the thing he knew best.

Every spring was the same. He would promise Vivian that this year he would return with her to Cuba, to mainland China, or to Russia. By the time June arrived, he would scare up some case to rescue him from his promise. As a compromise to three months in Europe, Vince went along on a two-week Mediterranean luxury cruise in 1980. "A God damn bore. That's what it was. Can you imagine, the highlights were forty-two meals with the same Orange County conservatives? I could have been in San Francisco defending armed bandits."

The nearest Hallinan ever came to wishful thinking was in his desire to go out with a bang. He did not want to go down the way he came up, with all those grubby cases from 1919 to the Egan breakthrough in 1932. Egan, Mansfeldt, Bridges, then all the political advocacy. Rather than slide back down, he kept looking for more work like that—work that would let him exit from the top.

Through the score of years during which most attorneys welcome retirement, Hallinan combined his desire to go out with a bang and his irrepressible urge to strike back and even old scores. The first and foremost was with the Catholic church. He still held the Church responsible for what he considered an emotionally joyless and intellectually barren youth, but even more for the wasted life of his sister. He also could not forget the abject shame his father felt because the Church would not bury Vince's younger brother.

Hallinan's first chance for revenge was doubly sweet. His old adversary, David Supple, the Grand Jury "expert," and "Mr. Knight of Columbus," died. So Vince bought out a portion of Supple's nephew's claim to the estate. The old bachelor had left it to the Catholic church. Hallinan contested the will on doctrinal grounds, claiming that Catholic teachings about heaven, hell and purgatory were fraudulent.

He maintained that Supple had been convinced by these false notions to leave his money to the archbishop and various Catholic charities in order that masses be said for his soul. The ostensible purpose behind it all was to prevent him from suffering the cleansing fires of purgatory and transport his soul quickly to God's presence, heaven. Hallinan, of course, denied all these spiritual entities.

Since the 1930s Hallinan had been convinced that Supple was a crook, just like his partners in the jury-packing business. Supple's well-publicized Catholicism made Hallinan's efforts at ridiculing his beliefs all the more satisfying. Hallinan pursued the case from the local courts through the California appeals process, all the way to the United States Supreme Court. En route he had a field day debating priests, rabbis, ministers, and an occasional infidel. He appeared on television, debated over the radio, and argued in court. Hallinan was at his best when citing scripture because of his exact memory. He enjoyed the accolades of disinterested observers, but there were too few of them. The avalanche of international mail came mostly from professional anti-Catholics and outraged believers of all faiths. He preferred the sanctimonious hate letters, because the anti-Catholics seemed too much like repugnant neighbors encouraging him to beat up his unworthy father.

The courts rejected his arguments at every step, refusing to rule on the validity of religious doctrine. He stuck with the case because, for him, it was fun. He liked saying that the Church kept Supple captive, in intellectual slavery, because he thought that was what his own teachers tried to do to him. He acknowledged that there was no evil intent on their part because, tragically, they believed their doctrine.

When the U.S. Supreme Court finally ended his joy ride, Hallinan revealed a more playful side of his character, but only to his private journal.

> All of this took seven years and, meanwhile, the Church was deprived of the use of the money while it was held by the Special Administrators. I believe it likely that while the

possibility of losing the bequest existed, the Church would not hand over from its "Savings Account" the indulgences which would permit David Supple's soul to enter heaven and that I had squared my grievances against him by holding him for so long a period in purgatory.

Meanwhile, as there was no such thing as David Supple's soul, heaven, hell, or purgatory, I had this small satisfaction without injuring him or anybody else.

Next Hallinan struck back against his concept of the prosecuting attorney hell-bent on conviction at any cost, the reactionary police commissioner, the brutal cop, the incompetent or venal attorney, and the judge who joins with the prosecution to insure convictions. He devoted a decade and a half to these tasks until all his grievances were settled and he defeated and outlived his antagonists.

Hallinan never heard of Robert Lee Kidd until the drifter's wife placed a bizarre ad in the *Examiner*. Gladys Kidd promised ten years of domestic service to any leading attorney who would help her death-row husband. Hallinan took the case for free when he discovered in the original trial transcript the indication of official suppression of evidence that demonstrated Kidd's innocence. He thought that Kidd was a good-natured slob, not a murderer. With ease Hallinan got him off death row, retried, and found innocent. Then Hallinan turned on the prosecutor. Although Ronald Reagan denied it, the force of Hallinan's letter to the California governor prevented Kidd's prosecutor from receiving a judicial appointment. Later, when the same man ran for a judgeship, Hallinan lined up the trial lawyers' association in support of the other candidate who won. And in the end Hallinan watched a new liberal district attorney replace most of the old guard with young liberals. The satisfaction Hallinan derived from the professional destruction of Kidd's prosecutor was about all he earned from the case. Kidd said, "Thanks," then asked Hallinan for free representation so he could divorce the stout blond wife who saved him from the gas chamber. When Vince declined, Kidd drifted away into the shiftless side of America from which he had come.

Thomas J. Mellon was a different sort of man. In 1960 as San Francisco police commissioner, he approved the high-pressure hosing of the City Hall protestors against the House Un-American Activities Committee. They were the students who began the northern wing of the American civil rights movement. Mellon's response to Hallinan's on-the-scene objections was, "You look after the Reds and I'll look after San Francisco."

Mellon's dignified appearance and law-and-order mentality reminded Hallinan of Commissioner Gordon in the Batman comics. Since in real life Mellon was likewise respectable, the most Hallinan could do was to harass him out of his job. According to the City Charter, commissioners were required to live in San Francisco. Mellon, however, enjoyed Marin County where he resided with his family. Hallinan kept after him in the press and in court until the commissioner resigned his cherished post rather than move his family back into the city.

The American courts never were institutions in which Hallinan sought abstract, impersonal justice. These were battlegrounds for individual clients and for his own griev-ances. Most importantly, the judiciary became the point of encounter between his mature radicalism and the legal system he tried to change.

The California Bar Association blocked the admission of Terence (Kayo) Hallinan to legal practice even though he passed the bar examination. Some said his father's unpopular politics were the reason. Others said Kayo's own history of youthful violence and early civil disobedience were the reasons. Whatever the reason, Vincent's legal persistence prevailed and the courts ruled on behalf of his son and against the State Bar. Young Hallinan promptly began his career by defending various protestors during the era of university campus disorders of the 1960s.

Once, at San Francisco State College, he intervened between a Tactical Squad policeman and a young woman who was being clubbed. Terence Hallinan's initiative earned him ten stitches across the crown of his head and a criminal charge of interfering with the police while they were discharging their duties. A conviction would mean disbarment and a foreclosed career.

Normally attorneys select other lawyers to defend their vital interests in order to maintain perspective and judicious restraint. Otherwise the danger of emotional misjudgment would be very likely. Nonetheless, Vincent Hallinan decided to defend his son and announced with characteristic modesty, "He deserves the best."

He won the criminal defense and then they sued the city and the police in civil action. In perhaps the best conceived and executed concluding statement of his career, Hallinan convinced the jury that the power which governing bodies confer upon the police must be exercised for the protection of citizens, not for the protection of individual policemen in the abuse of their authority. He convinced the jurors that for law enforcement officers to assault anyone without lawful necessity was a felony. He identified and exposed the actual conspiracy in this case whereby the police lied to cover each other's felonious and brutal actions. After the sober denials of any wrongdoing by the police, Hallinan sprang a film that required each officer to retract his sworn, perhaps perjured, prior testimony.

The charge of police brutality was an unpopular one which middle-class juries resisted. Campus protestors commonly were viewed as threatening the American way of life, which the police had to protect. Yet, Hallinan's summation was a model. In it he effectively masked his personal distaste for the police and his rejection of the entire American system. Step by step he brought the jurors from their natural assumption of police responsibility to the conviction that these particular officers viciously and wantonly brutalized Terence.

For his success in what was a classic though obscure case, Hallinan, then seventy-six, was selected to join four other living American attorneys as "Masters of the Courtroom." Instead of retiring on the honor, he announced his candidacy for the superior court against Carl Allen, the judge who had cited him for contempt in the original criminal defense of his son.

Hallinan campaigned in earnest and thereafter advised

every attorney who believed he had been unfairly treated in court to run against that judge at the next election. "It puts them to the bother and expense of campaigning and it scares hell out of them. The last thing they want is to have to earn a living trying cases in the courts they presided over."

He lost the election, but prized the editorial:

San Francisco has a nice habit of taking its radicals and problem citizens to its bosom aftrer they grow old, tired and tame. But when one of them reaches for the robes of judicial power, the question arises whether he is yet tame.

[Hallinan] is the only candidate for a judgeship in the history of California who: Has served two terms in a federal prison . . . ; Has been suspended from the practice of law by the California Supreme Court for a crime involving moral turpitude . . . ; Has been suspended from the practice of law by the California Supreme Court for practicing a deception . . . ; Has run for President of the United States as a candidate of a Communist-infested party.

Hallinan's best chance to go out in style came and went with the Patty Hearst case. The young heiress to the family publishing fortune was spectacularly kidnapped from her Berkeley student apartment by a radical terrorist group calling itself the Symbionese Liberation Army (SLA). Months later she appeared uniformed, armed, and in the company of known members and together they held up a branch of the Hibernia Bank in San Francisco.

In the meantime the terrorists were extorting a million dollars in groceries from her father, *Examiner* president Randolph Hearst. By the time the FBI apprehended Patty and her captor-colleagues, Vincent Hallinan and Randolph Hearst had come together. To this relationship Hearst brought his near-crushing fear for his daughter's safety and an understanding of Hallinan derived from little more than his own newspaper's editorials.

Hallinan brought to this association a lifetime of accumulated hurts. "The Hearst papers ridiculed everything I believed in and opposed everything I tried to do."

He also brought his personal hopes. He wanted the case. He wanted to go out by successfully defending the most internationally publicized celebrity of the day. Winning, he knew, would be easy. It would be the Mansfeldt defense over again. Only this time he would have all the advantages and none of the restraints. For the first time in his life he would be on the popular side. Patty was the victim. She did not ask to be kidnapped. She killed no one. And the drugs were forced upon her by young blacks who terrorized her.

How could he lose? The jury would like her just as the general public did. For that matter the public was starting to like Hallinan too. He realized that after the three street punks tried to mug him. The mayor attended his eightieth birthday party and the Board of Supervisors gave him a plaque. At eighty-five his party would fill the City Hall Rotunda and Harry Bridges would be the main speaker. Age was only an inconvenience in getting good cases, not in winning them. Jurors, for that matter, were so young that most of them did not even know what he was famous for and the young judges were giving him more and more latitude in argument and summations.

For the last few years he had been selecting lesser cases with care in order to keep up on the latest in medicine, psychology, and psychiatry. In quiet little courtrooms he kept sharp by dismantling expert witnesses from the University of California Medical School faculty and the San Francisco General Hospital psychiatric staff. He would need it in the Hearst case, he figured, because of his intention to try it with a legally up-dated and adjusted somnolentia defense.

To be innocent, Patty Hearst had to have acted while in a state of drug- and terror-induced psychosis. Since "innocent" was the only plea worth trying, psychosis was Hallinan's explanation for her actions.

Actually this was his son's case. Terence got them both into it because of his contacts and previous representations of convicts who claimed to know the SLA terrorists. Vince had taken Randolph Hearst to see some of these men in an effort to discover the whereabouts of Patty. That was another reason why Hallinan was in it. Hearst broke down on the ride over to San Quentin Prison and cried. "The power of a publishing empire didn't do much for him then. He was just like all the other scared fathers I've seen, poor bastards with their kids in trouble."

Catastrophe struck right after Terence represented Patty at her arraignment. Vince was busy on television seeding public opinion with the defense line. Unfortunately, Randolph Hearst looked elsewhere. The Hallinans were too radical for his establishment ways so he chose F. Lee Bailey and thereby compounded his daughter's tragedy.

Numerous attorneys who observed the actual court defense, including Charles Garry (developer of the diminished capacity concept), have stated that Bailey blew the case. "The defense Bailey chose presented the jury with an impossible problem. They couldn't acquit her!"

Bailey turned aside the Hallinan defense strategy and asserted that Patty participated in criminal acts due to compulsion and duress. Forty-two times the prosecutor poked holes in that story. Forty-two times, when he asked Patty to explain the obvious deficiencies, she took the Fifth Amendment. Forty-two times she did it in front of the jury.

Hallinan accused Bailey of malpractice at a luncheon for attorneys and journalists at the San Francisco Press Club. "It was like watching another doctor operate. As soon as he started I knew he was going to kill her. He kept at it and he did!"

Hallinan invited a law suit over his public remarks but, as he found so often to be the case, seasoned antagonists declined such bait.

In Hallinan's hands Patricia Hearst's last line of defense would have been the one that saved Irene Mansfeldt: "What you are telling me must be true, but I honestly don't remember it."

Hallinan told Shana Alexander of the "Sixty Minutes" television program exactly what he believed. "If you are going to give a client a defense, give her a believable one. In this case jurors were predisposed to acquit. A client's drug-induced psychosis could last as long as I want it to last. It could be total or selective. That's all the jury wanted to hear. They needed a rationalization to do what they wanted to do. Even though that sweet child called me 'a senile old fuck,' I would have saved her, because that's the thing I do."

True to his own experience, Hallinan never believed Patty the captive. He held fast to her case as long as he and Terence could. And he tried not to regret its loss to Bailey. But in the end all he got from it was his usual bit of private fun. When Shana Alexander's pop history of the case appeared in print she sent him an autographed copy. In it she wrote, "At seventy-nine, the old radical looked like an ancient but still alert Irish lizard, duded up in a sharp green suit and tie."

He was eighty-two by then and his old green suit looked at least half that age. Vivian was going to pick him up at his office before noon and together they would drive down to the airport. Hurriedly, then, Vince dashed off a letter to Alexander.

He thanked her for the book, quoted Silenus that *"nullae reptiliae in Hibernia sunt"* (There are no reptiles in Ireland), and concluded that if he had a choice though, he would rather be an ancient Irish lizard than a senile old fuck.

By the time he and Vivian boarded the flight for Hawaii for a swimming vacation on Maui, he had forgotten the big one that got away. In fact, he persisted in rehearsing his next one with Vivian. He could not get it out of his head.

A respected businessman had gotten into a curb-side dispute with two men over a parking space. He did not know it but they were plainclothes police officers. Foul language escalated to physical violence and ended with a total of eight police chasing and beating the man to the floor inside his own home. His regular civil attorney retained Hallinan to defend the criminal charge of resisting arrest as a preliminary to a million-dollar suit against the City of San Francisco for false imprisonment.

The case was half-comic and half-tragic. The lead cop had a long history of overreactions and injuries sustained in scuffles. These facts the police department attempted to keep hidden by engaging private counsel. The department also destroyed its tape of the victim's wife's phone call. When she saw two strange men beating her husband on the sidewalk, she phoned the police. It was her call for help that brought the other six.

Hallinan lined up two superior court judges and a black policeman as character witnesses and then he took detailed depositions from all the police. His thoroughness was aimed at preventing any change of story during the trial. During this process the plainclothesmen claimed that Hallinan's client began the altercation by telling them to go find their own "fucking parking space."

Gleefully Hallinan planned to splash them with a dose of the ridiculous by pretending in court that he was so old, he forgot what the word "fucking" meant. He thought it had something to do with sex. Then he intended to require the cops to define it for him in front of the judge and jurors, some of whom would be women. After that they would have to apply their definition to a parking space.

For his capstone though, he would rely on his own client. Hallinan had the facts to expose fully the eight officers who participated in the striking of a citizen, chasing him up his stairs, and terrorizing him in front of his wife and children. Hallinan's arrangement of the evidence supported this picture and the jury would be in his hand by the time he put the businessman on the stand to testify in his own defense.

Vincent's only question to Vivian was how audible would be the gasp from the jury when his client delivered Hallinan's arranged climax. "When they had me handcuffed and bleeding, face down on my kitchen floor, a police officer abused me, *sexually*, in front of my wife and daughter."

Three weeks later, when Judge William Mullins smiled down from the superior court bench, Vincent told the truth.

"Yes, Your Honor. I am ready for the defense."